THE ALIGNMENT FACTOR

The importance of creating a favourable impression is hard to overstate in all walks of life – in business it's vital for to achieve strategic goals. Customers, journalists, bloggers, investors, governments and other groups are all important stakeholders in an organization's performance and, by persuasively communicating a company's ethical and socially responsible behaviour, these groups can be kept onside.

Supported throughout by lively examples, this book contains guidance for implementing strategies that engage stakeholders – highlighting those organizations that employ communication professionals as key performers. Van Riel reveals how a dominant logic develops among executives that influences styles and techniques of trust-building communication.

The practical insights demonstrated in cases including Google, Unilever and Barclays make this book useful reading for MBA and other graduate classes, across areas such as public relations and reputation management, as well as for thinking managers across the globe.

Cees B.M. van Riel is Professor of Corporate Communication at Erasmus University, the Netherlands. His other publications include *Essentials of Corporate Communication* (Routledge, 2007).

THE ALIGNMENT FACTOR

Leveraging the power of total stakeholder support

Cees B.M. van Riel

Routledge
Taylor & Francis Group

LONDON AND NEW YORK

First published 2012
by Routledge
2 Park Square, Milton Park, Abingdon, Oxon OX14 4RN

Simultaneously published in the USA and Canada
by Routledge
711 Third Avenue, New York, NY 10017

Routledge is an imprint of the Taylor & Francis Group, an informa business

British Library Cataloguing in Publication Data
A catalogue record for this book is available from the British Library

Library of Congress Cataloging in Publication Data
Riel, C. B. M. van.
  The alignment factor: leveraging the power of total stakeholder
  support/Cees B.M. van Riel.
    p. cm.
  Includes bibliographical references and index.
  1. Business communication. 2. Corporations – Communication systems.
  3. Corporations – Public relations. I. Title.
  HF5718.R534 2012
  658.4′5–dc23
  2011037809

ISBN: 978-0-415-69074-4 (hbk)
ISBN: 978-0-415-69075-1 (pbk)
ISBN: 978-0-203-12453-6 (ebk)

Typeset in Bembo and Stone Sans
by Florence Production Ltd, Stoodleigh, Devon EX16 9PN

To Hanneke,
for your remarkable patience when
my thoughts drifted to the book during
social and family gatherings

CONTENTS

PART III
Key performance indicators in establishing alignment with corporate communication   **185**

PART IV
Epilogue   **211**

ILLUSTRATIONS

Figures

Tables

Boxes

FOREWORD

A defining piece of work

The modern corporation operates in an increasingly turbulent and crowded space, with an unprecedented range of people and institutions that are vested in its success, interested in the business or vigorously opposed to the firm's very existence. These 'stakeholders' may include employees, customers, investors, financial analysts, government regulators, elected officials, self-appointed activist organizations and, among others, the media. Earning the support of these various groups – or even simple neutrality – is the key to alignment, one of the most powerful factors in a corporation's ability to execute and fulfil its strategic intentions.

In *The Alignment Factor*, Dr Cees van Riel makes the case that a company can attain total stakeholder support only through exceptional corporate communication. Through a series of academic constructs supported by practical case studies – including the company for which I work, FedEx – Van Riel demonstrates the steps that are needed to persuade stakeholders to align with, or not actively oppose, a company's objectives. He also argues that, with total support across the stakeholder continuum, a corporation then has an 'unrestricted licence to operate'.

Although a metaphorical licence, it's a powerful permit: with total stakeholder support, a company often earns favourable regulatory treatment; has the trust of customers who admire and routinely purchase its products and services; holds a good reputation with the media; and, with a workforce committed to its strategies, has smooth, efficient and profitable operations.

On a more personal note, I'm delighted that Dr Van Riel has once again made a compelling case for the importance of the discipline in which I'm engaged. Only a couple decades ago, corporate communication was often viewed by line executives as something of a lightweight department that fed the company line to employees and kept prying reporters at bay. Compared with marketing, legal, human resources and other departments, 'public relations' had about as much gravity as the moon.

That's changed at many leading corporations, in part owing to the turbulence I've mentioned, and also thanks to the previous work by Van Riel and several colleagues, who introduced the critical nature of communication and influenced line management's thinking on the function. A professor of Corporate Communication at Erasmus University's Rotterdam School of Management in The Netherlands, Van Riel is most widely known for his research in the field of corporate reputation and strategic alignment. There, he created and leads an Executive Masters of Science programme in corporation communication, which many consider the best in the discipline, drawing senior leaders from companies worldwide.

In 1997, he co-founded the Reputation Institute with Charles Fombrun – formerly a professor at New York University – and is still active as the vice chairman of an organization that conducts research into, and measurements of, company reputations, and advises firms on how to manage their reputation among a complex set of stakeholders. Indeed, I'm personally familiar with its value, having worked with the Institute to successfully improve FedEx's internal alignment. It has built and maintains a strong link between business and the academic community, and it's one of the reasons Van Riel was honoured by the IPR's Pathfinder Life Time Achievement Award in 2011.

Dr Van Riel has also written numbers of scientific articles for prominent management and marketing journals, and several books on corporate communication and reputation, including the 2007 Routledge release, *Essentials of Corporate Communication*. But, in *The Alignment Factor*, he takes communication into a broader and deeper dimension by defining the notion of total stakeholder support, how it's earned, how it's leveraged and the benefits it provides an organization that harnesses such power. This book, in fact, is a defining piece of work.

It offers a sophisticated and holistic framework, including the different demands and approaches of earning internal alignment and external alignment, each of which poses discrete challenges. It also demonstrates two distinct approaches to forging alignment, including the application of *negotiating* and *confrontational* strategies. Whereas the dialogues and agreement from negotiating strategies are typically preferred by most corporations, Van Riel uses case studies to show the successful application of confrontation, which can include litigation, lobbying and vigorous public opposition to a stakeholder's grievance.

A long-time counsel to corporate leaders worldwide, Van Riel provides advice, examples and directions for professional communicators and senior corporate leaders, based on his dictum that 'corporate communication must first be corporate, and only then communication'. It is Van Riel's way of explaining how the discipline is different from mainstream journalism and other forms of communicating, in that business communicators must balance the beliefs and demands of corporate executives against the often-divergent opinions and behaviour of stakeholders. He also believes that a corporation's senior communication executive deserves a place in a firm's dominant coalition, with the chief executive officer, the chief operating officer and the heads of legal, marketing, human resources and other critical functions.

Informed by, and rooted in, metrics, modern corporate communication merges the art of persuasion with strategic intents, return on capital and the alignment that protects the company's most valuable asset, its reputation. In *The Alignment Factor*, Cees van Riel once again shows how it's done.

Bill Margaritis
Chief Communication Officer – FedEx

PREFACE

Organizations are lost without the full support of key stakeholders both inside and outside the company or institution. Support from employees is reflected in a high degree of motivation, which in turn stimulates the productivity that drives financial performance. Similar proof points confirm the value of solid relationships with the external world. When the viewpoints of outside stakeholders are in synch with a company's strategic intents, the benefits are manifest. For example, the organization may have access to cheaper capital from a lender and lower transaction costs from vendors and contractors, who enjoy doing business with a trusted partner. An admired workplace also attracts the most talented workers, who make products that customers not only purchase but rate highly, so critical in this era of social media. Most important, when elected officials and regulators view an organization in a favourable light, it has earned a sustainable and unrestricted 'licence to operate'.

Taken together, this is what I call *alignment* – a mutually rewarding relationship between a company and its key stakeholders that enables the firm to meet its objectives and realize its purpose. In the best of circumstances, *total stakeholder support* fuels the alignment. 'Support' can include employee actions to make a strategy happen, new government regulations that allow a business sector to grow, or simply a lack of interest or opposition from an external activist organization. Alignment and stakeholder support are the most powerful tools any company can have in its operational arsenal, providing leverage that opens markets, sells products and allows a business to thrive.

This book explores how managers can create a *road map* for building organizational relationships that align internal and external stakeholders, primarily through the coordinated actions of line and communication executives. As in all human interactions, forging this bond typically starts with persuading another individual or organization to recognize your presence and feel a positive attraction, but such relationships become sustainable only when both parties perceive it as mutually rewarding. Like interpersonal connections, maintaining an alignment between an organization and all of its stakeholders is an ongoing process, and one in which communication is critical to prosperity, stability and endurance.

Indeed, skilful corporate communication is fundamental in building total stakeholder support and alignment. It involves creativity, discipline and the use of numerous management tools, including key performance indicators. As illustrated in various case studies in this book, the framework for effective persuasion must be integrated throughout an organization, and yet also be actively led by the chief executive and his or her extended leadership team.

The practical insights that follow are based on academic research in the areas of reputation management and employee alignment, partly conducted at the Rotterdam School of Management of the Erasmus University in the Netherlands, and by a growing group of international academics interested in this relatively new field. Another important source of inspiration is rooted in a decade's worth of Reputation Institute studies of more than 2,500 corporations in forty-one countries, as well as the Institute's proprietary worldwide employee alignment studies for multinational firms. I am most grateful to my colleagues at the University and the Reputation Institute, and I would especially like to express my gratitude to my colleagues at the Corporate Communication Centre of Rotterdam School of Management/Erasmus University: Marijke Baumann, Guido Berens, Majorie Dijkstra, Mirdita Elstake, Ahong Gu, Mignon van Halderen, Patricia Heijndijk, Joke van Oost, Edwin Santbergen, Marjon Ullmann and Yijing Wang. At the Reputation Institute, Brian Craig, Charles Fombrun, Kasper Nielsen, Nicolas Trad, Ana Luisa de Castro Almeida, Marcus Dias, Beverly Nannini, Fernando Prado, Jussara Sant'Anna Belo, Natalie Elliot, Dominik Heil, Loren Schneid, Anthony Johndrow and many others helped me in getting this book written. Various representatives of companies have helped me with ideas, texts and illustrations that have been used in this book, for example: Richard van der Eijk (Unilever), Frank van Ooijen (FrieslandCampina), Hans Koeleman (KPN), Eraldo Carneiro da Silva (Petrobras), Secundino Muñoz Velasco (Gas Natural Fenosa Group), Angel Alloza, CEO of the Corporate Excellence Centre for Reputation Leadership, Peter van Minderhout (TNT), Jules Prast and Andre Manning (Philips), Frans Cornelis (Randstad), Bill Margaritis (FedEx), Ray Jordan and Craig Rothenberg (Johnson & Johnson), Jerry Steiner (Monsanto), Karen Beuk (ING), Paulo Marinho (Itaú), David Brilleslijper (Delta Lloyd), Jeroen Overgoor and Jolanda Ravenek (Eneco) and Khumo Mohlamme (Eskom). Last but not least, I would like to thank Jay Stuller, who helped me polish the text to produce correct, and above all crystal clear, English.

I've avoided extensive theoretical explanations and thickets of statistical data as much as possible. I've also attempted to write the book in a style that's common in executive teaching: fact based, rooted in research and hopefully expressing a point of view that is perceived as useful for executives, managers and communication professionals. Comments and suggestions for improvements are welcome on the website (www.corporatecommunication.nl/publications).

Cees B.M. van Riel
Rotterdam/Breda, March 2012

1

ALIGNING STAKEHOLDERS THROUGH CORPORATE COMMUNICATION

Visionary managers all have one thing in common: a strong desire to implement their ideas through actions that result in success. The abililty to divine an ingenious strategy and stimulate others to move down its path is the hallmark of great generals, winning coaches in sports and, of course, highly esteemed chief executive officers (CEOs). And yet, the most brilliantly designed and calculated strategy is absolutely futile, or doomed to utter failure, if the key stakeholders that the organization depends upon do not support it.

Alignment with those stakeholders is perhaps the most important factor in how well an organization conducts its business. *Total stakeholder support*, which is the strongest form of alignment, gives a company tremendous leverage that opens markets, wins government permission to do business and minimizes problems. The path to this objective, however, is one that's long, twisting and uneven, and it includes forks that can take a business in a wrong direction. Therefore, I frequently make reference to drawing up a *road map* to alignment. Most of the processes and ideas that follow are elements that will help an organization create that map.

Large corporations that touch on many aspects of society have numerous stakeholders, many more, in fact, than was recognized only a couple decades ago. The need to forge an alignment with employees, investors, customers, the financial media, elected officials and regulators is obvious. Today, however, that expanded list includes self-appointed advocacy groups that watch for corporate missteps; business partners and contractors; the general media, which now operate on a news cycle that never stops; and, of course, the collective power of individuals communicating through social media, which can send a small criticism of a company viral. Although companies clearly own the promise that's made by their brand, we now know that it's the internal and external stakeholders who own a company's most precious asset, which is its reputation.

Building alignment implies establishing a *relationship* with stakeholders, resulting in at least the willingness of both entities to listen to each other's arguments and assess the pros and cons of joining forces in ways perceived as being mutually rewarding. The ultimate goal of building alignment is to increase the perceived 'added value' of the company for customers, shareholders and employees, by creating synergies within the company and also between the company and its key external stakeholders.[1] Building those effective synergies requires senior executives to orchestrate the actions of managers in finance, marketing, purchasing, human resources, information technology and, perhaps above all, corporate communication.

The emphasis of this book is on the role of communication in building and maintaining alignment. Corporate communication managers can contribute substantially to the success of an organization by selecting the most appealing messages, which persuade internal and external audiences to be open minded towards a beneficial relationship. The messages crafted by communication managers have to be embedded in the purpose and overall strategic goals of the firm, and they also have to show recognition of the expectations of the key stakeholders.

This sometimes creates a schizophrenic position for corporate communication managers, as they have to balance the interests and demands of the internal *dominant coalition* – the few individuals who actually run a company, set its directions and dictate its abiding values and culture – versus the desires and beliefs of external groups. A communication executive must have the capability to offer serious, frank and even bold consultation to top management on potentially divisive employee beliefs or contentious external issues of reputation. What's more, to be truly effective, the communication executive needs skills comparable to those of a lead business consultant, so that he or she commands the full respect of the CEO and other line executives. In turn, and equally important, the CEO must fully appreciate that communication is no trivial or secondary matter and, in truth, may be as important to the company's success as a new product or highly productive factories.

The communication function does two exceptionally important things: first, it helps the executives draw up that *road map to alignment*, a clear and systematic set of steps that all departments of the company follow, on a path towards achieving alignment with internal and external stakeholders. Elements of the map and how it is created, interpreted and managed are found throughout the following chapters. However, in short, there are waypoints on the journey that involve intelligence-gathering, analysis, message creation, delivery and reiteration. And, although the map is very much an organized process, large companies must be inherently flexible with its use, as achieving alignment in today's very public world takes corporations into terrain where firms of forty years ago never had to travel.

However, once that alignment is achieved, and in particular with external stakeholders, the company will have earned what I've come to term an unrestricted *licence to operate*. It is the hypothetical product of a sterling reputation and reflects the quality of the performance of the firm in general and the contributions of the communication department specifically to organizational objectives.

Indeed, in abstract terminology, the licence embodies the organization's degree of success in obtaining and maintaining favourable relations with the permission-givers of society. It isn't a wallet-sized card bearing the corporation's photo and

FIGURE 1.1 Antecedents of licence to operate

its height, weight and age. In this context, licence has an exceptionally broad definition. But, in terms in winning permits, concessions or contracts with governments, a licence to operate can be quite literal and legally binding, the loss of which could put a firm out of business. When indirect stakeholders interfere with business operations, or create disfavour among consumers, the company certainly may not go out of business, but it will suffer wounds. To carry on the analogy of the privileges afforded a motorist by society and its laws, a person convicted of driving while intoxicated could lose his or her licence or be prohibited from driving at night or be limited to driving only to and from work – adverse stakeholder relations can put restrictions on a company's licence.

So, an unrestricted licence is perhaps an organization's most valuable asset, not unlike an individual's good personal reputation. For organizations that wish to earn or renew that licence, the formula shown in Figure 1.1 is the first stretch in the road map to alignment.

Put into words, what this means is as follows: the success of external corporate communication is the result of excellence in organizational performance, multiplied by excellence in communication, divided by the nature of the social context in which the organization operates.

The recognition of this dynamic presents the very idea of corporate communication in a very different light from in decades past. Although firms have always considered government relations a serious part of the business, 'public relations' was often viewed as fluff, a necessary-but-soft buffer between the company and the media and customer complaints. For many decades, it seems as if all too many executives believed that employees were lucky to have jobs, and, by and large, they were expected to perform tasks without any knowledge of how they contributed to corporate objectives, if they were even informed of the strategic intents.

Today, communicating with employees on all business matters is a vital piece of almost any major operation. Consequently, successfully fulfilling the communication executive's role requires having a deep knowledge of the organization and an understanding of the beliefs of internal and external stakeholders.

Perhaps my favourite saying about the discipline is that *the role of communication executives is foremost corporate, and only then communication*. What I mean is that, in working with line executives to draw out a road map to earning that unrestricted operational licence, the communication manager must have a general understanding of the business and, in fact, put the needs of the business itself above the

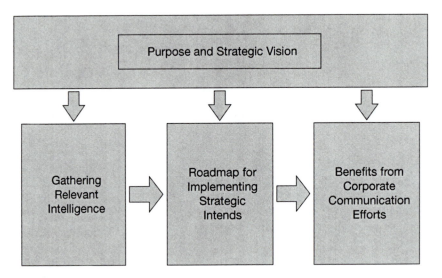

FIGURE 1.2 Three starting points in creating alignment with corporate communication

communication function. Although creating messages is clearly an important thing, the communication executive is much more than a message-maker, or even an image-maker. The tactical actions of communication are carried out in support of the strategic objectives of the corporation. Thus, the corporate role is foremost, and the communication element follows.

Once a strategic road map has been created, it must then be implemented. This is often done with departmental reorganizations, job shifts, new hiring programmes and the downsizing or elimination of entire departments, often done with the assistance of change management consultants who help the organization change without destroying the value of an initiative. All the physical and psychological changes, however, are facilitated through effective communication. These three basic characteristics of corporate communication in building and maintaining alignment are summarized in Figure 1.2.

Starting point 1: Gather relevant intelligence

Organizations gather intelligence in a variety of ways and using several specialists. Such experts usually identify information that is most useful for their own part of the organization. For instance, the research and development department searches for the most promising technologies and sciences that could improve the company's products and processes, whereas the legal department keeps watch on proposed legislation. Marketing looks for shifts in consumer behaviour and emerging needs. Corporate communication executives focus on more holistic types of information, which enables them to serve the organization as a totality. Communication managers have to know in detail what stakeholders know and believe about the organization. Gathering the required intelligence from employees and external groups requires substantial investments in time and money.

Gathering and using *external intelligence* can be distinguished at two levels. First, continuous tracking of social issues and beliefs about the company is aimed at understanding the reactions of these key stakeholders to the overall strategy and purpose of the organization. The information serves as input for decision-making about how to position – or adjust the positioning – of the company in relationships with corporate stakeholders such as financial analysts, governments and potential employees. Second, intelligence is needed to build alignment with stakeholders on specific strategic objectives that are extensions of the company's overall vision and purpose.

In order to implement a new strategy successfully, organizations depend on stakeholder consent, or at least a neutral position on the claims the company is making. Anticipating the beliefs and expectations of crucial external audiences requires serious investments in intelligence-gathering, both before introducing a strategy and after its launch. Especially large companies touch many segments in society; consequently, it is crucial for them to have a timely awareness of negative attitudes and even hostile behaviour of external advocacy and activist groups.

Creating alignment with external stakeholders is thus a matter of building and maintaining long-term relationships, a delicate matter indeed. Unlike with employees, external relationships are not greatly influenced by hierarchy or job security. Few external stakeholders have great emotional or financial dependency on a firm; investors, for example, can simply move their money elsewhere. Consequently, tracking the dominant trends in social issues – linked directly or indirectly to the new strategy – is one step towards developing a comprehensive grasp of the external context in which the company has to operate.

An organization also needs regularly to track its reputation at several levels, including its relative position within an industry and in each of the countries in which it does business. An essential aspect of using the intelligence wisely is frequently comparing the realities against the expectations of the company's managers. Knowing the gaps between desired strategy and facts and figures about external beliefs and behaviours is a crucial starting point for effective interventions, both in general executive actions and specific tactical communication.

Gathering intelligence aimed at understanding the external context in which a new strategy has to be implemented requires tracking and tracing the beliefs and behaviours of crucial *external* stakeholders – before launching the strategy and during its implementation.

For an illustration, let's look at Barclays, the giant financial institution based in the United Kingdom. Barclays' strategy is, according to its website: to achieve good growth through time by diversifying its business base and increasing its presence in markets and segments that are growing rapidly. This is driven by the ambition to become one of a handful of universal banks leading the global financial-services industry, helping customers and clients throughout the world achieve their goals. Barclays applies four strategic priorities: build the best bank in the UK; accelerate the growth of global businesses; develop retail and commercial banking activities in selected countries outside the UK; and enhance operational excellence.[2]

Becoming recognized as a leading global financial service company requires intelligence-gathering in retail and wholesale banking to see if key stakeholders hold an opinion of Barclays similar to the company's aspirations. This suggests that the bank also tracks the beliefs of customers, investors and government officials on whom the company depends to realize its ambition. In addition, one must assume that the company carefully monitors trends in public opinion regarding the role of banks in society at large.

In the aftermath of the first great recession of the twenty-first century, large segments of society are rightly suspicious of the financial services industry. Does it earn a fair profit and pay fair dividends to investors, while making loans that help businesses, consumers and society? Or, is it primarily dedicated to extracting large sums of money from the system, so that senior employees are handsomely compensated? There are important questions that have not yet been answered. But it seems to be understood clearly by Barclays, as the company shows purposeful illustrations of socially responsible behaviour on its website and in press statements. One example is a Social Intelligence report entitled 'Carbon capital: financing the low carbon economy'; another is recognition by the United Nations on community banking.

In addition to the overall beliefs people associate with Barclays, the bank also needs to gather intelligence on one extension of its strategy, which is to 'build the best bank in the UK'.[3] This requires specific intelligence, such as consumer demand for certain products and services, expectations around community involvement, and taking responsibility for helping customers understand the pros and cons of investing in complicated financial products. Evidence of being aware of those roles can be found too on Barclays' website. In addition to sponsoring the England and Wales Premier football league, various examples of community involvement and solutions to the financial illiteracy problem can be found in Barclay's publications.[4]

Another example is Philips, an electronics giant that, at the start of the twenty-first century, purposely shifted its product and market categories, which included lighting, components in computers, mobile telephones and consumer electronics such as televisions and compact discs, towards a health-care company that is also active in consumer lifestyle products. Category changes such as this can be explained easily to shareholders. Revenues from health-care products are substantially higher than from traditional consumer electronics and are less volatile than sales in the component market. However, explaining these changes to employees, some of whom may lose their job or be forced to work in an entirely different discipline, is exceptionally difficult.

Similar problems will be faced with retail chains, suppliers, local governments and various others who fear the negative consequences of a major strategic business shift by a large and influential corporation. In general, all companies that move out of well-established business lines and shift into others take intelligence-gathering seriously, simply to understand the viewpoints of stakeholders, who can make the

FIGURE 1.3 Barclays' sponsorship of the Premier League

change successful or delay its implementation. However, understanding does not mean that organizations have to adapt to the beliefs and preferences of those stakeholders.

In fact, companies have the right and even the obligation to be stubborn. Suppose that Philips asked consumer goods retailers about developing a health-care profile? Many might have objected. Visionary companies make their own choices, most of the time far ahead of current stakeholders. Intelligence-gathering should be focused on what stakeholders know and believe right now, combined with assessments about how they might react in the future when confronted with specific new developments.

As mentioned, explaining major changes to employees can be difficult. However, quite often they are a company's most crucial stakeholder group: the larger the gap between what top managers want employees to believe about a new strategy, and what survey data show about actual employee attitudes and behaviour, the more intense *internal* change processes have to be.

Gathering *internal* intelligence can be distinguished at two levels. The first relates to organizational characteristics, and the second to employees. Managers need to understand the identity traits that typify their organization. (Chapter 2 includes a detailed discussion of these traits, some of which are common to industries and others specific to companies.) Companies also need to understand employee attitudes, behaviours and support for strategic objectives. When management launches an internal programme aimed at stimulating desired actions, it is essential to measure the degree to which employees show supportive behaviour for the strategic objectives.

Table 1.1 summarizes the key elements for gathering internal and external intelligence.

The intensity of the degree of information gathering differs from situation to situation. However, a general rule of thumb on how much time and effort should be spent in elaborate intelligence-gathering is as follows:

TABLE 1.1 Gathering relevant corporate communication intelligence

Internal intelligence	External intelligence
Overall organizational identity traits	Issue scanning
Specific organizational identity traits	Stakeholder beliefs
Employee attitudes and behaviours	Specific intelligence

The more the strategic intentions of an organization require a fundamental shift in the existing dominant identity and reputation, the greater the necessity to spend time and effort gathering elaborate intelligence, to simplify a decision-making process that incorporates points of view of all crucial internal and external audiences upon whom the company depends for the new strategy to succeed.

Starting point 2: Select the right road map

There are two different road maps to alignment, each with variations in reaching either an internal or an external audience. But, in general, executives can choose either a negotiation-focused or a confrontation-focused approach to building alignment. Both extremes require different types and intensities of support from corporate communication professionals.

Explaining the strategy to stakeholders and adjusting its implementation and nuances in response to feedback characterize the negotiation model. An often-applied technique is *consulting* with crucial stakeholders to discover how prepared they are to support the company, or whether they'd offer little or no opposition. In addition, *dialogues* can be used to reach a mutually rewarding understanding or agreement. Building alignment with negotiation techniques usually engenders better and longer-lasting relationships with stakeholders, both inside and outside the organization.

That's not to suggest that a confrontation-based road map isn't useful, and even preferable in many cases. Confrontation techniques often involve a combination of low-risk interactions between company management and stakeholders, including a pair of techniques known as *mirroring* and *power play*. Mirroring is essentially selling a story about the strategy, using the persuasive techniques common in advertising and political communication. In a *power play*, a company might file a lawsuit against an opponent, hire key talent away from a competitor or take a firm stand in a public debate.

Clearly, the confrontational approach creates enemies, especially with stakeholders the company attacks. But it does not automatically mean that all other stakeholders react negatively. On the contrary, confrontation can generate respect for an organization that is expressly sticking to its values. An interesting example is the way producers of luxury goods – including Gucci handbags and Rolex watches

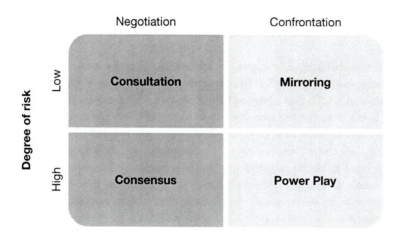

FIGURE 1.4 Road maps in creating alignment

– have attacked Chinese companies for their lack of respect for intellectual property, by producing inexpensive knock-offs of these products.

A mixture of negotiation and confrontation is also used with internal stake-holders. Most managers lean towards negotiation when trying to align colleagues with new strategic ideas. But confrontation-focused road maps are useful in crisis situations. For example, during the first few months of a merger – or in the case where a regulator forces a company fundamentally to shift its strategy – confrontation-based techniques, such as ordering employees to handle new or different tasks, without question and in a hurry, simply can't be avoided.

Developing an effective road map to internal and external alignment requires a balanced approach between negotiation and confrontation. Selecting the most appropriate road map requires managerial courage, but in combination with relevant intelligence about stakeholders and a clear anticipation of their reactions to the road map's style.

The four basic choices managers can apply in building alignment are summarized in Figure 1.4. The differences and details explaining which techniques can be distinguished and how they work are explained in Chapter 3 (internal road map to alignment) and Chapter 6 (external road map).

Starting point 3: Benefit from corporate communication efforts

Negotiation-focused strategies generally require a different type of support from communication professionals from those employing confrontation. In most negotiating strategies, the number of stakeholders is fairly limited. This allows managers to interact directly with group representatives. In these situations, the work of communication professionals mainly involves informing internal and external audiences of what has been done and why it's relevant, through common communication tools such as press releases, newsletters and additions to the organizational website.

When confrontation strategies are applied, the need for communication support increases exponentially. The reputation risks also rise, if only because the organization is taking up a bold and blunt position with a stakeholder. In addition, there is the potential for a confrontation to cascade, spilling over and attracting stakeholders who are even more threatening than the original adversary.

Truly effective communication professionals not only support executive management in media relations, but also help them develop sophisticated, long-term interactions with key stakeholders. Some industries have more elaborate experience with this approach than others. Banks, for example, were not that accustomed to the harsh and intense criticism that was levelled at them in recent public debates. When confronted with a bombardment of negative reactions following the 2008–9 fiasco over derivatives and bankruptcies, financial institutions were not fully prepared to react adequately.

Some industries are more accustomed to criticism and consumer activism, including food manufacturers and automotive, pharmaceutical and petrochemical companies. They increasingly seem well prepared for any challenge, showing advanced skills in reducing reputation damage. Such companies employ experienced professionals who are trained and practised in the arts of *issue management, public affairs* and *crisis communication*, the ultimate warriors in corporate firefighting, especially when dealing with confrontation applied from outside the company.

Confrontation strategies also need internal communication support. Employees need to be aligned with the company's identity and strategy long before any conflict arises, which is why employee communication is another important sub-speciality of the corporation communication function. However, organizations grow extremely vulnerable when their own employees do not fully support the claims made in confrontation strategies.

Employee communication professionals succeed – and are perceived by senior management as adding great value – when the organization's employees know, feel and act voluntarily in line with strategic intents. Such specialists are most often found in organizations that depend largely on their employees to create a competitive advantage. Service-oriented organizations, including airlines, retail and brokerage firms, often have large and extensive employee communication organizations, with subgroups devoted exclusively to dispersed business units.

Another communication speciality that is highly useful to senior management is *investor relations*. Often listed as an entity separate from corporate communication, the investor relations group deals with business journalists and handles the sensitive relations with financial analysts and regulators. Regulations require companies to communicate openly about highly technical financial topics, and, under several types of disclosure law, in an even-handed, timely and uniform manner with all audiences, so that no individual can take advantage of hearing the inside knowledge first, trading stock for profit before others hear the news, good or bad. Communicators in investor relations add organizational value when they not only successfully disclose financial information that's relevant to external stakeholders, but do so in a manner that enables analysts and journalists to understand and appreciate the choices made by the firm, and in turn write favourably about it or recommend the stock to clients.

Business-to-consumer companies in industries such as retail, food and automotive have a great deal of practice in *marketing communications*. These communicators create product awareness and appreciation that maintain and increase sales. The value added by the function is mainly supporting sales and increasing brand value for the company.

All these specialists in communication jointly provide support in building and maintaining internal and external alignment in two complementary ways. First, communication specialists have to establish lasting *foundations*, used as a starting point for developing communication activities about the company in general. This is done in four steps:

1   The first is codifying the basic *rules and directives* of the corporation's communication, introducing nomenclature (house style, naming etc.), launching handbooks for branding or sponsorship policies, and defining daily routines in media relations.
2   The second step is the *organization of the communication function*. This requires clarity about the way tasks and budgets are allocated, plus the procedures used to link the commercial processes to the communication roles.
3   The third step is *gathering intelligence* for the company. Other departments also gather intelligence, including strategic planning's studies of competitors, or marketers who collect data about consumer satisfaction. However, communication specialists watch for general trends inside and outside the organization, scanning for threats that might derail the firm's position or progress. Corporate communication specialists look at a wide variety of issues and reputation research.
4   The fourth step in developing a distinctive *corporate positioning* is the use of a corporate story to illustrate the organization's nature and purpose. GE's ecomagination campaign puts the company at the forefront of the technologies that produce power from environmentally clean and sustainable sources. It tells stories about creativity in wind, solar and other forms of power production, and the imagination that can be applied to conservation. Whereas GE is a massive company, making everything from military jet engines to sophisticated medical devices, ecomagination projects a company that's devoted to servicing society and the environment in which its people live.

A second key role for corporate communication managers is developing tailor-made strategic *communication programmes* aimed at building external alignment about particular strategic objectives. This is most often done in five steps:

1   Setting the starting points that have to be used as a logical consequence of the *overall corporate-branding promise* and *determining* which structure is dominant: monolithic, branded or endorsed? The second step in this phase is simply determining *which competitors* have to be taken into consideration, and what, in comparison, are *their* strongest characteristics.
2   Gathering *additional* specialized intelligence in the context of the nature of the strategic objective; for instance, gathering data about genetically modified (GM) food requires different intelligence from knowledge aimed at improving shareholder value.
3   Deciding how to *position* the communication support in the overall context of the road map that the company is applying regarding a specific strategic objective.
4   Transforming the choices into messages than can be used in the *execution* of the communication support. All these decisions result in messages that have to be implemented.
5   *Evaluating* the successes and failures of this specific communication programme, resulting in adaptation aimed at increasing the degree of alignment around this specific issue.

The conditions under which corporate communication managers can contribute most successfully to the creation of sustainable alignment can be summarized as follows: benefiting from effective corporate communication efforts requires creating lasting *foundations* of corporate communication and using them in a consistent way

FIGURE 1.5 GE's ecomagination advertisement

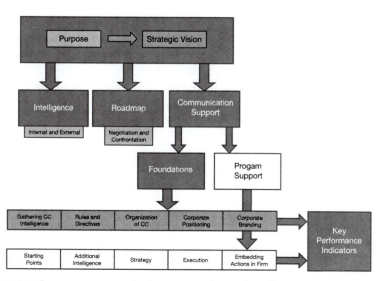

FIGURE 1.6 Corporate communication support in creating alignment

in *specific communication programmes* aimed at building enduring alignment with internal and external audiences.

The two roles of corporate communication are visualized in Figure 1.6.

Finally: the never-ending pursuit to create alignment

Building and maintaining alignment around core strategic issues are difficult for organizations, as they require a high degree of trust among a large variety of stakeholders. Even the most trusted organizations can be hit by reputation problems, be it through actions that are illegal or considered immoral or simply through a huge mistake in business judgement. Hard-earned reputations can, however, recover from unforeseen events that shed an ill light upon an organization, mainly because of the care and effort that have gone into building relationships and alignment with a wide range of stakeholders. No matter whether the institution is a for-profit company, a non-profit advocacy group or a government entity, all are being judged by a number of interested parties.

If a highly rated reputation facilitates an organization's interactions with stakeholders and, in turn, helps the institution meet its goals, alignment is the desired behavioural consequence of reputation. An organization that is able to align with internal and external stakeholders is given much more latitude and the benefit of the doubt, should the organization's acts or behaviour ever be questioned.

Given this dynamic, it behoves corporations to include professional communication experts in all business discussion, elevating the discipline to the same level as legal, human resources, strategic planning and operations. In turn, professional communicators must help the organization define its core mission with the most authentic and resonant description possible. While developing the organization's key messages for various audiences, professional communicators must also anticipate on issues in the social context of their firm that can either be a threat or an opportunity and that enable an organization to create a thought leadership position with factual proof points and appealing communications. This should guide most of the corporation's interactions with stakeholders and will enable an organization to build and maintain sustainable alignment with crucial stakeholders it depends upon.

Notes

1   R.S. Kaplan and D.P. Norton, *Alignment. Using the balanced scorecard to create corporate energies*, Boston: Harvard Business School Press, (2006).
2   Barclays Group website, http://group.barclays.com/About-us/Who-we-are-and-what-we-do/Our-vision-and-strategy (accessed 5 March 2011).
3   Barclays Group website, http://group.barclays.com/About-us/Sponsorship (accessed 5 March 2011).
4   Barclays Group website, http://group.barclays.com/Media-Centre/Barclays-news/News Article/1231784854970.html (accessed 5 March 2011).

PART I

Building internal alignment

2

GATHERING INTELLIGENCE INSIDE THE ORGANIZATION

Generating internal support for new strategic objectives requires having fundamental intelligence about the organization. Specifically, three discrete clusters of information must be, not only gathered, but also tested, to allow understanding of the fit between the new objectives and the existing beliefs plus actual behaviour of employees.

Cluster 1 focuses on the overall identity characteristics of an organization. Most organizations have one of four holistic identities, which are more or less common to a specific sector or industry. Some large corporations may contain more than one of these characteristics, especially when there are departments or operating companies with diverse missions. Still, individual organizations mostly fall into one of the following categories: *bureaucratic, accountability, shared meaning* and *ideology*. Each of these paradigms speaks volumes about employee motivation and behaviour and the kinds of message that resonate in the specific culture.

Cluster 2 focuses on specific identity traits that are desired, projected and perceived. These traits are characteristics *unique* to an individual organization. Albert and Whetten[1] state that such specific identity traits have to express the organizational core in continuity, centrality and distinctiveness. For example, *continuity traits* are those traditions, practices and expressions that show a link between the past and the present. *Centrality traits* show the degree to which certain characteristics are evenly spread throughout the organization. Finally, *distinctiveness traits* are those characteristics that are almost unique to a given organization and that are not found at competitors or similar-sized firms. Although seemingly dry on the surface, these terms actually represent the lifeblood of any corporation or institution. Only by understanding the feelings, emotions, motivations and behaviours that flow from these traits can communicators build an authentic and compelling story – or stories – that helps generate acceptance of, and support for, a strategy.

Cluster 3 focuses on attitudes and behaviour that are already aligned with strategy, and the degree to which employees show their support. Something of an acid test, the third cluster reveals whether alignment has actually taken place, and it's something that can be tested only after the launch and implementation of a strategic initiative. A summary of the three levels of internal intelligence-gathering is shown in Table 2.1.

Let's illustrate the consequences of intelligence-gathering, using the purely hypothetical example of the American express-delivery company FedEx and the introduction of its Access strategy. Although the following analysis of what might have happened around that introduction is merely an informed assumption, the actual Access strategy is explained on the company's website: see Box 2.1.

Competitors of FedEx in the logistics and delivery industry, including UPS, DHL or TNT, all offer logistic services enabling customers to ship physical products from points A to B in a safe, transparent and cost-effective way. In many respects, they all focus on improving worldwide trade. However, FedEx clearly has taken a variety of initiatives, supported by appealing communications, that make the company a thought leader in stimulating global free trade. The company has even created a public index gauging the degree of trade access in countries around the world and, through lobbying, actively promotes it.

The basic ideas behind Access are simple and can be easily understood, at least from an intellectual point of view. However, the key problem seems to be how to communicate this to lower levels of employees in such a way that it provides a clear idea of what, for example, couriers should *do* to show behaviour that supports the Access concept. For obvious reasons, FedEx used a simpler message in explaining the strategy to couriers, the so-called 'Purple Promise' to 'make every FedEx experience outstanding'. Easy, yes, but there is depth in the identity beneath the simple slogan.

Let's now apply those three clusters to FedEx, starting with an assessment of its *overall identity*. The company is well known for the following traits: FedEx has a strong identification with its CEO. There is clear recognition and support for the future direction of FedEx, inside and outside the company. There is also a high degree of self-determination at the business unit level. And last, but not least, the vision embodied by Access is perceived as an appealing example of thought leadership in the world of global trade. This tends to suggest that FedEx could be characterized as having a *shared meaning* overall identity.

Shared meaning does not exactly fit with the company's structure and the self-determination of business units. Such decentralization and independence seem to run counter to the identity descriptor. Consequently, any communication programme must be built around a powerful narrative, one that skilfully argues that the units of a decentralized organization can work well together if they embrace and act in alignment with the ideals expressed by Access.

Let's also assume that research about the *specific identity traits* reveals that the gaps between the desired and the projected identities are limited. And, although the distinctions between the desired and the perceived identities are not enormous, they do show a fundamental difference in traits as 'hierarchy', and again

Table 2.1 Internal intelligence

Internal intelligence	Focus points
Overall organizational identity	Bureaucracy
	Accountability
	Shared meaning
	Ideology
Specific organizational identity	Desired organizational identity
	Projected organizational identity
	Perceived organizational identity
Supportive employee attitude and behaviour	Employee engagement
	Employee alignment

Box 2.1 FEDEX ACCESS STRATEGY

Access is the force that makes all forms of interaction and exchange possible between people, businesses and nations.

Access, put simply, is the ability to connect. Access is powered by anything that makes it easier for people and businesses to connect with each other – whether it's a smartphone or a computer or the ability to ship a package overnight to anywhere in the world.

When Access expands, it empowers people with the ability and confidence to improve their current conditions and future prospects. Access creates new opportunities, accelerates and simplifies global connections and changes what's possible.

Access gained its force from the collective efforts of many people and businesses, but FedEx has been the driving force behind many milestones and advances in Access. Express delivery was a historic breakthrough in Access, collapsing the time and distance between places and connecting people everywhere.

FedEx is a tireless advocate for Access and the opportunities that come with it, because FedEx knows that Access drives positive change. Our company has become a student of Access, analyzing its impact on everything from global corporations to remote villages.

FIGURE 2.1 FedEx Purple Promise

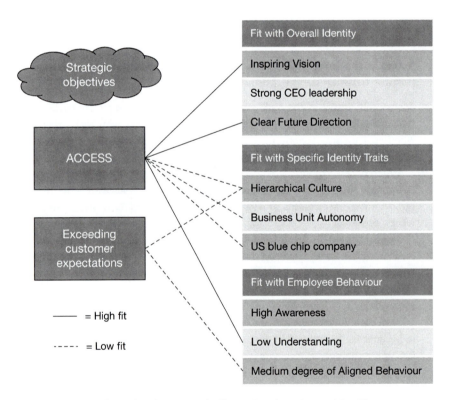

FIGURE 2.2 Hypothetical FedEx example illustrating three internal intelligence approaches

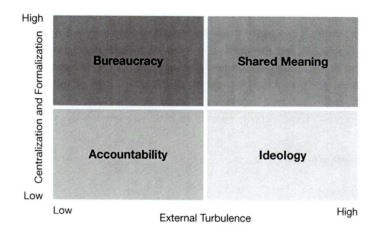

FIGURE 2.3 Four types of overall organizational identity

decentralization, with a prevailing desire for specific operations to be seen and treated as autonomous business units.

Finally, a test is required to measure *supportive employee behaviour*, in combination with the degree of awareness, understanding and supportive attitude, all of which together drive that behaviour. Again, imagine the study reveals that many lower-level FedEx employees simply don't understand the strategic objectives, or, more specifically, do not have full clarity about what it means for their daily routines and what, if anything, they're supposed to do differently. To resolve this issue, the company must frequently expose those employees to corporate messages, carried in simple success stories that embody a splendid execution of the strategy. Moreover, this can be combined with training opportunities and/or dialogue sessions where the implementation is regularly discussed. The three types of internal-intelligence approach are summarized in Figure 2.2.

Overall identity traits

In academic and managerial literature, many classification schemes can be found typifying organizations in categories that are coloured by a specific dominant culture,[2] structure[3] or by a resemblance of characteristics assumed to be typical of ancient Greek gods.[4] As I am focusing on the role of *communication*, I have developed a new classification. Although inspired by the previously mentioned types, mine is significantly based on the degree of external pressure to which organizations are exposed, combined with the nature of the internal organization. In my opinion, each organization type has a common collection of identity characteristics that are crucial to a communication professional developing an attractive story about the organization and the specific strategy.

Of course, organizations are living organisms that continually change. For this reason, it's unlikely that many would fit perfectly within only one of the quadrants seen in Figure 2.3, but the division is intended to help understand which basic types exist. Executives responsible for initiating major changes in a company's culture and business practices would be wise to search which type of organization they are today, and which type they desire to be in the near future. The characteristics of each organizational identity, mentioned here, can simplify this search process.

Accountability

General traits

Exposed to limited external turbulence or advocacy-group conflict, such organizations are generally decentralized and informal.

Management vision

A high-performance organization in which employees decide how to create substance around their tasks and are stimulated by clear, predetermined rewards for reaching their goals.

Overall organizational intent

There are strong, performance-based mentalities here, with employees holding a high level of autonomy.

Characteristics

A clear rewards structure for professionals, with either short or extremely long careers. The organization focuses strongly on its own market sector. Specific department objectives are primary, with low identification with overall organizational goals.

Communication demands

Very clear key performance indicators (KPIs) of what someone is expected to contribute individually, so that it is clear whether an employee is successful or not. Success is rewarded, for example, by a partnership in a law firm, or tenure for a university professor. Success typically correlates with a high level of job satisfaction. In an ideal situation, an employee sees him- or herself as an independent entrepreneur within the larger context of the organization. Supervisors must communicate exactly what is expected of the individual during annual performance reviews, in combination with regular feedback sessions where KPI scores and ways to improve numbers are explored. Motivating and involving people here occur mainly through a one-to-one dialogue, although it is sometimes complemented by a more mass-media approach. Communicators emphasize proof of how clear accountability leads to the organization's success.

Examples

The accountability identity is often seen in large law, industrial, accounting and consultancy firms. At Chevron, the California-based international oil giant, employee performance is typically measured over several dimensions, including those of the individual, the business unit and the corporation as a whole. Financial measures are balanced against safety performance, both individual and collective, and there is an emphasis on matters over which managers and rank-and-file employees have control. Bonuses vary greatly and rise sharply as an employee moves up in pay grade, but the payout is based on a numerical formula that is quite clear, especially for managers and executives. Meanwhile, people in refineries think little about colleagues in offshore exploration. Identification is much more centred on a specific business unit, rather than the corporation – except for the relatively small number of employees reporting to the corporate centre. Such accountability is common to the petroleum industry.

Bureaucracy

General

Low external turbulence combines with a high level of centralization and formalization.

Management vision

This is a primary process that increases the predictability of outcomes and strengthens the support of internal forces – and the officials who are directly served – as well as that of the external political environment.

Overall organization intent

This is to contribute to a greater cause that improves the quality of life in a society.

Characteristics

Equality in providing services is a democratic right and a democratic duty, where transparency in actions is necessary to stimulate and reinforce a sense of justice and a mutual dependency on the political climate.

Communications demands

It is necessary to establish clear and detailed guidelines about what the members of the organization must do, with the ultimate goal of gaining external support for the organization's continued and largely unchanged existence. Internal consensus is based on the belief that following rules generates external legitimacy, which is then the organization's *raison d'être*. Communication is frequently top–down and includes instructions that are audited by line managers who report back up on the fulfilment of the orders. Members of the organization need to know exactly how they can give substance to the daily routines that shape the primary processes. Identity is stimulated by emphasizing the disadvantages facing those in organizations without clear rules and where there is not the same degree of job security.

Examples

Many government organizations operate in this manner, including the military, public ministries, police and fire departments. To a certain extent, this is also apparent in semi-public organizations, such as in the fields of health care and social work.

Shared meaning

General

There is a high degree of external turbulence in combination with a high level of centralization and formal operations.

Management vision

When members of the organization experience the leadership and especially the vision of their organization as inspiring, they will be more stimulated to put in active and appropriate effort for their company.

Overall organizational intent

This involves strong identification with the president or CEO and the dominant logic that he or she articulates about the organization's unique values and trust in the future. The culture here is strongly 'in-group' versus a real, manufactured or even imagined 'out-group'.

Characteristics

Organizations will be more successful if employees are inspired by the thought leadership expressed by the most senior executives, resulting in a high degree of self-determination to expend discretionary personal time and effort to stimulate organizational performance.

Communications demands

These concern pointing out a clear future direction that is convincingly 'sold' to members of the organization by middle managers, such that they are able to address the right issues successfully. The capacity of management to make front-line employees feel as if they are an important part of the operation (self-categorization), that their contributions are appreciated (self-enhancement), forms the critical success factor. Self-categorization comes with the idea that, 'if you do not embrace the shared meaning, you are not part of the group'. Self-enhancement is developed through introducing a compelling and codified version of: the company's shared principles, which is the case at 3M; its core values, which is done at Sony; or through a credo, which is the case at Johnson & Johnson. Communication professionals support top management at town-hall meetings and through websites and corporate publications, which frequently reiterate the firm's values and the role of a charismatic CEO.

Examples

Many companies try to reach a strategic consensus in this manner. One good example is Southwest Airlines, a high-performance organization where employees are encouraged to be individuals with a sense of humour, even as the airline has one of the best on-time departure and arrival rates in the business, offers low-cost fares and doesn't charge extra for bags. The humour and generally pleasant, shared atmosphere around this airline enable passengers to overlook crowded compartments, older aircraft and bare-bones service – trivialities compared with the total offering.

Ideology

General

This involves high external turbulence in combination with a low level of centralization and formalization.

Management vision

A strong ideology is almost always sufficient to inspire people, individually and collectively, to perform what the organization requires. Thus, management can focus nearly all of its energy on its goal, with less time devoted to managing people than in other types of organization.

Overall organizational intent

This is an idealistic and almost dogmatic operation, where all employees have a clear distinction between what they believe is right and wrong, while having little room for, or patience with, differing opinions.

Characteristics

Open, democratic societies are entitled to have professional advocates focusing on the promotion of one issue, whether it is a respect for animal rights, preserving ancient forests or pressuring an undemocratic nation on its human rights policies, or lack thereof. Clarity in the organization's key goal simplifies internal coherence and identification among volunteers and employees, who are all fully aligned with the objective. Internal conflicts never focus on the nature of the goals, but only on the speed and the nature of the means to achieve them.

Communications demands

The core elements of the ideology need to be supported 100 per cent at all times. Messages make it implicit that differing from the ideology would lead to removal from the organization through social control mechanisms, although this can be an unspoken given. Success in the external arena is repeatedly featured and quoted in internal communications. Influencing public opinion is seen as not only serving an internal goal, but also contributing to society. Communications repeatedly define what needs to be seen as ideologically correct.

Examples

Greenpeace, Oxfam, the Sierra Club and many other idealistic groups use these principles to publicize their ideals worldwide. Yet another good example is the Body Shop, where its late founder, Anita Roddick, set out five abiding values for the organization: stand against animal testing; support community trade; protect the planet; activate self-esteem; and defend human rights. For the people who work at the Body Shop, the organization's ideals could not be clearer.

Fit between strategic issues and overall identity traits

The first step in gathering intelligence about overall identity traits is determining the present dominant paradigm. The second step is deciding whether or not a shift is necessary towards a new, more desirable paradigm, given the demands that are linked to the nature of the strategic objectives. The accountability model can typify, for example, most global law and consultancy firms, such as Baker & McKenzie, PricewaterhouseCoopers (PwC) or KPMG. Key identity traits include 'working with a clear performance and reward structure at individual level', 'having either a long career and becoming a partner' or a short one, facilitated by valuable professional experiences, that leads to a well-paid position elsewhere. These traits all fit with the central belief notion of the *accountability* perspective: that performance will be higher when employees feel and act like owners in their daily work.

Many consultancy and law firms in the twenty-first century are shifting towards a more globally integrated structure and culture, which is a form of centralization.

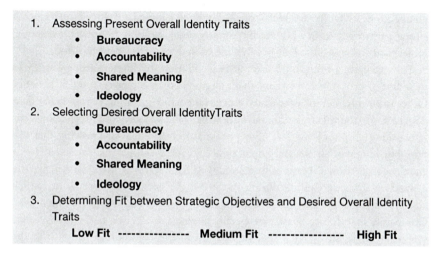

1. Assessing Present Overall Identity Traits
    - **Bureaucracy**
    - **Accountability**
    - **Shared Meaning**
    - **Ideology**
2. Selecting Desired Overall IdentityTraits
    - **Bureaucracy**
    - **Accountability**
    - **Shared Meaning**
    - **Ideology**
3. Determining Fit between Strategic Objectives and Desired Overall Identity Traits

    Low Fit ---------------- **Medium Fit** ----------------- **High Fit**

FIGURE 2.4 Assessing fit between strategic objective and overall identity traits

As a result, local autonomy is replaced by a broader, regional market focus, combining specialists from various countries into teams that aim to serve global clients in an effective way. This way of working requires identity traits that are more in line with the *shared meaning* perspective, stimulating employees by presenting them with a unifying, inspiring idea such as a Baker & McKenzie type of change programme. The new paradigm requires the introduction of driving forces rooted in what I call 'collective sense-making mechanisms'. And yet, its introduction will of course create conflicts, as it challenges the old driving forces that were built on individual rewards and, above all, recognition.

Such problems, in my opinion, are no reason to stick with the old paradigm. If management is convinced that a new strategy will yield a competitive advantage, then one has to accept the consequences of the shift towards another paradigm. The final decision on whether or not to change is made in the third step – honestly assessing which overall identity traits best fit the requirements of the strategic objectives. In the example of the global legal consultancy firms, a set of traits, such as working with 'one vision', and a regional decision-making structure are good arguments for shifting from an accounting paradigm towards a shared meaning perspective. A summary of these three steps can be found in Figure 2.4.

Specific organizational identity traits

Besides the four clusters with overall identity characteristics, organizations also have more specific customs, traditions, routine behaviours and even an occasional bad habit, which gives them a certain kind of individualism, not unlike a person. Although groups of companies may share more similarities than differences, each is one of a kind, at least in some dimension. If a company is to differentiate itself from its competition – whether for recruitment, retaining talented employees, earning the closest partnership with a community or any other business advantage – it should understand and make the best possible use of those specific characteristics.

For example, a firm could take pride in offering the highest average salary in its industry, or a mid-level salary that's augmented by a generous set of benefits. Other firms might emphasize casual attire and encourage employees to bring their dogs to work, today fairly routine in California's Silicon Valley high-tech and social-networking corporations. Still others provide free meals, well knowing that this promotes long work hours and a tight, symbiotic relationship between the employee and the corporation. Occasionally, a Southwest Airlines flight attendant will practise a stand-up comedy routine during the pre-flight safety announcements, which actually attracts more passengers to listen and lightens the day of fellow employees. Companies that donate heavily to specific charities, or, better, free employees for volunteer work thus have a specific identity in the community and also in the minds of those who are employed, or who are considering employment.

A person attending a job interview will be first and foremost interested in the specific job that's being offered. Soon thereafter, the applicant will want to know in what kind of company he or she will be working: is it large or small, national or international? In what types of business is it involved? Although these kinds of objective issue can be easily researched on the Internet and understood by prospective employees, the true personality of the organization is never wholly obvious nor easily discovered. However, it's that personality that will ultimately determine if a prospective employee will be attracted to the firm and, later, if a job offer is tendered and accepted, and if he or she is inspired to make maximum effort.

That does not automatically mean that a fundamental change in strategy will hold appeal for all employees, especially if they perceive a misfit between the nature of the organizational identity and the demands arising from the new strategy. That is why it is vital to understand in-depth beliefs of employees and their collective opinion about the organization's most important traits.

Wikipedia rightly typifies an organization as a social arrangement that pursues collective goals, controls its own performance and that has a boundary separating it from its environment.[5] In order for the organization to be successful, there needs to be an agreement between people to start a joint undertaking in which the members of the organization collectively pursue targets. In other words, the members are jointly responsible for the final performances that will be delivered. However, all are restricted by the boundaries their environment imposes on them, including demanding regulations or competitors slowing down the firm's growth potential by capturing an increasing market share.

The applicant mentioned earlier will have to deal with the ramifications of this arrangement, including matters of organizational trust and discretionary effort. When an employee signs a contract or employment agreement, he or she has entered a social arrangement. The contract itself is not that meaningful, in that more and more people perceive a job as a temporary interruption to the ultimate career they envisage. Conversely, an increasing number of employers seem to prefer temporary employment contracts to lifelong employment. Still, no social arrangement will succeed unless all parties are convinced they will somehow benefit by it. Because there is interdependence between the collective and the individual, neither can function without the other. Thus, the professional communicator understands the foundations of the relationships between the organization and its people and creates messages that resonate with the implicit and explicit aspects of the bond.

Which specific identity traits have to be used?

Creating a company's specific identity characteristic list can be a relatively easy task, especially if it's drawn up by a CEO in consultation with a communication director, with the caveat that both have spent enough years with the firm fully to appreciate its cultural subtleties. Experience in management consulting has taught me that the vision of senior management is decisive and most often predominates in the development of communication content and materials. However, I've also learned that ignoring the opinions of managers and employees in lower echelons will have a negative effect on the speed and completeness of implementing any kind of change.

Simply put, there will be a variety of visions within any organization about its most typical characteristics, even at the board of management level. What this suggests is that any organization probably has multiple identities. Although this need not be a problem, it can become an issue when senior management and communications professionals do not realize or acknowledge that multiple identities exist, or if they do not reflect and make use of those traits in stories, advertisements, position papers and marketing collateral that present the company to stakeholders.

Such traits will typically fall into three *perspectives*, which are usually differentiated into two clusters. The first cluster is influenced heavily by senior management's vision and can be labelled as *desired* and *projected* identity. The second reflects the employee perspective, which is the so-called *perceived* identity. Each results in a description of what is seen as typical for the organization (see also Figure 2.5).

Each perspective results in a list of words. Although such lists are partly overlapping, there are also vital differences. Being aware of these similarities and distinctions is an important stepping stone in finding a road map that will create alignment of employees and strategy.

To illustrate a working example of three perspectives, consider data gathered for Postbank, long a widely admired brand in the Netherlands. Postbank was one of the three firms that merged in 1991 to create the International Netherlands Group, or ING. Today, ING has become a commercial powerhouse, with 105,000 employees and worldwide recognition. The ING corporate name was originally used only with financial audiences. At first, it borrowed Postbank's iconic blue lion symbol, but then converted it to the Netherlands' national colour, orange.

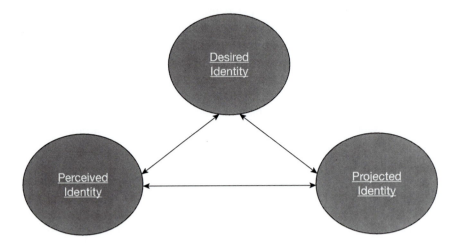

FIGURE 2.5 Identity traits in three perspectives

As the ING brand became increasingly recognized – and used commercially around the globe – its management began to question the need for, and expense of, maintaining a separate Postbank brand and identity.

The ING board of management signalled their intentions for Postbank during the first decade of the twenty-first century, when all of Postbank's advertisements and literature described it as 'a member of the ING Group'. This generated a great deal of emotion among Postbank employees, who were aware that ING was considering the elimination of the brand. Examples for the three perspectives of identity shown here were gathered in surveys taken during that time of uncertainty and organizational stress, as no final decision about eliminating the Postbank brand had yet been made.[6]

Postbank operated independently in the Dutch market, with a strong focus on customer service, an extending product portfolio that served not only traditional retail needs but increasingly the commercially attractive business-to-business market. The fears of Postbank employees came to a head in 2007, when ING eliminated the Postbank brand and integrated the institution into a newly created entity under the name ING. External stakeholders expressed anger, including customers and even Dutch branding experts, who accused ING of destroying one of the nation's most esteemed brands. The ground truth, however, came from market research, which showed that, although Postbank's brand was highly appreciated by the majority of the Dutch population, most of the bank's customers simply used their accounts to deposit salary payments and pay bills – low-value stuff in the world of finance.[7] Postbank's commercial value had been waning for years, which made the value of maintaining the brand economically questionable. Although misperceptions drove public criticism of ING and its board for a period of time, the numbers supported a wholly pragmatic and sound business decision.

Orange lion   Blue lion   Orange lion   Orange lion

FIGURE 2.6 ING and Postbank lions

The case study that follows deals with the period before ING Group decided to delete the Postbank brand. Elstak *et al.* (2010) carried out three studies to assess the special identity characteristics – *desired*, *projected* and *perceived* – of the bank and evaluate them in the context of the new strategic objectives, which were improving customer focus and extending product portfolio to more attractive offerings.

Desired organization identity

Compiling a list of desired organizational identity characteristics is absolutely essential, as these reflect the wishes of senior management. Few strategic objectives are ever reached without the support of an organization's leadership team. Most often, the executives know exactly what characteristics they'd like to predominate in the organization. However, in taking a closer look at the words used by the leadership team to describe the desired identity, we often find that their terminology can be shared perfectly with the board of management and other top managers, but is harder to explain to people in lower echelons. It's not for lack of intelligence, but context. Executives function in a realm full of jargon and code words with meaning to someone who has a well-informed and macroscopic view of a corporation's business. And yet, those words often say little to rank and file employees.

The desired identity traits can be gathered in focus-group sessions with top managers, for example by using the so-called consensus method. This method systematically maps what executive participants see as crucial organizational characteristics. To give a brief outline, such a meeting will generate a list of characteristics that map the eight leading identity characteristics that focus on 'how we judge our performance at this moment' versus characteristics that focus on 'how it should be' in the organization. This provides a first indication, in quantitative terms, of

TABLE 2.2 Desired organizational identity of Postbank

Characteristic	Present situation	Desired situation	Gap
1 Commercial	6.0	7.7	1.7
2 Close to customer	5.5	7.5	2.0
3 Service driven	4.7	7.0	2.3
4 Extending product portfolio to high-end market segment	5.2	7.5	2.3
5 Expert in retail banking	7.8	8.7	0.9
6 Independent	8.2	8.2	0.0
7 Excellent in mass production	7.5	8.0	0.5
8 Job security	7.9	7.5	−0.4

what management believes to be the essence of the desired organizational identity. An example of the outcome of such a focus-group meeting at Postbank can be seen in Table 2.2.

Projected organizational identity

Projected identity can be described as the self-presentation of the organization through communications, expressing the traits that management believes – or wants to believe – are typical of the organization, both explicitly on websites and in corporate brochures and speeches, and implicitly through the architecture of buildings, quality requirements of vendors and in the design of messages. The projections are fairly easily deduced from an analysis of a few key expressions. The 'About us' section on the website is most telling, as are stories in the company's internal magazine and its annual report.

The projected identity of a centralized organization is quickly obvious and consistent throughout a well-run operation with a skilled communication function. When an organization operates in a more decentralized way – and especially if it is active in multiple product-market combinations and in a number of different countries – it becomes more complex to develop a list that shows consistency of purpose.

I encountered a practical example during a recent visit to PwC in New York, where I listened to a lecture on the credit crunch and what PwC believed it could do to assist companies to minimize the consequences. On departure, everyone who attended received a beautiful set of brochures, stating the causes of financial crises and what PwC could do to assist. Upon my return to the Netherlands I found that the local PwC office had worked on a similar brochure. Although it described similar causes and offered more or less similar solutions, it was clear that both brochures were produced independently. Consistency would have saved the

TABLE 2.3 Projected organizational identity characteristics of Postbank[8]

Projected organizational identity items for Postbank
1   Postbank's products are suited for the self-reliant customer
2   Customers who are self-reliant are well served by Postbank
3   At Postbank, employees do not stand above the customer; they work together with the customer
4   Postbank is the ideal bank to take care of your finances from home
5   As a customer, you can fully trust that Postbank will take good care of your finances
6   At Postbank, customers can conduct their financial activities in a safe and secure environment
7   Postbank communicates straightforwardly
8   Postbank communicates transparently
9   At Postbank customers get value for their money
10   Postbank is accessible for the customer
11   Postbank is innovative
12   Postbank works with the state of the art in technology
13   At Postbank, we abide by the rules, not because we have to, but because we want to
14   At Postbank, we always conduct our business in an honest and fair manner
15   At Postbank, we offer financial services to retail and business-to-business prospects
16   Postbank is honest and open to the customer about the risks of our products
17   At Postbank, customer satisfaction is a top priority
18   At Postbank, our service revolves around attention, speed, simplicity and accuracy
19   At Postbank, we strive for structural, profitable growth
20   At Postbank, we aim for a stronger sales force
21   At Postbank, we will do everything to make sure that our core processes run smoothly
22   At Postbank, we will do everything to enhance quality and lower costs
23   At Postbank, we try to work as efficiently as possible
24   At Postbank, the customer is central
25   Postbank makes things easy for the customer
26   Postbank keeps its promises
27   Postbank treats me fairly

organization time and money and also decreased the chances of conflicting messages on a sensitive topic.

Although national differences are understandable, company-wide research into what's wanted in a projected identity could prevent undesirable or inconsistent messages from being introduced. No matter how diverse and multinational a company might be, the authenticity and consistency of corporate-wide internal beliefs are important to the faith employees have in their employer, who in a sense is representing them to the outside world.

Listing projected organizational identity characteristics is therefore extremely relevant. What's more, it is frequently an eye-opener for all those involved to see the diversity of descriptions that are being used in their own organization. Table 2.3 shows a selection of projected organizational identity traits at Postbank.[9]

Perceived organizational identity

One can look at specific organizational identity traits from the perspectives of both management and employees, simply by asking them to describe the traits they believe to be most typical of the organization. For communicators, the perceptions of employees are crucial, as they are the targets of messages conceived and articulated by senior executives. And the insights are most reliable if they are taken from a cross-section of employees throughout the organization.

Such perceptions are naturally coloured by the position each subject holds, but especially in hierarchical institutions where supervisors have a strong influence over what subordinates perceive and believe. Critical too is the length of time the person has been active in the organization, as veteran employees have seen numerous strategies and initiatives come and go. The nature of an individual's personal and social identity also carries weight in their perceptions. That is, a person will describe the organization in positive terms when it corresponds with his or her personal and social identity preferences, or in more negative terms in cases where it deviates.

An example of the kinds of characteristic people mention about Postbank in the context of perceived identity can be found in Table 2.4. It is apparent that, for workers at this firm, some of the perceptions differ greatly from what the company attempts to project. The most striking differences focus on the willingness to stay independent. Apparently, employees did not believe that Postbank was acting autonomously. Neither did they believe that the bank offered a broad product portfolio, at least not yet. Such mixed feelings and jarringly opposing sentiments are, of course, common to a large cross-section of people in most institutions. But management needs to know to what degree these mixed feelings are broadly spread throughout the organization.

Fit between strategic issues and specific identity traits

The Postbank case illustrates the complexity of implementing a new strategic objective internally. Aiming at increasing the degree of customer focus, plus extending the product portfolio towards more attractive, high-end market segments may sound logical and obvious, but appears to be received internally with less enthusiasm than management expected. This was partly caused by the perceived threat among employees that the holding company (ING Group) would abandon the autonomous Postbank brand and wrap the operation into a more integrated ING brand. Employees also appeared to be less positive about the qualities of the bank compared

TABLE 2.4 List with perceived organizational identity characteristics[10]

Perceived organizational identity characteristics

1   Postbank is good at mass production of simple products

2   At Postbank, you have job security

3   Employees often stay with Postbank because of the attractive secondary benefits

4   At Postbank, procedures are followed in detail

5   At Postbank, ambitious managers get the chance to prove themselves

6   At Postbank, maximizing profit has the highest priority

7   Postbank is a dynamic company

8   At Postbank, you get a lot of responsibility

9   At Postbank, you have the freedom to develop your own ideas

10   Postbank is arrogant

11   At Postbank, you have to put yourself out there and be visible in order to get ahead

12   At Postbank, nepotism plays a big role in your career

13   At Postbank, you have good internal career opportunities

14   Postbank suffers from a generation gap; there is a big difference between the younger and the older employees

15   Postbank has a complex structure, which makes it difficult to see where the responsibilities lie

16   At Postbank, you often have to work together with departments that have conflicting interests

17   It is good for your career with the parent company (ING) to have worked at Postbank

18   Important strategic decisions are made by the parent company (ING) and not by Postbank

19   It is important for Postbank to be part of the parent company

20   It is important that we keep the Postbank brand

21   Adding 'part of the parent company' in our corporate communication is of added value to Postbank

22   At Postbank, we say 'act as normal as possible'

23   At Postbank, we work very hard

24   Postbank has a flat organizational structure

25   Postbank is unique in Dutch financial services

26   At Postbank, employees have a tendency to evade their responsibilities

27   There is a pleasant work atmosphere at Postbank

28   Postbank becomes increasingly individualistic: everyone for him- or herself

29   At Postbank, we work in teams; you are not supposed to go about on your own

30   Postbank has a strong consensus culture; everyone is involved in everything

31   At Postbank, all your activities are monitored; it's like 'big brother is watching you'

32   It is very important at Postbank that you meet your personal targets

33   Postbank is an underperformer; we are not the best in class

1. **Assessing Specific Organizational Identity Traits**
   1. Desired Identity
   2. Projected Identity
   3. Perceived Identity
2. **Analyzing the Gaps**
   - Gap 1 Desired versus Projected
   - Gap 2 Perceived versus Projected
   - Gap 3 Desired versus Perceived
3. **Selecting the final list of traits to focus on in corporate messaging pursuing employees to implement the new strategic objectives**

FIGURE 2.7 Fit between strategic objective and specific identity traits

with perceptions among management. Next to the gaps between management views and employees' perception, the intelligence gathered internally about specific identity traits also revealed that the projected claims to fame were not all rooted in firm beliefs held by employees, an almost unbridgeable gap when launching the new strategic objectives.

As explained in Figure 2.7, assessing the degree of fit between the intended strategic objectives and the specific identity traits is done in three steps. In step 1, the actual traits are gathered for the desired, projected and perceived identity, followed by step 2, an analysis of the gaps between those three specific identity traits. More specifically, it's necessary to focus on the similarities and differences in the three lists. In step 3, managers have to decide which traits will be focused on in developing a common narrative for communicating with employees about the intended strategy.

Fit with employee behaviour

Managers have a range of instruments to monitor the progress of support for a new strategic focus. The most obvious one is carefully observing what people do and say in meetings, at parties and on trips. The higher a manager is placed within an organization, the easier it becomes to observe basic trends, if only thanks to travel and cross-functional exposure.

However, the work of Hambrick et al.[11] has revealed that senior executives are often blinded by 'bounded awareness'. That is, either consciously or unconsciously, they are not always aware of what is really happening in the organization. In part due to a failure to see relevant things in time, it is also a manifestation of corporate silence, that fear-induced spiral that explains why employees seldom speak about relevant trends. This double-edged sword – it's double-edged because some managers prefer the tranquility of ignorance – creates many problems in organizations, ultimately leading to a lack of employee support. That is why early-warning systems are no luxury investment.

Employee behaviour: tracking engagement

Managers at the top of the organizational pyramid mostly acknowledge the patience that is required to implement a strategy, to get all relevant employees involved in the actions that are needed to make it click. However, few employees automatically understand or fully appreciate the many steps needed to create competitive advantage. This is especially true if employees perceive the new steps as illogical, if only because they are inconsistent with previous corporate messages.

For a strategic change to succeed smoothly, it is vital that the actions and decisions of all employees are in accordance with the desired change. This requires compliance, but also a willingness to cooperate enthusiastically. It's why many organizations are interested in their employees' degree of engagement.

Many engagement studies measure this among all employees and are comparable with employee-satisfaction research, enabling executives to see which units have fully involved people and which need improvement. Tracking engagement also allows executives to see which line managers are performing and which are not. This is why the outcomes of engagement studies are often linked to appraisal and compensation systems. One often-used instrument is Gallups' Q12 tracking tool, which focuses on the twelve questions in Table 2.5.[12]

TABLE 2.5 The Gallup Q12

The Gallup Q12 questions	
Q01	I know what is expected of me at work.
Q02	I have the materials and equipment I need to do my work right.
Q03	At work, I have the opportunity to do what I do best every day.
Q04	In the last seven days, I have received recognition or praise for doing good work.
Q05	My supervisor, or someone at work, seems to care about me as a person.
Q06	There is someone at work who encourages my development.
Q07	At work, my opinions seem to count.
Q08	The mission or purpose of my company makes me feel my job is important.
Q09	My associates or fellow employees are committed to doing quality work.
Q10	I have a best friend at work.
Q11	In the last six months, someone at work has talked to me about my progress.
Q12	This last year, I have had opportunities at work to learn and grow.

Employee behaviour: tracking alignment

Elaborating insights into engagement is a good starting point, but I don't believe it is enough. Here's a comparison with consumer research: data about what a consumer knows and feels are essential, but when they are not linked to purchase intentions – or, in other words, to behaviour – they are much less useful to a marketing manager. The same logic is true for involving employees in an organization's new strategy. Winning employee hearts is an essential and necessary starting point, but managers can't rely on attitudinal data alone.

Creating aligned behaviour among employees is not an easy task. However, if scores are positive, benefits for organizations appear impressive. A study by the Corporate Executive Board (CEB) of 2007 showed that, 'the extent to which employees commit to something or someone in their organization and how hard they work and how long they stay is a result of commitment'.[13] In this study, the CEB introduced the so-called '10:6:2 Rule'. It means that every 10 per cent improvement in alignment increased an employee's effort level by 6 per cent, which in turn generated a 2 per cent improvement in the employee's performance. In addition, every 10 per cent improvement in commitment can decrease an employee's probability of departure by about 9 per cent.

Retaining employees spares companies the inevitable risks and costs of hiring and training new talent. Evidence also suggests that offering employees a sense of meaning, fulfilment and happiness in their work does more than keep them on board, and gives a tangible boost to a company's performance over the long term. From 1999 to 2008, a portfolio made up of *Fortune*'s '100 best companies to work for' yielded a 4.1 per cent annual return beyond that of a broader group of companies, a figure reported by the Centre for Research in Securities Prices (CRSP), which is the economics research arm of the University of Chicago's Graduate School of Business.

In short, if an enterprise is ever to generate its maximum value, it is clearly in its best interest to align and engage its employees. If a company can focus the power of its individual members together towards a common strategic end, it will transform from a sterile legal construct into a living, breathing and ultra-competitive organism. What's more, a concern for employee attitudes and commitment levels should not be overlooked during volatile economic periods, market woes and other distractions. In fact, companies should double their efforts to invest in and align employees during a downturn. This will inevitably solidify a degree of loyalty, enhance engagement levels and perhaps keep valued talent on board when conditions reverse and alternative job options are more plentiful.

Success in mobilizing employees to increase the performance of their organization requires understanding and reliance on hard numbers of what people actually *do*. What employees really do is measured with instruments that assess alignment, such as the RepTrak™ Alignment Monitor, developed by the Reputation Institute.[14] The Strategic Alignment Monitor is based on an internal survey, with a questionnaire that is typically sent out via e-mail to a stratified sample of

Box 2.2 ESKOM

Looking inward first: a case from South Africa

Eskom is South Africa's largest utility company, a state-owned enterprise that produces 95 per cent of the country's electricity, which is approximately 45 per cent of the electricity used in Africa. With some 33,000 employees, Eskom faced many of the internal and external issues common to energy companies. A RepTrak Deep Dive survey of both external and internal stakeholders confirmed that the general public had a negative perception of the company, and that employees were not particularly supportive of Eskom's key strategic objectives.

To understand why, according to Khumo Mohlamme, Reputation Management Specialist – Eskom Holdings Ltd, South Africa, the company used, the RepTrak Alignment Monitor to identify three internal strategic priorities and describe the gaps that existed between employee understanding and implementation of the strategies. In a survey of workers who had online access, it was found that priorities involved financial and funding plans, supply-chain quality and a plan for capacity expansion. It was also discovered that most employees felt excluded when decisions were made, and only divisions with engaging managers were aware of what the company was doing around these key objectives. Silos were very evident among divisions, teams and initiatives.

Moreover, as these business concepts are complex and even esoteric, it's not surprising that employees didn't have a great understanding of the strategies – and never would without significant management and communication attention.

With the key drivers of alignment now clear, Eskom developed a road map to build more supportive employee behaviour. It started with an internal communications campaign. After providing employees with a great deal of information, subsequent studies showed that most now feel that they are consulted, included and informed of strategic priorities and, most important, about key decisions that affect day-to-day deliverables. What's more, Eskom's people are now engaged in one of the more important external reputation-building tasks, acting as brand ambassadors for the company, which is the start of converting those negative public perceptions into positives.

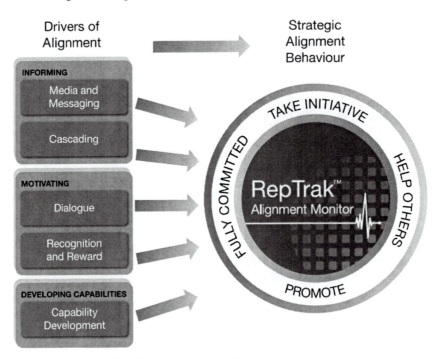

FIGURE 2.8 RepTrak™ Alignment Monitor (Reputation Institute)

an organization. The basic outcome of such a study is a number varying between zero and one hundred. A score of fifty or lower indicates that a workforce's alignment is low; above sixty it becomes sufficient; and numbers that exceed seventy represent world-class alignment.

Experience with this type of research has taught me that not many companies move easily above a score of sixty. Creating aligned behaviour among employees appears to be rather difficult. However, if scores are positive, benefits for organizations appear to be impressive. A model illustrating the mechanics of the RepTrak™ Alignment Monitor is shown in Figure 2.8.

The general assumptions behind the model start with *supportive behaviour* for strategic issues. This is measured by asking respondents to indicate on a scale to what degree they perceive their colleagues are personally acting in accordance with the organization's initiatives, and whether the collective is helping each other implement the strategic goals.

Individuals will buy into a core strategic issue only if they are *aware* and familiar with it, express positive feelings about the intents, and completely *understand* what the strategy means. Various studies have shown that this is the tightest bottleneck when creating aligned behaviour. Even highly educated people often appear to lack an understanding of strategic goals, mostly because the organization has not invested substantial time and effort in explaining the intents.

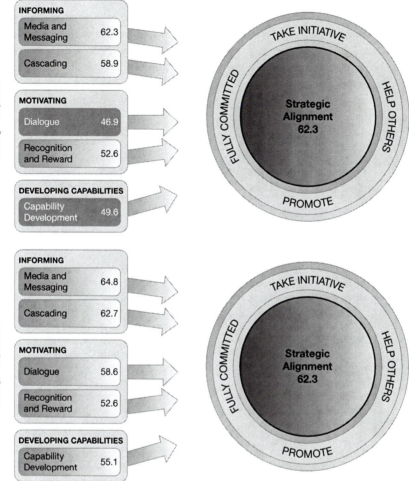

FIGURE 2.9 Overall results of Reptrak™ Alignment Monitor

Alignment can, however, be stimulated by three managerial actions: informing, motivating and capability development. Informing consists of two drivers: the first is aligning *media and messages*, that is, creating a similar look and feel for all internal media. The second aspect of informing is involving middle management in the strategy, through *cascading* principles. Motivating is distinguished in *dialogue* efforts and *recognition and rewards* investments. Finally, *capability development* consists of managerial efforts aimed at training and coaching employees in the context of the strategic objectives.

The gathered data are reported in two ways. One is an overview of the results of the company, showing comparisons between relevant units – be they regions, divisions, business units or demographic segments – which enables executives to see if age, tenure, gender or job level influences alignment. The second shows data comparing the specific company with a *benchmark*, based on the results of previous studies among thousands of respondents at hundreds of companies around the world. This enables an organization to identify relative strengths and weaknesses in the alignment drivers, including the quality of the contributions of individual managers and employee communication specialists.

A short summary of an application of the RepTrak™ Alignment Monitor at two companies is shown in Figure 2.10.

PHILIPS

From archipelago to aligned company

During the 1990s, Philips had to transform itself in order to save the company from bankruptcy. Cost reduction programs were set up, followed by initiatives to increase customer focus. The product portfolio was refocused to healthcare, lifestyle and technology and the new strategy emerged: Sense and Simplicity.

However, commitment with Philips was limited at the beginning of the 21st century, due to the long-lasting cost reduction programs. RI's Strategic Alignment Monitor was used several years in a row to globally track commitment among Philips' employees. This provided Philips with a clear overview of which communication initiatives worked to boost commitment and which ones did not.

Avoiding the cascading trap

The first alignment study at TNT took place in 2005 and assessed alignment with the major goals among all employees at TNT (from postmen to top) all over the world. The study revealed that cascading was not working perfectly: TNT had to involve its management first, before spreading the word to the whole company.

In 2007 the Strategic Alignment Monitor was applied for a second time, this time only among TNT's management to assess their alignment with the major goals. Results revealed that managers were now sufficiently aware, and motivated to support TNT's major goals.

FIGURE 2.10 Practical examples of a strategic alignment monitor study at two multinationals

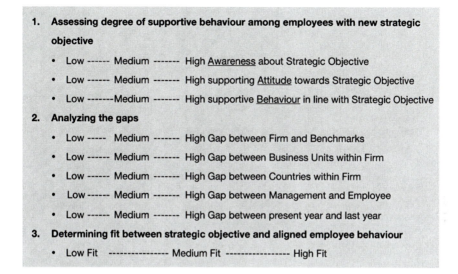

1. **Assessing degree of supportive behaviour among employees with new strategic objective**
   - Low ------ Medium ------- High <u>Awareness</u> about Strategic Objective
   - Low ------ Medium ------- High supporting <u>Attitude</u> towards Strategic Objective
   - Low -------Medium ------- High supportive <u>Behaviour</u> in line with Strategic Objective
2. **Analyzing the gaps**
   - Low ----- Medium ------- High Gap between Firm and Benchmarks
   - Low ------ Medium ------- High Gap between Business Units within Firm
   - Low ------ Medium ------- High Gap between Countries within Firm
   - Low ------ Medium ------- High Gap between Management and Employee
   - Low ------ Medium ------- High Gap between present year and last year
3. **Determining fit between strategic objective and aligned employee behaviour**
   - Low Fit   --------------- Medium Fit ---------------- High Fit

FIGURE 2.11 Fit between strategic objectives and employee behaviour

Fit between strategy and employee behaviour

Determining the fit between strategic intents and actual employee behaviour is done in three steps, as is shown in Figure 2.11. Management has to be provided with a firm figure showing what employees know and the degree to which they feel and act positively regarding new strategic objectives. Management also has to analyse in depth the problems that can be seen at specific levels when there's a low degree of fit. This can be done at business unit, country or hierarchical level, comparing an organization with a relevant benchmark, or simply with the current situation against the recent past. With these steps, one can then make a more holistic assessment when evaluating satisfaction – or lack thereof – with support and alignment. The poorer the fit, the greater the need to intensify managerial efforts to stimulate acceptance of the strategy.

Integrating the three clusters of intelligence data into a road map

This chapter has shown how management can gather intelligence about typical organizational traits that have to be taken into consideration before implementing various efforts aimed at increasing alignment among employees. Three clusters of traits are relevant. Two apply to identity traits, both overall and specific. One cluster applies to the degree employees already appear to show behaviour aligned with the new strategy. Summarized, the three internal studies will provide the following input for decision-making about an internal alignment programme (see Figure 2.12).

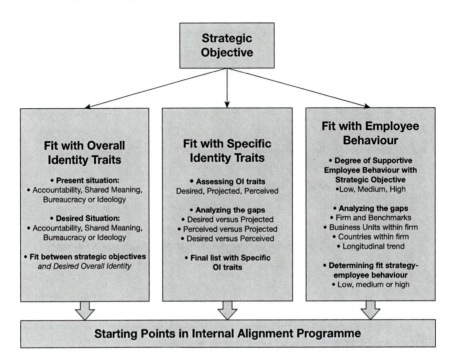

FIGURE 2.12 Three internal intelligence sources

The three internal studies provide managers with a priority list of where to focus and also upon whom. Focusing on a limited number of acute topics is highly pragmatic. It avoids doing too much about largely irrelevant issues. When a high degree of resistance can be expected – say, because it will dramatically change existing patterns of work, to which employees are accustomed – a more sophisticated road map is needed. In the end, however, one notion remains vital to remember, whatever the outcome of the studies: employees will only become aligned when the persuasive offers made to them are perceived as mutually rewarding.

This requires more than purely understanding the obstacles: an organizational change process may demand a fundamental attitudinal shift from top management too. That is why, in addition to gathering intelligence about what employees feel, believe and do, it's also highly relevant for top management to do some soul searching. What are senior executives willing to change personally to make strategic objectives a success? When employees become aware of this change in attitude among their executives – and, more importantly, experience the consequences in the daily behaviour of top management – the chances that they, as employees, will follow this example will increase tremendously.

Notes

1 S. Albert and D. Whetten, 'Organizational identity', in L.L. Cummings and B.M. Shaw (eds), *Research in organizational behaviour*, Greenwich: JAI Press, 1985, pp. 263–95.
2 K.S. Cameron and R.E. Quinn, *Diagnosing and changing organizational culture*, Reading: Addison-Wesley, (1999).
3 H. Mintzberg, *Organisatiestructuren*, Schoonhoven: Academic Service, (1992).
4 C. Handy, *Gods of management, the changing world of organizations*, London: Souvenir Press, (1978).
5 Wikipedia website, http://en.wikipedia.org/wiki/Organization (accessed 3 May 2010).
6 M.E. Elstak, C.B.M. van Riel and M.G. Pratt, 'Why identify? Self-enhancement and self-consistency motives in organizational identification', *Working Paper*, Rotterdam School of Management, (2010).
7 G.A.J.M. Berens, C.B.M. van Riel and G.H. van Bruggen, 'Corporate associations and consumer product responses: the moderating role of corporate brand dominance', *Journal of Marketing*, (2005), vol. 69(3), pp. 35–48.
8 Elstak, van Riel and Pratt, 'Why identify? Self-enhancement and self-consistency motives in organizational identification', *Working Paper*, Rotterdam School of Management, (2010).
9 Ibid.
10 Ibid.
11 D.C. Hambrick, 'The field of management's devotion to theory: Too much of a good thing?', *Academy of Management Journal*, (2007), vol. 50(6), pp. 1346–52.
12 Gallup website, www.gallup.com/consulting/121535/Employee-Engagement-Overview-Brochure.aspx (accessed 11 July 2011).
13 Corporate Executive Board website, www.clc.executiveboard.com (accessed March 2011).
14 C.B.M. van Riel, G.A.J.M. Berens and M. Dijkstra, 'Stimulating strategically aligned behaviour among employees', *Journal of Management Studies*, (2009), vol. 46(7), pp. 1197–227.

3

DEVELOPING A ROAD MAP FOR INTERNAL ALIGNMENT

Generating internal support for a new strategy requires a clear understanding of an organization's various identity characteristics, both overall and specific, plus an awareness of the degree of employee support for the objectives. Although senior executives typically lead a strategic initiative, corporate communication professionals make critical contributions to its creation, deployment and, most certainly, to a successful implementation. The communicator's efforts should not only be closely aligned with top executives, but also fully integrated with counterparts from marketing, accounting, information technology and human resources. In fact, pulling together a well-aligned workforce demands joint leadership from – and execution by – nearly every function and discipline within an organization.

Starting a new strategy transformation is one thing. Creating *sustainable* support for it requires building and executing a road map that combines the efforts of managers from various fields applying a sophisticated mixture of demands and incentives. There are two main sets of tactics. One can be labelled *negotiation*, which includes *consulting* with representatives from internal groups and *dialogues* with internal decision-makers. The other set is *confrontation*, and the use of *power play* and *mirroring* that was initially described in Chapter 1.

Strategy implementation processes mostly start with negotiation with internal stakeholders. In Europe, for example, it is vital to win the support of trade unions and working councils before taking action. This requires meetings and explanations that clarify any consequences a strategic change would have on job security, increased demands on job execution, new organizational structures or new appraisal systems. These negotiations are often led by senior management, with assistance from human resources. The next step towards implementation is starting to build internal support by articulating the strategy in management meetings, followed by dialogues with larger groups of rank and file employees, using IT-based dialogue sessions and town hall-type discussions. Here again, senior management is in the lead, supported by corporate communication.

TABLE 3.1 Techniques for creating internal alignment

Negotiation	*Confrontation*
Consulting	**Mirroring**
• Presentations and negotiations with unions • Presentations and negotiations with working council(s)	• Unavoidable exposure by internal messaging • Using external corporate ads to persuade internal audiences • Allocating coaches to key managers aimed at adjusting role behaviour
Consensus	**Power play**
• Town-hall meetings • Management meetings • Jam sessions	• New organizational structures and decision-making procedures • Appointing new managers in key roles • Capability development in internal training programmes • New appraisal rules

Confrontation tactics often commence with the introduction of changes in organizational structures, new appointments, even the replacement of existing management. At the same time, adjustments to the appraisal system – if needed in the new system – are also introduced. This is a typical power play, as employees are forced to accept the changes or look for work elsewhere.

A more informal method of persuading employees to show aligned behaviour involves confronting them with unavoidable messages, through internal communications and even corporate advertising aimed at external stakeholders. This is mirroring, as it confronts employees with the realities of the new strategy. Moreover, one of the newer tactics being used in a growing number of companies is the hiring of consultants to 'coach' executives and managers in delivering the new messages. I've even seen professional actors train executives to be more persuasive speakers, both in person and through online videos. Although some elements of leadership may come naturally to the gifted few, many others can benefit from communication coaching and training.

There are, however, various levels of risk that accompany these techniques. Consulting and mirroring will be less risky than having dialogues with employees aimed at creating consensus, and certainly less so than applying a power play. A summary of the approach is given in Table 3.1.

Employees are hard to convince

Creating a workforce aligned with new strategic goals requires much more than the use of the 'right' tactics. No matter how hard management pushes and pulls, it is individual employees who will accept, reject or interfere with change, and resistance is a natural response for both long-tenured workers and younger employees. Veteran workers tend to cherish the comfort zone of existing routines and often have little desire to adapt to new and seemingly unpredictable patterns of activities. Younger generations are also hard to convince, but for different reasons.

This restlessness has been compounded by widespread cynicism and mistrust of business among employees of all ages. Fraud committed by employees against their own companies has rocketed recently, now comprising 21 per cent of all calls to whistle-blower hotlines operated by The Network,[1] a US-based compliance company serving large, multinational companies. This begs a couple of questions: have corporate irresponsibility and the global credit crisis chipped away at employees' loyalty to their companies? Or, are companies reaping the consequences of their own policies toward workers, actions that clearly stated loyalty had less value than in times past?[2]

An aligned workforce does add value. Resistance to change and cynical attitudes towards commitment have to be taken seriously when managers are on the brink of starting a change process. There are many examples of successful change and sustained employee alignment for a new vision, but it always requires substantial work and management that takes employee concerns seriously.

Management may well be asking a great deal of world-weary and even sceptical employees to behave instantly like loyal professionals in a corporate collective, willing to put in discretionary effort and even personal time for the sake of its success. However, an aligned organization is characterized by a high level of employee engagement; an entrepreneurial spirit across all levels; and authentic relationships between managers and employees, who agree on a strategic road map and believe in their combined power.

Picture a rowing team, training with its sights set on a gold medal at the next games. Success – and pushing ahead of any competing sculls in the water – depends on all rowers moving their blades in unison. Although individual rowers may vary in strength, it is the simultaneous and collective movement that generates full speed, and commitment that differentiates also-rans from medallists. While a team is only as strong as its weakest member, it is the collective that counts most. All the while, a lasting emotional bond is forged between the team members on board, including the coxswain at the helm issuing inspirational shouts to the rowers. The end result is pride in communal membership that transcends a sense of individual accomplishment.

Companies that succeed in transforming individual ambitions into an aligned collective have the opportunity to achieve the following:

- Previously unconnected parts of the organization are brought together, creating a higher degree of competitive power.
- Employees are bound by a common aspiration and are clear on how their individual efforts contribute to the company's overall strategy, and how they will be rewarded for furthering corporate objectives.

FIGURE 3.1 Integrating individual ambitions into one collective goal

- The company gains a focus on achieving something relative to an outsider, most often a competitor, resulting in a stronger focus on an integrated market approach, as well as responsiveness, and increasing customer satisfaction in the process.
- The company's training and learning processes are kept on course.
- The highest-calibre talent is attracted and retained; in this way, 'One-Company' becomes self-perpetuating, enhancing competitiveness over the long term.

Road map to internal alignment

Aligned organizations are more adaptive to evolving circumstances, more resilient in weathering downturns and more capable of retaining top talent and establishing industry leadership in a fast-changing world. However, changing *mentalities* does not happen overnight. Humans have a natural tendency to resist change, especially drastic change. Experienced managers know this and must provide catalysts that inspire the adoption of new ideas more quickly and smoothly.

Let's first focus on the requirements of the four managerial efforts that have to be executed:

- *informing* employees about the new strategy, its intent, what it might mean for their daily activities and career and the organization's future;
- *motivating* employees by emphasizing individual opportunities and positives, while clearly articulating the expectations of managing ongoing work while implementing the strategy;

- *capability development*, enabling a workforce to implement and execute a new strategy by training and coaching crucial people, teaching them to adjust to the new requirements;
- *tracking and tracing results*, showing managers what did work and what failed in the implementation of the change process, using clear and achievable benchmarks and milestones.

These four managerial efforts have to be executed in different styles depending on whether the emphasis is on either negotiating internally or confronting employees with strategic choices that are no longer debatable. This has been visualized in Table 3.2 and is illustrated with some practical examples.

The efforts described in Table 3.2 are most frequently implemented by middle managers of various disciplines, although the role of senior executives does not stop with the announcement of the new strategy. By the nature of their leadership position, executives always initiate the intent and attempt to sell the vision in a compelling and consistent way. But an executive who introduces a strategy at a major town-hall meeting and then figures his or her work is done will probably not see the plan attain its full value. As the implementation goes on, executive participation probably grows ever more important, especially in showing commitment to the strategy in daily behaviour, and with a leadership style that supports managers and front-line employees. During the most difficult days of implementation – before positive incoming results reinforce and reward efforts – hands-on, supportive senior leadership is essential to stimulating aligned and allied front-line execution.

CEOs and presidents also must focus on the firm's middle managers, emphasizing a belief and confidence in the relevance of using tracking tools – such as balanced scorecards – linking the outcomes of the work to bonuses and promotions. What's more, various disciplines bring useful skills and perspectives to the change. Marketing managers, for instance, are crucial because they communicate to employees the claims and promises the company made to the market, most often through external corporate advertising campaigns. Seeing external marketing campaigns actually provides employees with a perspective of what is expected from them.

Another marketing management technique used to stimulate internal alignment is the introduction of key account management. This is an instrument that forces marketing people to integrate their sales efforts closely with other disciplines, avoiding fragmentation and forging an integrated marketing approach. Key account management requires a different decision-making structure from that found in an individual function, with reporting lines that criss-cross conventional silos. Finally, marketing managers must evaluate the success of their communication actions by measuring changes in the awareness of employees of the strategic intent, and their level of commitment to alignment.

IT managers are also important to stimulate and cement employee alignment. Their role is naturally focused on providing an information infrastructure that allows

TABLE 3.2 Road map to internal alignment

Tactics	Negotiation		Confrontation	
Managerial efforts	*Consulting*	*Consensus*	*Mirroring*	*Power play*
Informing	Top management explains a new vision. Might result in adaptations regarding consequences for employees.	Top management tests the new vision in dialogue sessions. Might result in changes.	Unavoidable exposure to successes of the implementation of the new strategy by testimonials and hard facts. Corporate advertising revealing the desired behaviour.	Announcing new structure, appointments and appraisal rules.
Motivating	Providing hard facts showing necessity to support new strategy.	Discussing KPIs and conditions needed to create success in specific business segments.	Transparency about rewarding successes.	Showing successes. Rewarding successes.
Capability development	Announcing training opportunities.	Specifying training opportunities.	Introducing account management in sales.	Providing relevant training and coaching.
Tracking and tracing results	Benchmarking successes of comparable firms.	Benchmarking successes of comparable firms.	Measuring outcomes.	Measuring outcomes.

employees to exchange information, even as the new strategy demands some systemic changes. These communication vehicles and venues are especially necessary when the new strategy requires not only horizontal but also vertical integration.

A similar logic can be formulated for finance and accounting managers. Like IT, these disciplines provide a form of infrastructure, although here the emphasis is on financial reporting standards. Such standards, of course, should correspond with the success criteria derived from the new strategic objective. The vital role of finance and accounting becomes clear when one realizes that this structure dictates success or failure internally; in other words, it dictates whether one gets a bonus or no bonus.

Communication and human resources play a complementary role in aligning the workforce. Communication's role boils down especially to informing and motivating employees, whereas human resources is focused on capability develop-ment, either through training, hiring or bringing in consultants. It is crucial that a communication group guarantees consistency in its one-way communication, but also builds in mechanisms for two-way dialogue about the strategy between rank-and-file employees and senior executives. For human resources, training and rewarding people in ways that don't always involve money are also vital, including special assignments, trips to conferences and exposure to new advancement opportunities.

A case study: reinventing Philips

Founded in 1891 by Gerard Philips, ironically a cousin of Karl Marx, Royal Philips Electronics of the Netherlands is a corporation that practically defines capitalism. One of the largest and most widely recognized electronics companies in the world, Philips employs more than 125,000 people, operates in more than sixty countries and, in 2011, generated sales worth roughly US$40 billion. And, although it struggled, like most other manufacturers, during the global financial crisis, Philips is emerging from an exceptional and successful transition, a purposeful transformation from a corporate culture based on accountability, to one in which the company's people are aligned around shared meaning.

In the process, the company shifted from a conglomerate of independent divisions, focusing on consumer electronics, domestic appliances, lighting, medical systems and computer components, towards an integrated health-care, lighting and consumer-lifestyle company. This reinvention, if you will, changed not only the way in which the company was organized, but also how its people worked with each other. In addition, the new identity perceived by employees manifested itself in a culture dedicated to integrating technologies and design into customer-centric solutions, and a brand that promises, in the company's own words, 'sense and simplicity'.

For much of its 120 years of history, Philips was organized around strong divisions that operated as more or less autonomous units. Employees excelled within their own business units and very likely linked their identity much more closely to their specific division than to the corporation. The very idea of a 'One Philips' philosophy undoubtedly struck employees as strange and foreign. Bringing the concept into reality required a step-by-step change-management initiative, led by Philips President and CEO Gerard J. Kleisterlee in the first decade of the twenty-first century.

Born in Germany and raised in the Netherlands, Kleisterlee was educated at a Jesuit-run high school and at the Eindhoven University of Technology and became an electrical engineer. Like his father before him, Kleisterlee has worked for Philips his entire adult life. After working in, and managing, several of those fiercely independent business units, Kleisterlee became the corporation's president and CEO in April 2001.[3]

Throughout the 1990s, Philips' company-wide strategy was often an amalgamation of incongruous, individual divisional strategies. Still, because the corporation developed excellent technology and products that sold in high volumes, the company often grew by at least 10 per cent annually. That changed dramatically in 2001, when the market for semiconductors collapsed, and it became clear that the margins on consumer electronic products were too low to sustain the company, given its relatively high production costs. Philips' profitability suddenly fell to dramatically low levels.

Kleisterlee viewed Philips' existing business units as an armada of independent ships, each with its own identity. He was 'determined to change them to one effective fleet, joining forces with the aim of serving customers' needs in an integrated way'. Consequently, he started by changing the company's product portfolio, shifting away from high-volume businesses to high-profit market segments – such as those serving the health-care business, consumer lifestyles and lighting – and demanding more growth within Philips' medical division. And, for the first time, Philips took a more integrated marketing approach, especially regarding key customers in the automotive, retail and government sectors.

In 2002, Philips began seriously to cut costs. High-volume activities were jettisoned piece by piece, with the company striking deals to exit from its computer-monitor and mobile-phone businesses, culminating with the 2006 sale of its Components Division for US$8.3 billion and, six months later, the sale of Taiwan Semiconductor Manufacturing, valued at US$3.36 billion. At Kleisterlee's direction, Philips cut its number of factories from 269 to 160, sold low-growth businesses such as fax machines, and forced divisions to share services.

With cash in hand from its divestments, Philips was able to purchase the health-care assets of Agilent and Marconi and, in 2005, a trio of health-care companies. It also made a handful of other acquisitions for its Lighting, Consumer Electronics and Domestic Appliances and Personal Care (DAP) divisions. Near the end of 2007, Philips made its largest acquisitions, including the US health-care company Respironics, for US$5.1 billion; the US lighting-fixtures manufacturer Genlyte, for US$2.7 billion; and the medical systems and services provider Visicu, for US$430

Box 3.1 KEY POINTS IN PHILIPS' NEW STRATEGY

PHILIPS

Mission

Improve the quality of people's lives through timely introduction of meaningful innovations.

Vision

In a world where complexity increasingly touches every aspect of our daily lives, we will lead in bringing sense and simplicity to people.

Values

Delight customers – Deliver on commitments – Develop people – Depend on each other

Brand promise

We empower people to benefit from innovation by delivering on our brand promise of 'sense and simplicity'. This brand promise encapsulates our commitment to deliver solutions that are advanced; easy to use; and designed around the needs of all our users.

---

million. These acquisitions were funded by the repurchasing of up to US$5 billion of Philips' own stock, a signal that Philips' top executives had strong confidence in the corporation's future.

Today, Philips is the largest lighting manufacturer in the world, competing globally and with small and regional companies. It is one of the top three health-care companies in the world, competing with General Electric and Siemens. It is Europe's largest consumer-lifestyle company. Said Kleisterlee, in a 2006 interview with *Global Entrepreneur*: 'If we look at Philips' more than one hundred years of history as a novel, the title for the chapter that I am in is "Repositioning".'

Indeed, Kleisterlee repositioned the company into a market-driven, customer-focused organization, structured around three product-market combinations – health care, lighting and consumer technology – which were selected as much for their stable growth in sales and revenues as for Philips' ability to make products that would provide simple but attractive solutions for its customers' needs.

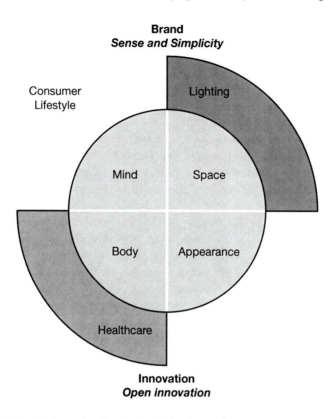

FIGURE 3.2 Positioning of Philips in the Kleisterlee era

Philips' changing portfolio and more intense market focus were supported by an external advertising campaign based around one unifying theme. The campaign expressed the company's new outside–in focus, in contrast to the previous inside–out approach of the 'Let's make things better' era. The key promise of the company to the market is embodied in 'sense and simplicity', a slogan that expresses two key points: first, that Philips is determined to launch products that make sense to customers. And second, that, above all, technology should be delivered to the end-user in a simple way, not as a high-tech solution only decipherable to consumers with an engineering background.

The message always starts from within

Such changes did not come forth fully formed, but rather were the product of a fairly lengthy evolutionary process. Engaging internal stakeholders in the 'sense and simplicity' paradigm was not easily accomplished. Two main obstacles had to be overcome before Kleisterlee and the other architects of the strategy could stimulate a supportive attitude among broad organizational layers.

First, the new strategy had to be *explained*, both before and during its launch. This was done with what Philips called 'Touch Point workshops', where all employees were asked to: (1) give examples of advanced solutions that their department could provide; (2) explain why those solutions would be easily experienced (implying: simple); and (3) explain how that end solution could be designed around the customer. The workshops yielded a huge and remarkably reinforcing set of proof points for the 'sense and simplicity' paradigm, illustrating exactly how the new slogan could be translated into tangible products and services that made sense for Philips customers. The Touch Point workshops were followed by sessions for the company's upper ranks, about 1,000 top executives, who were then asked to cascade the ideology downward to the next level of about 8,000 managers.

Second, the *dominant logic* that prevailed at Philips for nearly two decades had to change. Although the quasi-independent divisions had been the key factor in the company's steady success, the growth covered an underlying flaw. Divisional performance was a mix of occasionally dramatic successes and outright failures. Some divisions contributed enormous profits, while others ran huge deficits. Kleisterlee wanted a more consistent performance across all divisions, an objective that created a need to cease high-volume and low-margin activities and increase synergy. And achieving synergy meant busting the old business-unit silos.

Key decision-makers had to accept and, in turn, champion the new dominant logic. In the evolving paradigm, Philips would shift from a financial holding structure replete with stand-alone divisions assessed on their individual performance, into a strategic holding company that focused both on the contribution of its divisions to the company's overall performance and on its success in servicing global purchasing chains. Philips adopted a global account-management approach, where both the customer and the company benefit greatly from the integration. This simplifies life for the purchasing departments of global conglomerates in market segments such as retail, automotive and health care. This was stated by executive vice president and executive board member Gottfried Dutiné:

> Now they can deal with one Philips team instead of dealing with competing divisional representatives that all focus solely on their own product-market combination. Actually, I think that if we had not integrated our sales efforts towards the huge global purchasing conglomerates, they simply would have kicked us out.

Appointing apostles of change

Kleisterlee believed that profitability and less volatile returns on investment lay in the up-and-coming categories of health care, lifestyle and consumer technology. The autonomy of entrenched divisions had to give way to an integrated offering, through key account management. Moreover, he felt that divisions should engage in joint research and development.

FIGURE 3.3 Advertisement used in the Sense and Simplicity campaign

Simply saying there will be change is not enough to ensure it happens throughout a business as global as Philips. At the board of management level, Kleisterlee appointed division directors and changed their scope of responsibility and bonus structure to ensure that they were as invested in the company's overall results as they were in their own sphere. Money talks, and Kleisterlee soon had a highly supportive group of apostles pushing the new Philips philosophy, executives who had previously held the trust of independent divisional leadership and who retained that trust, despite the changing work arrangements. It was only a matter of time before Philips' internal media began regularly to contain messages in support of the new strategy, issued from the management rungs far below Kleisterlee, providing a clear cue to employees that both executives and management were on board with the new strategy.

Still, at the beginning of the Kleisterlee era, employee support for Philips' strategy was limited, and doubt was only exacerbated when the Internet bubble burst, resulting in yet another round of Philips' cost reductions. Support for the initiatives increased along with improved stock performance, as being part of a winning team is always a plus. But the greatest inroads were made through the attitude of Kleisterlee himself, who worked ceaselessly to stimulate dialogue while keeping an open mind for initiatives that fitted the sense and simplicity ideal.

Philips had long had a culture dominated by an engineering mindset. More often than not, concrete proof points were needed to win employee acceptance of just about anything. However, products that were well received in the marketplace – such as a simplified coffeemaker called Senseo, which offers its user only the options of 'one cup' or 'two cups' – was indeed proof that sense and simplicity ideas could generate sales.

Some of the initial dialogues at Philips took the form of 'Challenge and Connect' workshops, in which more than 1,500 top executives participated in sessions chaired by a member of the executive board. The workshops were aimed at developing individual action plans to implement 'One Philips' at both division and business-unit levels. Building on the success of those, in November 2007, a Simplicity Day was organized, in which all 120,000 people then working at Philips were asked to provide ideas and suggestions about how to implement 'simple' solutions to the day-to-day problems they encounter in their jobs – an initiative that applied Philips' external messaging to its internal workings. Initiatives such as these appeared to increase the presence of a supportive communication climate, as was shown in annual alignment studies.

The cascade trap in understanding

The inward-looking culture at Philips during the 1980s and 1990s did not stimulate strong corporate communication or human resource management functions. However, following the replacement of the old divisional structure with a vertical integration into three complementary business lines, Philips' corporate communication group launched several communication platforms with a strong focus on corporate goals, instead of divisional goals and achievements. The department then created a more consistent look and feel for its internal media, which feature key corporate messages. When research revealed that a lot of the internal media was hardly read by employees, Philips made a logical, albeit drastic, cut of many divisional- or country-focused magazines.

Corporate communication pushed content focused on the group strategy, both over the company intranet and in the global employee magazine. Meanwhile, the performance of the divisional communication managers was judged by how well corporate issues were covered in 'local' media, with bonuses given accordingly.

In addition to conventional media, Philips also applied the cascading technique of town-hall meetings, in which top management would speak directly to employees about the strategic focus. Unfortunately, internal research revealed that the meetings

FIGURE 3.4 Dialogue sessions at Philips

alone were not enough to get employees at all levels to understand what was expected of them. The annual alignment-tracking monitor revealed that employees at various hierarchical levels were not sufficiently capable of describing in their own words what the new strategy actually meant.[4]

Philips' management tried to solve the lack of understanding by increasing platforms where managers could discuss and explain the new strategy and its application in individual employee settings. The company started to organize intensive dialogue sessions to stimulate the adoption of the new corporate focus, in which top management discussed suggestions from employees to implement the sense and simplicity philosophy.

Despite the orchestrated efforts by general management and corporate communication specialists, many front-line employees at Philips still did not understand the strategy well. Even worse, the results of the second measurement of the alignment monitor showed that the degree of understanding had decreased.

This can be explained by what I call the 'cascading trap'. As divisional management tried to explain the new corporate strategy, the diffusion of the messages was invariably – although not always on purpose – coloured by the individual manager's definition of business priorities, which naturally modified the desired message. Based on these results, corporate communication eventually supplied managers with quotes that expressed the 'correct' interpretation of the goals and recorded this in a corporate video. Although not the most trusting of remedies, it was necessitated by the circumstances.

Applying other functional support

Integrating *marketing* into a key account management system was partly inspired by Gottfried Dutiné's previous experience at Motorola, and partly a reaction to severe criticism by important customers. For example, Wal-Mart was quite vocal about not wanting to be bothered by a legion of salespeople from different product divisions, but instead wished to be served by a single account manager representing Philips. The company also found that the integrated approach ensured a firmer grip on corporate governance: an integrated marketing system creates more certainties for regulators and shareholders, indicating that the company for example has control over child-labour law and sustainability issues.

Prior to its transformation, Philips had long been accused of poor performance in marketing efforts. After all, the research and development department, which invented great products, dominated the firm's psychological hierarchy, and there's truth in the contention that Philips lacked the marketing skills to win all battles in the open market. The failure of Video 2000, Philips' take on the VCR, is one classic example. However, as marketing integrated a global branding campaign under the 'sense and simplicity' tagline, the external narrative helped the internal dialogue resonate.

As Kleisterlee continued to seek new ways to draw more employees into the strategic discussion, he spoke with former IBM CEO Lou Gerstner, who revealed that *his* biggest worry was always about aligning employees around strategy. While facing a similar problem at IBM, Gerstner's *IT* department helped set up a series of online 'jam sessions' – brain-storming exercises involving a large number of employees, facilitated by IBM's corporate intranet. Division-centric Philips did not immediately have the infrastructure to handle such an exchange. However, Kleisterlee made sure that global online communication was part of Philips' €32 million IT investment, a function that, ever since, has supported communication on strategy.[5]

Meanwhile, *human resource* management focused on developing the skills of employees responsible for implementing the company's strategy and embedded an appraisal system that accounted for promotion of the plan within its regular review system. In contrast to the past, where career advancement was often based on seniority, Philips developed a more performance-based evaluation to locate and place high-potential employees. A new performance assessment system was created for managers that rewarded them for contributing to the performance of the organization. Even the *accounting* function joined in the effort, creating a methodology to define and capture a division's or group's corporate contribution, in addition to the reported numbers for the specific function.

Messaging and measurement

Aligned organizations are upheld by consistent communication from the organization's senior management, with messages that cascade both vertically and horizontally to keep all employees engaged, aligned and actively participating. However, if top management is not willing to put itself in the firing line to create an honest dialogue, alignment can be a risky, uphill struggle. What is said and believed by those on the front line is *sine qua non*, because these are the people who have the vast majority of interactions with external stakeholders, including customers. Consequently, executives need to know.

At Philips, senior management cascaded the 'One Philips' strategy through town-hall meetings, where Kleisterlee explained the new approach in a series of two-hour sessions to relatively intimate groups of 50–200. Today, he holds such meetings fifteen to twenty times a year, fielding questions that can be sent in by employees in advance. This kind of personal executive commitment to the cause is essential. The more genuine employees perceive the corporate messaging to be – and the more they believe they can play a role in shaping and supporting the corporate strategy underlying it – the more credible and attractive a proposition it will be.

Although a workforce may appear aligned, due diligence means that management should routinely test that assumption. Values are, by definition, soft and nebulous, and so an organization must look past rhetoric and quantify progress wherever possible. Philips uses two tools, an employee-engagement index and the alignment monitor, to gauge the feelings and actions of its people. Senior management tracks results closely and sets specific, longer-term targets. As US President Ronald Reagan famously said of weapons treaties with the former Soviet Union, 'Trust, but verify'.[6]

The tools enable Philips to quantify strategic awareness, attitude, understanding and actual behaviour at divisional and country levels. They can identify specific areas where employee actions do not align with, and drive, corporate strategy. In essence, the indexes hold senior management accountable for keeping itself focused on its people. This attention seems to be paying off: despite market turbulence, Philips' employee-engagement score increased 5 per cent to 69 per cent in 2009, very close to its targeted goal of 70 per cent, and alignment scores went up to 62 per cent, showing an increase of 5 points in a period of three years.[7]

Lessons learned from the Philips experience

A *first* important lesson found in the Philips experience is that an allied effort is an absolutely necessity in creating an aligned workforce. The key challenge for executives is not necessarily devising a brilliant strategy, but implementing it success-fully. This requires the full support of a strong leader navigating the company in the desired direction and keeping it on track. The leader will only succeed in a sustainable way if he or she is supported by motivated specialists in marketing, corporate communication, human resources, IT and finance and accounting.

These managers will be more successful when they can work with the best and most compelling strategies that are based on an inspiring purpose and strategic vision. Corporate communication managers have an essential role in creating awareness and understanding regarding the strategy among employees, contractors, vendors

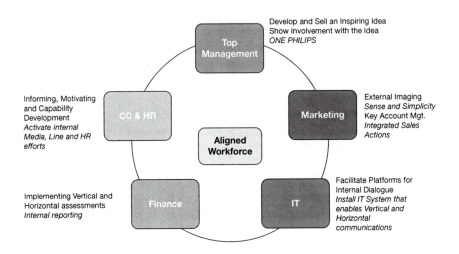

FIGURE 3.5 Roles of five groups of managers in creating 'One Philips'

and other non-commercial stakeholders. However, their success relies heavily on the efforts of colleagues in other fields. Human resource managers, for example, have to ensure that the appraisal system is in line with the strategy, and that employees are able to develop the necessary skills. The role of marketing management is to present the company to commercial stakeholders, but, in the case of Philips – and many other companies – it also plays an integrative role in implementing a customer focus through key account management. IT supplements the role of corporate communication in facilitating the transfer of information throughout the organization, and, finally, accounting plays a vital role in controlling the performance of the organization and its divisions in implementing the strategy. The key roles of specialized groups of managers are shown in Figure 3.5.

A *second* important lesson of this case – from an employee-alignment point of view – is the necessity to combine internal with external communication when a company decides to shift dramatically to a different product portfolio. Philips had to make daring decisions regarding disinvestments in components and production facilities in the Netherlands and other European countries. This allowed the company to be more focused and, above all, less volatile in terms of financial results. Shifting the emphasis towards health care appeared to be a great success. However, it also implied that employees who were working in the divisions that were disinvested lost their jobs. This is a reality communication people have to take seriously and it requires a balancing act. Explaining the good and the bad news is a serious challenge for communication specialists, especially when the relative distinctions between internal and external messaging are lacking. An important lesson learned from the Philips case is that, in addition to being transparent about the 'what and why' of the new strategy, one can't avoid having to apply a confrontation intervention strategy expressing negative and sometimes bold messages for the new vision.

A *third* important lesson is the necessity to be *consistent*: be consistent regarding internal demands and external claims and stay consistent in expressing beliefs about the intended strategy. At the start of his presidency, Kleisterlee was confronted with economic disasters that forced him to start programmes aimed at reducing costs. The temptation to shift to a safer strategy might have been suggested to him by advisors. However, Kleisterlee firmly maintained his plan to create one integrated Philips in three lines of business: health care, lighting and consumer-lifestyle products.

Concluding observations

An aligned workforce is clearly the product of a concerted effort, by participatory executives, middle managers and front-line employees. A variety of departments, including human resources, marketing, IT and others, play a key role in its creation, development and maintenance. Noble value statements, however, can't simply be pulled out of thin air, but must represent authentic beliefs that are widely held throughout an organization. Once the values have been articulated and a new strategy has been introduced, the process of building and maintaining internal alignment is only getting started.

Long-term and multidimensional discussions between executives and internal stakeholders on the process and progress of internal alignment are mandatory if a company is to succeed. But, even if executives are hearing what they want to hear in meetings, cold, quantitative studies are essential to confirm conclusively the evolution of alignment and strategy.

During all phases of the change process, corporate communication plays a specific role that no one else feels capable of or responsible for. This is articulating messages that bring the abstract strategy to life, in words and pictures that evoke emotional appeal among employees. Words express beliefs and values and inspire actions. Words and feelings are what connect employees with a company and its strategy. Words form that critical connection – the point at which employee self-interest and corporate interests fuse – that is the cornerstone of an aligned organization.

Notes

1   The Network website, www.tnwinc.com/index.aspx (accessed 3 May 2010).
2   R. Cookson, 'Employee fraud causes on the increase as bad times fuel crime', *Financial Times*, 11 May 2009.
3   Wikipedia website, http://en.wikipedia.org/wiki/Gerard_Kleisterlee (accessed 3 May 2011).
4   Reputation Institute, RepTrak™ Alignment Monitor applied at Philips in 2006.
5   L. Dorsett, M.A. Fontaine and T. O'Driscoll, 'Redefining manager interaction at IBM', *Knowledge Management Review*, (2002), vol. 5(4), pp. 4–8.
6   Wikipedia website, http://en.wikipedia.org/wiki/Trust,_but_verify (accessed 3 May 2011).
7   G. Kleisterlee, *Annual shareholder speech*, March 2009.

4

CREATING INTERNAL ALIGNMENT WITH EFFECTIVE INTERNAL COMMUNICATION

Building internal alignment starts with gathering relevant intelligence, followed by a mixture of negotiation and confrontation techniques. In applying this road map, corporate communication specialists play two important roles, the first of which is the development of a 'corporate story' that expresses the firm's distinctive brand position. Some brands and stories endure with little or no change, such as Coca Cola's. But, for most companies, a well-crafted story and brand presentation are useful for between five and ten years, after which a change in product lines or a new strategic direction demands either a revision of the story or one that's totally new.

Story development and corporate-branding efforts are embedded in what I call the *foundations of corporate communication*. This involves five clusters of activities: (a) continuously gathering intelligence on emerging issues, reputation and alignment measurements; (b) establishing consistency in messaging strategy by launching rules, directives, guidebooks and the like; (c) creating or reorganizing the communication function, including lines of authority, well-defined tasks, goals and budgets; and (d) defining a desired corporate position over a long term, which is distinguished by the corporate story and the corporate brand.

A detailed discussion of these foundations is presented in Chapter 7. Here, we'll examine the second role of corporate communication, which I call *programme support*. In daily practice, most corporate communication activities are centred on supporting programmes that may change annually and that are focused on promoting specific strategic objectives. As with overall strategic change, a key objective is creating internal alignment, and, for communication professionals, the work in both areas is similar. Effective programme support involves intelligence-gathering, positioning an activity in the context of the corporate brand, and executing messages that inform, motivate and develop capabilities plus providing charity about task allocation.

A summary of the two roles of corporate communication, embedded in the overall approach of a strategic change process in an organization, is shown in Figure 4.1.

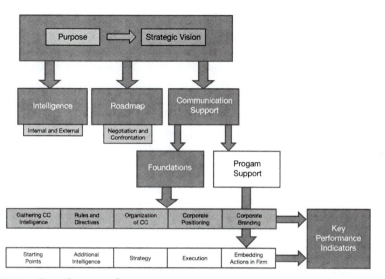

FIGURE 4.1 Contributions of communication in creating internal alignment

Communication support in programmes building internal alignment

As we have seen in the previous chapter, Philips stimulated support among employees for its overarching objective to create 'One Philips'. However, many other programmes were derived from the core concept, some aimed at the top 1,500 leaders in the corporation, others directed at all Philips employees, and yet another devoted to generating cooperation between divisions within research and development and the purchasing and sales departments. Likewise, while the company routinely pulls together basic data about engagement and alignment, it also gathers *additional intelligence* for specific programmes aimed at special strategic objectives. A programme for the top 1,500, for example, was based on information acquired from other global firms that had previously dealt with the challenges of creating a shared meaning organization.

When sufficient intelligence has been gathered, a key decision has to be made regarding the *positioning* of the programme. It is vitally important that the programme is in line with the overall strategy, and not presented as a brand new initiative that demands employees adopt a totally new way of working. Consistency, or – probably more important – perceived consistency, increases the potential for alignment tremendously. Another step is *executing* a series of messages aimed at building and maintaining internal alignment. Finally, *evaluating* the programme during a crucial phase of the implementation process enables managers to make *adaptations* to improve its impact.

The execution phase of an internal alignment programme can be simply summarized: internal corporate communication professionals impact the successful establishment of internal alignment by executing three managerial efforts: *informing*, *motivating* and *capability development*. All three of these efforts can be broken into four communication-process dimensions: *structure, flow, contents* and *climate*. More specifically, communicators must select *the most relevant structure for communication channels*; the most effective *flow* or *direction* of the material; the specific *content* that best tells a compelling story; and the degree of respect employees perceive they get within the firm, and the so-called *climate* in which the message is presented.

The nature of the choices within each of these four dimensions, of course, is influenced by an organization's predominant overall identity, whether it is bureaucracy, accountability, ideology or shared meaning. A summary of the roles is presented in Table 4.1. After the concepts used in this table have been explained and clarified, Table 4.1 will no longer show empty boxes, but will reveal the tasks demanded of internal communication once a company has decided to adopt one of the four identities.

Using soft- or hard-wired tools in building employee alignment?

American corporate managers are annually surveyed by the Conference Board, which asks what they see as their biggest threat at that specific moment. In 2003, shortly after the Enron collapse and the introduction of the Sarbanes–Oxley law, the Conference Board published a report entitled 'Forging strategic business alignment'. Although the amorphous title could lead to a myriad of interpretations, it dealt with executives' fears about their own employees not acting in accordance with boundaries prescribed by law. This created sleepless nights for American executives, who felt ill-equipped adequately to manage the new demands.[1]

In its 2003 report, the Conference Board referred to two types of instrument to ensure legal compliance. One fell under the heading of *hard-wired tools*, which meant restructured organizations, reporting lines and reward systems that put a premium on ethical governance. The others were called *soft-wired tools*, which involved training and internal communication.

In a sample of top managers, the majority believed that an emphasis on soft-wired tools was the best way to develop alignment. This may seem odd at first glance. However, although hard-wired tools are essential and indispensable, they will only be effective for a few months. Obviously, you can't continue firing people and setting up new reward structures, although stressing rewards for ethical practices should have some lasting effect. The soft-wired tools, however, are most effective in allowing individuals to decide for themselves to do those things they are meant to do. In practice, strategic consensus can only be reached when both hard and soft instruments are deployed. However, seen from a longer perspective, soft-wired tools appear most effective.

This conclusion creates high expectations about the contributions of internal communication in improving the strategic alignment of employees. Internal communication specialists implement three interrelated efforts: *informing, motivating*

Table 4.1 Building blocks of internal communication when creating employee alignment

	Informing					Motivating					Capability Development				
	Structure	Flow	Content	Climate		Structure	Flow	Content	Climate		Structure	Flow	Content	Climate
Bureau-cracy														
Account-ability														
Shared meaning														
Ideology														

and *capability development efforts*. As is explained in Table 3.2, they are also responsible for tracking and tracing the results of these three efforts. However, this is especially relevant for the communication managers themselves and is not something employees will notice when confronted with internal motivation programmes. Each role can, under specific conditions, contribute to strategically aligned behaviour.

Informing efforts

Stimulating aligned employee behaviour starts with providing employees with three different types of information:

1   information aimed at creating a positive mindset about the organization, especially within the context of the new strategic objective;
2   information about the strategic objective itself, including a short summary of the key goals and proof points of how the collective organization can make it happen; and
3   information about what the individual must contribute if the strategy is to work.[2]

Such information is relevant for a couple of reasons. It provides employees with sufficient opportunity to perform the desired behaviours, reducing natural feelings of uncertainty regarding the new or changing job. And, when employees feel less uncertain, they are more likely to feel committed to the organization, which usually improves performance.

A practical first step in informing employees adequately involves exposing them to a consistent look and feel of the key message that, in a condensed way, explains the strategy's essence. Such 'primary thematic messages' can have a powerful impact,

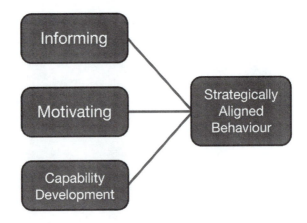

FIGURE 4.2 Drivers of strategically aligned behaviour

shaping the company's image among employees and their beliefs about the company they work for. Typically, the themed messages will dominate internal communications for as long as necessary for employees completely to absorb the intent.

With the primary thematic idea in place, a second step is to cascade the supporting key messages through the organization, using senior line management. In such town-hall meetings, senior managers personally cover the core elements of the strategy, embedded in presentations that have an understandable and appealing corporate story, summarized in a memorable way. The meetings must be led by a respected executive who keeps the messages consistent and fairly basic.

The same story – repeated consistently in corporate media – will also be supported by other functional managers in business unit-specific town-hall meetings, following much the same formula as the top executive. This is called cascading, and it's an effective means to involve mid-level managers and front-line employees in a strategy. As has been shown in the Philips case in Chapter 3, cascading has disadvantages too – for example, the most unconscious adaptation line managers make while passing on the corporate headquarters message to their reports.

Motivating efforts

Another antecedent of desired employee behaviour and performance is the degree to which they are motivated to perform their assigned tasks. Several characteristics of motivation correlate directly with positive aligned behaviour. For example, describing clear and attainable goals – *which must be within either the employee's individual and direct control or that of the group in which he or she works* – increases motivation and performance. I emphasize that last, italicized point, as rewards are too often based on total corporate earnings, or the safety performance of an operating unit in a different country, neither of which most individuals could influence. Being judged by measures over which one has no control is one of the most demotivating practices in business.

Providing clarity about the strategic goal increases motivation, but so does providing information about the goal in a specific way. When a clear rationale is given for how certain actions will help the organization reach its goals, motivation and performance are at a higher level than when pure instructions are given without any justification. In addition, allowing employees to participate in the decision-making process, adding input to the goals and processes, also leads to greater personal responsibility and commitment. Smidts et al.[3] explain this by arguing that stimulating a communication climate that is characterized by openness, participation in decision-making and supportiveness will increase employee identification with the organization. For an employee, it enhances the sense of belonging through self-categorization, as well the self-enhancement that develops when an individual feels he or she is an important member of the group. In turn, such employee identification can lead to greater efforts to show supportive behaviour regarding the new strategy.[4]

On the negative side, research on 'organizational silence' has shown that, when management does not stimulate such participation or acknowledge employee opinions, a 'climate of silence' is created, in which employees are reluctant to speak out on important issues.[5] Silence is caused by the fear of ridicule, censure or the threat of poor performance reviews by managers who don't respond well to critical observations or questions, however obvious and logical. Such a climate develops when management does not routinely solicit feedback, or typically responds negatively or dismissively to suggestions. The silence is also caused by managers who react brusquely to any semblance of criticism, owing to a belief that employees are dominated by self-interest and care little about the company's affairs.

Employee silence can have disastrous consequences. It can lead to less effective organizational decision-making and poor error detection and correction, which inhibit the success of change processes. In turn, this decreases employee commitment and employee alignment and ultimately increases employee turnover, as people tend to leave organizations where they perceive a hostile climate.[6]

An ideal way to engage and motivate employees is through organizing a dialogue. The rationale of starting a dialogue with employees is to solicit suggestions about how to implement the strategic objective *most effectively in a local context*. In other words, the strategic objective is a given; implementing it is allocated to local managers. Dialogues enable managers to raise an employee's need to understand the broader picture of the strategy process and, more specifically, what his or her role is in that process.

Participating in dialogue sessions can boost employee motivation, especially when managers are prepared to listen and react openly and honestly. An interesting illustration of this style of working is the 'brutal honesty' approach in dialogue sessions at TNT (see Box 4.1), a mail and express-delivery company with its head-quarters in the Netherlands, which employs more than 152,000 people worldwide, operates in more than 200 countries and has revenues of about US$18 billion.

Peter Bakker, TNT's CEO, told CNN in 2005 that he takes a very hands-on role in motivating people in the organization, spending a great deal of time communicating through a cascaded system. Although the company issues numerous print publications, Bakker personally stresses 'a lot of getting out there and listening'. He hosts regular chat sessions on the Internet, where hundreds of employees from all ranks and countries are free to join the conversation. He also convenes about fifteen meetings annually, at different locations round the world, relatively intimate gatherings that average about 250 employees.

In a bit of a break from the traditional tone of many town-hall meetings – though very much in keeping with TNT's commitment to 'brutal honesty' – Bakker calls the meetings 'shoot to kill' sessions. He invites, encourages and practically demands that employees ask the toughest questions imaginable. Culturally sensitive, he also confines this exercise to employees 'only in countries who can handle a bit of direct language'.

While companies that hold such dialogues try to involve as many employees as possible, limited IT capabilities are a decided hindrance. The most aligned organizations appear to have IT systems that allow for a company-wide dialogue between

---

Box 4.1 BRUTAL HONESTY AT TNT

Alignment and engagement of all of TNT's management and staff are essential in successfully serving the interests of all the company's stakeholders, contends Peter van Minderhout, the company's director of corporate communication. A widely shared, understood and supported sense of direction, coupled with a deep sense of belonging, provides the basis for the company's corporate culture – the ties that bind. Van Minderhout pointed to Tim Collins' book, *Good to great*, as a real inspiration. 'The book inspired us all, especially his findings that successful companies have a culture of brutal honesty and – at the same time – are confident that they can overcome all problems they face,' he said. 'Integrity, honesty and pride. That became the mantra for all we do.'

---

all parts of an organization. Wanting such dialogue to flow beyond hierarchal levels and throughout a geographically far-flung organization, IBM Chief Executive Sam Palmisano has pushed for recurring 'jam sessions'. The intranet-based communication channel draws large audiences, including plenty of employees willing to express bluntly a helpful point of view. 'I am a big believer in our jams', Palmisano has explained, in that they allow IBM employees 'at every level to share their ideas and suggestions . . . and make a real difference.' Palmisano also said that the sessions enabled the company to find important business issue patterns and themes.

These discoveries helped simplify the transformation of IBM from an accountability model firm into a shared meaning management system company, leveraging customer-facing employees who deal with the end-users of IBM's services-oriented business model. Many companies around the world have followed in the footsteps of Big Blue, stimulating dialogue with employee groups aimed at informing them about strategy; motivating them to explain the conditions they see as crucial to making it work; and pushing them to show the behaviour that supports strategic success.

Motivation is also stimulated by recognizing and rewarding employees in the context of the strategic objective. An interesting example of rewarding employees is at FedEx, where high-performing employees are recognized with the 'Purple Promise' award for delivering outstanding customer support (see Box 4.2).

Capability development efforts

Capability development is a collection of efforts aimed at improving employee job performance. Naturally, the degree of alignment displayed is dependent on whether workers have the capabilities needed to carry out an assignment. Capabilities can

Box 4.2 FEDEX'S PURPLE PROMISE

 At FedEx, it comes down to a wide range of couriers, pilots, customer-service agents and package handlers who work as part of a global team to deliver a level of service that customers expect from a logistics company. FedEx rewards those team members who deliver extraordinary customer service with the annual Purple Promise awards.

Fred Smith, FedEx chairman, president and chief executive, reiterates his company's commitment to the corporate message often:

> We've been working hard to make every customer interaction a point of differentiation, whether at our website, on the telephone, or during the pick-up and delivery experience. Now, we are even more committed to keep our Purple Promise, which states simply, that all of us at FedEx will do our best to make every FedEx experience outstanding.

include skills, habits and tacit or explicit knowledge. For managers charged with implementing strategy, capabilities might include leadership and communication skills, planning skills, and knowledge and expertise in the disciplines to which the strategy relates, such as new-product development or customer-relationship management. Developing such capabilities can include formal or informal training programmes, or the organization-wide dissemination of specific knowledge and resources, such as a booklet on a new computer system.

In addition to building relevant employee knowledge and skills, management attention to capability development can result in secondary and tertiary benefits. Indeed, training that gives portable and flexible job skills suggests to employees that their organization and its leaders care about their individual well-being, and for the long term. Such feelings can stimulate motivation and initiative and, ultimately, alignment. An effort to develop capabilities also gives employees the sense that management is truly committed to implementing the strategy. And, aside from the effect of employees' actual capabilities, Bandura's self-efficacy theory suggests that the degree to which employees perceive themselves as capable can be an important motivating factor.[7]

Efforts aimed at motivating, informing and developing capabilities interact with each other, in the sense that the effect of any one of these types of effort is strongly diminished – or even goes absent – when the other two types are not present. All three communication-focused efforts are necessary, as the effectiveness of one action is slight when the other actions are not engaged in full. Therefore, not only should managers pay attention to all three types of action, they should also use internal surveys to measure the collective impact.

TABLE 4.2 Processes and instruments in internal communication

	Processes			
Instruments	Structure	Flow	Contents	Climate
Informing	By which channel?	In which directions?	With which contents?	To what degree open?
Motivating	By which channel?	In which directions?	With which contents?	To what degree open?
Capability development	By which channel?	In which directions?	With which contents?	To what degree open?

The timing of the communication efforts is also important. For example, once employees have already been adequately informed about the company's strategic objective, it might not be necessary to give them further information. Instead, communicators should focus on engaging employees and stimulating capabilities. Conversely, when employees know or understand little about the strategic objective, it's too early to focus on capability development, as employees might not yet see the relevance.

Increasing impact of internal communication

Informing, motivating and capability-development efforts all use four key characteristics of internal communication: the *structure*, including the formal and informal channels through which internal messages are conveyed; the *flow*, or those processes through which internal communications move through an organization vertically, horizontally and laterally; the *content*, including the specific messages in communications; and the *climate*, which is the emotional environment of the organization and which determines how open, frank and comprehensive successful communications might be. The result of these considerations is a disciplined and methodical approach to communicating to employees through verbal and written messages, actions and consequences.

There are a number of critical success factors for each process dimension. Moreover, the three managerial efforts and the four process characteristics work in different ways with the four distinct types of organization described in Chapter 2. This will be explained in detail in the next paragraphs.

Internal communication: structure

Any internal communication structure tends to follow that of the organization. That is, organizations frequently arrange themselves in terms of specialized tasks, be it engineering, IT or accounting; the formal process of who is responsible for what; and whether an activity is to be done by a core group in a central location, or by people dispersed geographically or in business units. All of these considerations influence the ways in which people will have the greatest or least contact with each other.

Most communication experts agree that information spreads in three distinctive ways within an organization (see Figure 4.3). Proprietary or closely-held business information is normally dispersed and appropriately watered down at each step in the line reporting structure, through what's called 'formal communication'. Such communication is thought to follow an organization chart step by step. The CEO informs the extended leadership team of a desired action or outcome; they in turn explain things to middle managers, who then create memos or hold meetings with front-line employees. The reverse, sending employee messages up the line to senior management, is also considered formal. However, as the number of links increases, so does the chance of message interference, including misinterpretation and misunderstanding.

Organizations attempt to negate the potential effects of such interference through 'parallel media'. This can include internal magazines, intranet sites, message boards and meetings. On the surface, the choice of tools seems to vary with the flavour of the month, but in truth follows technology. Some years ago, video clips broadcast over a firm's intranet became one of the most popular means of executive communication. Although this leaves little room for dialogue, it's an excellent use of executive and employee time, especially where issues and information not requiring discussion are concerned. Today, executive blogs are well entrenched and, by the nature and 'rules' of social media, require at least some executive response to employee comments. But, although there are few large companies that can afford to do without an intranet, an executive's in-person communication still trumps all other forms.

Indeed, a third way in which information is rapidly spread throughout an organization is through rumour, yet another in-person and often viral form of interaction called 'the grapevine'. With the first two forms of message dispersion, management has a dominant influence over content, form and timing. The uncontrolled and mostly uncontrollable grapevine, however, is 'owned' by an organization's lower echelons.

Literature on the topic, by Johnson et al.,[8] suggests that line communication is seen by employees as more valuable than parallel media. According to the authors, this can be explained because information given through personal contact can naturally be better adapted to the needs of the speaker and listeners. As the propositions are coming straight from a supervisor's mouth, they are easier to understand and sound more credible.

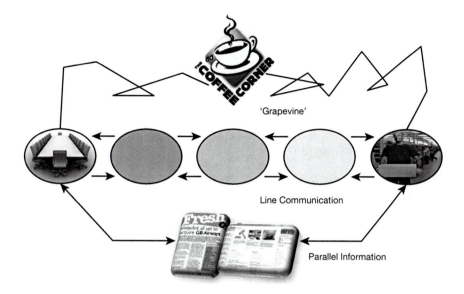

'Grapevine'

Line Communication

Parallel Information

FIGURE 4.3 Internal communication structure

This does not mean that parallel media can't be effective. On the contrary, repeated exposure to a message clearly impacts the perceptions and behavioural intentions of employees. Parallel media are, according to Dutton et al.,[9] essential conditions that 'force' the exposure of organizational members to the goals, norms and values of the organization. Analysts, including Dutton et al., believe that parallel media can intensify exposure to, and awareness of, the message. This is not surprising, as we see a similarity with advertising research: repetition leads to more familiarity with, and especially higher appreciation of, certain commercials, including their underlying intentions.

From a typical employee viewpoint, parallel media are most appreciated when they provide feedback about the employee's own performance or that of his or her work group; when the time spent with the internal media is entertaining or rewarding; and when the vehicle and its messages are considered trustworthy. Satisfaction with internal instruments is mostly measured in terms of *usefulness, reliability, timeliness* and the degree to which employees believe the organization really makes an honest, open and authentic effort to inform them.

Without doubt, the *audits* applied to measure such things will reveal which channels score best. It seems illogical, however, to suppose that the conclusions from such studies provide a reliable judgement on the quality of internal communication. It is nothing more or less than a judgement on the quality of the specific channels, where true communication is in fact broad, diverse, complex and holistic in nature.

Box 4.3 GAS NATURAL FENOSA

gasNatural
fenosa

Two companies, a merger and 'Our energy' at Gas Natural Fenosa

When Gas Natural acquired a controlling stake in its rival Union Fenosa late in 2008, it was clearly a 'transformative deal' for the two companies head-quartered in Spain. With some 20,000 employees and operations in twenty-three countries, the consolidated natural gas and electricity producer would have sufficient strength to remain a domestic force and fend off acquisition by a predatory, non-Spanish buyer. But it was clear from the beginning that managing the merger's *emotional* impact on employees was more important than any *operational* detail.

Merger integration is a demanding art, according to Secundino Muñoz Velasco, internal communications director of Gas Natural Fenosa Group, as it involves continuing the daily output at both companies, planning and implementing numerous departmental and regional reorganizations and managing the change so that mistakes aren't made and a great deal of money isn't lost in the process. During mergers, employees in both companies naturally suffer anxiety, fears of rejection and worries about their jobs and futures. When merger-related events transpire without sufficient information and lead-time, behavioural paralysis is a natural workforce development.

Launch of 'Our energy'

24 April: A banner accesible from any computer for Gas Natural and Unión Fenosa lets you see the launch commercial that marks the opening of the 'Our energy' platform. The launch of the platform is accompanied by posters that can be seen in the company's centres.

The initial content of 'Our energy', such as the speech by the chief executive or the video allowing you to see the headquarters of Gas Natural and Unión Fenosa, received around 48,500 visits on its first day.

Recognizing this dynamic, Gas Natural and Union Fenosa focused on internal communications even before the integration commenced. The idea was to transform those anxieties and fears into enthusiasm, involvement and contributions to the new company. Managing uncertainty to keep employees from rejecting changes meant generating a positive image for the merged firm, in a transparent way that encouraged workers actively to *participate* in the communication process. To earn support and alignment, the merger integration communication team believed it was critical to create a 'new concept', or a reference point that showed the validity of the merger, an identity that expressed a positive future with new opportunities for all. The term was 'Our energy' and it was the first of four pillars upon which the communication effort was built.

'Our energy' enabled the company to respond to employee doubts, give them direct access to information on the integration and ensure that workers could play a leading role in the process of unifying the two firms. Communication, then, led directly to operational changes. Following are a few highlights of the integration process:

1   Internal communication campaign: 'Our energy':
    (a)   reproduces the mechanisms of a product-launch campaign;
    (b)   has the purpose of creating an attractive image;
    (c)   has as its product the new, extraordinary company Gas Natural Fenosa;
    (d)   serves as the union of all messaging and through all channels.

2   Direct communication:
    (a)   occurs face-to-face through cascading;
    (b)   is the principal channel preferred by employees.

3   Interactive intranet:
    (a)   is the 'Our energy' platform;
    (b)   has attractive content with journalistic treatment;
    (c)   provides information in an often unsure and changing environment.

4   Feedback/'listening thermometers'
    (a)   are a necessary element of internal communication;
    (b)   include surveys, focus groups, interviews to regularly determine the organization's situation and mind frame;
    (c)   offer capacity and knowledge to react.

In practice, one of the keys to what turned into a successful integration was direct communication, which unfolded into results generated by the following activities:

Box 4.3—*continued*

- *closeness*: through visits by the chairman, chief executive and new company management to different headquarters and countries;
- *preparedness*: cascade communication has made it possible for the different levels of the company to receive the most important information from their immediate supervisors, directly;
- *participation*: bottom–up communication through focus groups and questionnaires included in cascade communication, which reflected employee concerns and doubts;
- *training*: off-sites, events and meetings have created the necessary focus of attention on key elements of the integration process.

If the communication goal was enthusiasm for the merger, then alignment with the merged company's strategies is clearly reflected in the following employee comments.

- 'I would simply like to send you my congratulations as an enthusiast of communication policies and strategies for the brilliant management of internal communication you are carrying out in such a short time. Congratulations!!'
- 'As an employee of the group and head of human resources in one of its businesses, a big THANK YOU to all the communication team for working so hard to keep us informed. I think that you are key players and have a critical mission at what is such an important time for our company. Once more, THANK YOU for helping us to integrate.'
- 'The platform manages to transmit enthusiasm for what will be a great company.'
- 'I love this campaign.'

Internal communication: flow

The majority of communication happens between people who have a direct functional relationship. Therefore, vertical communication – both top–down and bottom–up – occurs much more frequently than horizontal or lateral communication. Perhaps ironically, more information flows upward than down. The contents of the upward-directed information deal mostly with accountability to leadership, including financial reporting, sales figures and personnel data.

Research by Trombetta and Rogers,[10] however, shows that, although negative information flows slowly upward, it flows down in a rather peculiar way, as if pulled by some psychological gravity. Apparently, managers have less difficulty communicating bad news to subordinates than vice versa, although they are particularly willing to share information upward when they have good news and a trusting relationship with their superiors. A similar mechanism appears when people suppose that the person they communicate with can influence career opportunities: the larger the perceived influence, the more one will endeavour to pass positive information to this person.

Internal communication: content

Satisfaction with the contents of internal communication can be ascertained with a few questions and assessments. First, are the contents timely, readable and clearly understandable, and to a degree where employees find they receive sufficient information? Various studies provide an interesting finding, namely that people seldom indicate they have been given 'sufficient' information. Apparently, more is better,[11] even though employees frequently tune out the missives when their frequency and repetitiveness interfere with work.

Second, the content of internal communication can be clearly judged by the perceived 'feedback value' of the information being presented: do employees agree that the information contributes clarity on their role in the organization? Employees' self-confidence will increase as they better understand the end results of their contributions and are appreciated for it, which also improves involvement.

Clampitt and Downs[12] have proven, however, that the hierarchical position in the organization influences judgement on the usefulness of communication. 'The higher the position of an employee', they observe, 'the more positive their evaluation of the usefulness of the information they received from and about their organization.' We also know that positive personal feedback on the employee's contribution has an uplifting effect on job satisfaction[13] and individual productivity.[14] So, good employee communication is a blend of print, broadcast, new social media, executive presentations and also discussions between employees and their managers.

It is also important for the organization identification that employees receive reliable information about important matters occurring elsewhere in the organization. Internal articles, videos and reports on charitable works, remarkable

FIGURE 4.4 Communication contents

operations and special achievements by colleagues bring the company's extended world home. The *in-group* phenomenon becomes more prominent through such information, giving an employee more explicit things in which to take pride and with which to identify.

Third, the content of internal communication can be additionally tested by the degree to which employees experience the authenticity of the information. That is, does it sound like a massaged and biased viewpoint from the top, or does it have the look and feel of an independently produced piece in a mainstream newspaper or magazine? Most readers and viewers can tell the difference. Company stories that are one-sided and never mention difficulties – other than the euphemistic and neutered 'overcoming challenges' – almost scream their lack of that authenticity. All good story-telling, whether fiction or non-fiction, contains dramatic tension and conflict. Even if a piece or film contains a point of view, which you'd expect from a corporation, political entity or advocacy group, it loses persuasive value if the tone is perceived as insufficiently authentic. Corporate communication that honestly reflects natural tensions – including critical dialogue on important issues – gains an almost incalculable measure of credibility. This requires guts, plus a combination of strategic and creative skills among communication managers.

Internal communication: climate

Communication climate refers to the degree of openness in an organization. Redding[15] states that the characteristics of a positive communication climate include a supportive nature, participative decision-making, trust, confidence, credibility, candour and above all the application of high performance goals. The latter stresses the necessity to join forces in achieving corporate goals successfully. Various authors deem the communication climate to be the most important dimension of internal communication, because a positive climate demonstrably increases employees' commitment to their organization, improves trust in senior management[16] and, as a logical consequence, leads ultimately to improved productivity.[17]

A positive communication climate is typified by a two-way dialogue and gives routine employees a sense of being able to play an active role in the internal decision-making process. At least as important, a good climate is the ideal condition in which to create a positive self-image for employees, which in turn strongly improves feelings of importance. Again, the authenticity and quality of the communication either contribute greatly to a warm-and-yet-temperate climate, or are the result of one. If a company's psychological atmosphere and culture are marked by distrust and an intolerance of questions – based on the presumption that any enquiry signals disloyalty – good communication is unlikely to grow.

Aligning internal communication in each of the four overall organizational identity types

The four organizational identity types discussed in Chapter 2 obviously have quite divergent cultures and climates, with beliefs and behaviours that shape the tone and flow of effective communication. An anecdote or story that might be appealing to a bureaucracy – reinforcing, for example, the worth of checks, balances, double checks and deep layers of hierarchy that maintain internal order – probably wouldn't resonate well in an ideology-based organization. Conversely, making a difference on its targeted cause comes before all else, with bookkeeping and housekeeping lower on the list of priorities. As a result of these differences, internal communication must be adjusted for each type, if it's to stimulate strategically aligned behaviour.

Bureaucracy

The key managerial belief in a bureaucracy concerns managing primary processes so that outcomes are predictable, resulting in internal and especially external political support, especially in the political realm. Because specific rules and directives are logical characteristics of a bureaucracy, communication will focus heavily on informing employees of opportunities to do the right things, while motivating them by stressing the elite nature of the work they are ostensibly doing for the common good. Capability development is often aimed at the skills and attitudes that contribute order, accountability and discipline to society at large.

Many informing efforts are downward focused, and line communication is vital here, both in delivering instructions and checking the quality of the implementation of rules. Parallel media are needed, especially when the organization's size requires that additional information be disseminated to large groups of widely dispersed employees. The content of internal communication is mostly focused on topics stimulating employees to do the right things for the organization. The climate is symbolized by taking employees seriously. But, in the typically rigid bureaucratic context, employee input on forming and implementing policy is inherently limited.

Accountability

In this managerial system, employee performance increases if there is a crystal-clear process that rewards individual contributions to the organization's overall performance. The informing component of communication is thus most concerned with the organization's KPIs. Motivating efforts, however, are crucial in this organizational type, in which there is a common and widespread belief among employees that they have the potential to join the elite levels of management one day.

In reality, only a limited group of employees manage to qualify for a partnership or the rewards and perks that accrue for executives. But, because the overall performance of the firm depends on high employee performance, this little half-truth is embedded in rank-and-file beliefs. Enlarging the potential executive-management pool implies a substantial investment in developing capabilities, especially for new employees. In truth, the organization is spurring them to add value as quickly as possible, while also identifying those who can go on a true high-potential list.

Line communication in this structure is vital, whereas parallel media actually have limited relevance. Senior executives at headquarters do not intend to interfere with partners or business-unit leaders, respecting local entrepreneurial autonomy. Communication flow is mainly upward and focused on delivering results, so that desired performance is rewarded with the requisite bonus. The climate is in part a cubbyhole culture and includes a bold honesty about who can go up or who can't, at least among the fortunate.

Shared meaning

This philosophy is captured by the description that: 'Employees will perform better when top management shows a leadership vision that is inspiring.' Such a culture will coalesce only if employees strongly identify with the leader and the dominant logic that is promoted by the CEO. Even more than an accountability organization, a shared meaning organization often features a strong in-group versus out-group dynamic, which dominates the culture.

Both informing and motivating are done by line management and are supported by intense parallel media. Dialogues are crucial and have to be repeated, particularly for new employees. Stimulating and maintaining shared meaning undoubtedly require the most intense and most expensive employee communication, including support from human resources on capability development.

Shared meaning, of course, requires information flow between all parts of the organization, including the traditional vertical exchange, but also horizontal and lateral. Much of the content is about 'we' topics, or the nature and purpose of the organization and its mission. The climate, therefore, has to be open-minded, a place where employees feel that they can co-design a strategy and its implementation. As a consequence, employees should be made to feel that they are taken more seriously than is needed in other organizational types.

The nature of this model puts an inherently large degree of pressure on communication professionals, who have to be fully aware of the magnitude of the demands. Not unlike the power behind the throne, communication specialists here provide acutely vital support to the CEO and others, building and highlighting their charisma, while making executives symbols of the belief system.

Ideology

This management view can be simply summarized as follows: 'A strong ideology is enough to inspire people to do the right things.' Indeed, in an ideology, goals are non-debatable. Joining this type of organization means the employee is self-selected and already follows and cares deeply about its purpose. Although deviations from the collective beliefs will not be tolerated, most potential deviants know better than to take a job in a place where they're unwanted.

Peer influence here is large and demands little or no management concern beyond scattered and local matters. Informing and motivating are mixed. That is, most content confirms success stories that simply reinforce what employees already believe. Capability development is cognitively focused: what does one need to know to do a better job? The structure of employee communication is strongly typified by parallel media and intense dialogues in the line between employees and management, at business-unit or country level. Flow is mainly horizontal and vertically upward, centred mostly on actions that need to be orchestrated. The climate is highly stimulating for individuals who feel as if they belong to an elite cadre of believers who contribute to a better world.

Differences in paradigms require different approaches in internal communication. In other words, communication aimed at building and maintaining internal alignment does not fit a 'one size fits all' perspective. Within each of the four overall organizational identity paradigms, different requirements regarding internal communication have to be taken into account. The four process elements of employee communication – flow, structure, content and climate – have to be applied differently in each of the four paradigms. In addition, these elements are set against the three managerial efforts that go into facilitating change, including informing, motivating and capability development. The different demands put upon internal communication special are described in Table 4.3.

Looking at these factors across a matrix may at first appear complicated. But it does not really take long to grow accustomed to the combination, and to see how the interplay between the elements starts to align with an organization's identity.

TABLE 4.3 Different demands on internal communication per overall organisation identity

Paradigm	Flow – Upward – Downward – Lateral	Structure – Line – Parallel – Grapevine	Content – Me – We	Climate – Participation (P) – Openness (O) – Seriousness (S)
Accountability	• Mainly upward • Reporting results	• Line is vital	• Focus on Me	• Goal oriented • Cubbyhole culture • P, O medium; S high
Bureaucracy	• Downward and lateral EC	• Line is vital • The larger the organization, the more parallel media are needed	• Focus on We • Me only relevant as control	• Regulated; rigid, plans/policies • P, O, S low to medium
Shared meaning	• All directions; however, only if this will stimulate acceptance for core values	• Strong parallel media and persuasive • Line EC	• Focus on We • Me only relevant as part of the award system	• Visionary: one company, one vision • P, O, S high
Ideology	• Mainly upward and lateral	• Strong parallel and grapevine • EC/hardy line EC	• Clarity about We, Me topics irrelevant; only the ideal counts	• Innovative/intimacy/cooperative • P and S extremely high

Note: EC = employee communication.

From this web, executives and internal communication professionals can gain great clarity about the organization's needs and challenges; insight on what's required in the messaging; and, while developing a roll-out plan, the kinds of managerial element most needed for stimulating company-wide alignment around a new strategy.

Four scenarios in building and maintaining internal alignment

The building blocks to facilitate internal alignment, and the role of corporate communication, are clear. What remains is providing insight on using this information in a practical context. In order to provide a general idea about what mangers can expect when they decide to apply the suggested approach of this book, I have selected four scenarios that often develop in real corporations. Each starts with a key shift from one overall identity paradigm to another, which demands a transformation in desired identity traits and changes to the perceived and projected identity and in the required behaviour of employees.

All scenarios suggest the use of a specific road map, illustrated in Table 4.3. Each has specific demands made upon internal communication managers, to help implement the paradigm shift. Please note that the scenarios are examples of what happens when a company is drastically changing its strategic direction. It is during these moments of organizational truth that communication professionals can best demonstrate their added value. The four overall shifts in organizational paradigms embedded in the introduction of a new strategic focus are summarized in Table 4.4.

Scenario 1: From accountability to shared meaning

New strategies that will be highly demanding require substantial changes in the daily routines of either a large subset of employees, or a small but key group of people in the organization, such as the rainmakers in a law firm. This is especially true when the strategic intents demand that the organization shift from an accountability paradigm towards a shared meaning perspective. Trends in global consultancy and law firms illustrate this clearly. Until recently, the majority of these firms tended to focus on driving forces that rewarded individual (partner) performance. Since the turn of the century, there seems to be a shift towards a more group-focused reward system. A successful implementation of this vision requires the application of a road map where a combination of negotiation and confrontation techniques unavoidably exposes internal groups to the intentions of corporate leadership.

This requires internal messaging where the 'One company' vision is stressed continuously and consistently, in line with the vision and preferably with convincing proof points of the shift's added value. During the introductory phase, perceived identity traits will most probably show an enormous gap between the projected

TABLE 4.4 Four scenarios in shifting from one overall organizational identity to another and the consequences regarding identity and alignment

Desired identity	Projected identity	Perceived identity	Aligned behaviour
Paradigm shift			
From accountability to shared meaning			
• Shared vision • Integrated structure • Rewards based on contribution to the collectivity	• Charismatic leadership as source of inspiration	• Worries about losing autonomy and individual rewards plus fear of becoming a less entrepreneurial company	• Awareness is mostly high, attitude is formally positive, but degree of understanding and aligned behaviour are negative and require substantial investments
From bureaucracy to accountability			
• Typical for public-sector organizations that want to become more market driven • Introduction of new reward systems (bonus, differentiation in payments), emphasis on performance that can be quantified	• Language becomes filled with terminology from the private sector (clients instead of civilians; return on investment instead of adding value to society etc.)	• Many employees feel a gap between the old world and the new (desired) world and tend to be sceptical about the new vision and the way it is implemented	• Awareness is high, but attitude and especially understanding plus actual aligned behaviour are mostly negative and not in line with the dreams of top management or their political leaders

From bureaucracy to shared meaning

- Organizations with a high number of rules and directives understand that their employees will be more inspired if they are confronted with BHAG ideas.[18] For example, insurance firms that take customer satisfaction 100% seriously by being open about their offerings and the way they handle claims is a nice example

- This type of organization focuses messaging on an inspiring idea that creates excitement and a higher degree of involvement with the organization
- Interesting example is the Cooperative Bank in the UK or Rabobank in Holland; both explicitly state they are not focused on profit but on serving members (not clients)

- Friction here will focus on the daily routines in the business versus the ideals presented in corporate messaging
- Appealing as these messages will be, employees will especially have doubts about the exact meaning of the claims in their daily work setting

- Again awareness will be high, just as attitude is
- Understanding and actual supportive behaviour will take time too

From shared meaning to ideology

- This is a dangerous shift. It often suggests a situation where the visionary leader takes or is pushed into a more or less ideological role

- Leadership is presented less and less critically, expressing a person and/or a leadership group as the best the firm has ever experienced

- Employees often are enthusiastic about the leadership as long as success continues, both at macro level and at their own micro level.
- As soon as success turns into failure employees feel like actors in their own emperor's clothing fairy tale

- During success most employees know, understand and fully support the strategy. As soon as failures come up, their support is reduced fast

FIGURE 4.5 The introduction of the new *Strategy As One* at Deloitte Netherlands

and desired identities. Long-standing partners will probably adhere to the old, dominant logic of the accountability paradigm, convinced that what worked in the past will continue to work in the future. It takes leadership courage, time and, above all, proof points to convince entrenched employees to start believing a new vision.

In line with this trend, supportive behaviour – measured in alignment research – will most probably be low. But shifting towards a shared meaning paradigm has become very popular over the last decade. The investments needed to implement this successfully do not always seem to be fully realized at the start of the process. (Investments, by the way, are not only financial, but include a psychological shift from, say, the rainmakers, to accept a system where group rewards take precedence over the individual.) This scenario probably includes the highest expectations of corporate communication, if the change is to succeed.

Scenario 2: From bureaucracy to accountability

Public-sector organizations in many Western countries have been confronted with a growing belief among politicians that applying market mechanisms increases the effectiveness of what were once government-owned institutions, including tele-communication companies, utilities and railways, as well as other segments that used to be part of the public sector. This has resulted in the launch of new strategies, initiated by politicians and top civil servants, to become more customer focused. The change also includes adopting internal reward systems comparable to the private sector and openly distinguishing high-performing employees from the laggards who were protected in a bureaucracy. Typical in this shift is an emphasis on quantifiable KPIs, with less attention paid to qualitative criteria such as supporting society.

Obviously, this results in the projection of messages that look and feel like private-sector communications. Among employees with long tenure, this will evoke a feeling of disorientation. The new, dominant logic will be hard to accept for those who have lived for years with the ideas of pure bureaucracy developed by the German philosopher Max Weber.[19] Resistance from some employees will be high, both explicitly and above all implicitly. Thus, stimulating customer focus and converting a bureaucracy into an accountability model organization is quite a challenge for senior management.

An important driver of employee support involves finding specific identity traits that are seen as realistic, relevant and inspiring by a majority of the key people. The process starts with analysing perceived identity traits and comparing them with the desired ones of top management. Increases in aligned behaviour will require the application of both negotiation and confrontation techniques and will come to fruition when management succeeds in finding a satisfying balance between perceived and desired identity traits. Employees are moved positively by internal messages that show respect for their contributions in the past, but that also provide them with hope for an inspiring future. However, in line with the logic of the accountability paradigm, internal messaging will also convey the importance of KPIs, explained through a variety of communication vehicles, including in-person conversations between managers and employees.

Indeed, line managers play a crucial role, as they are the ones who assess the quality and quantity of the contributions of individual employees through appraisal discussions. Shifting to accountability no doubt includes the use of confrontation techniques for those employees who don't fit in the new vision. In a shift from bureaucracy to accountability, appraisal discussions and salary treatment – including

Box 4.4 REPSOL'S SHIFT TO ACCOUNTABILITY

At Repsol, we're working hard to adapt the entire organization to a work culture and climate that boost efficiency and stimulate new ideas.

This involves responding to business needs, while, at the same time, sharing specific values that define Repsol's own style – our unique way of doing things. With this as our objective, we are working on several initiatives that deal with: executive leadership; diversity; equal opportunities and work–life balance; attracting talent; training; mobility; performance assessment; innovation and improvement processes etc.

In all of these projects, the employee is considered to be the main stakeholder in the creation of the company's reputation. In fact, their opinion is so important that, every two years, a climate survey is carried out on the entire staff, approximately 22,000 workers worldwide. In the last survey, presented in July 2011, eight out of ten Repsol employees claimed to be proud to form part of the company, showing a 7 per cent increase compared with the previous survey and confirming the importance of working towards cultural alignment in the organization.

The opening of a new headquarters in Madrid, planned for early 2012, will undoubtedly help to substantiate the values that comprise Repsol's culture, given that it will house almost 5,000 people and has been designed to develop new interpersonal relations. The building has been awarded with a sustainability certification and is made up of four interconnected buildings, all looking over a large central garden. Emphasis has been placed on the creation of spaces for interaction and professional and personal facilities for employees.

the denial of a raise, counselling and even the threat of demotion or termination – becomes a vital form of communication in its own right.

Scenario 3: From bureaucracy to shared meaning

The bureaucracy paradigm is not exclusive to the public sector. Many organizations that are coloured by rigid rules and directions fit this paradigm too. Businesses where safety is clearly an issue, such as the chemical industry, or where standardized administrative procedures are crucial for success, as with banks, often are dominated by bureaucratic identity traits. A shift towards a shared meaning paradigm requires identifying other inspiring traits, along with concrete instructions from top management for implementing this new ambition in daily routines.

Success in generating employee support for the new strategy will increase when the desired traits fit with the perceived identity traits among key groups. Many employees will be easily inspired but lack self-confidence to implement the vision in their daily activities, simply because they don't dare to do it or, more likely, don't know how to start working in a different way. Various alignment studies have shown that, when employees don't understand the new strategy well, supportive behaviour is weak.

Negotiations and confrontation techniques become most effective when they include testimonials, showing unconvinced employees how others have successfully incorporated the new vision in their daily routines. But shifting from bureaucracy to shared meaning includes some risk, as the key identity traits typifying each are quite opposite. Although such a transition is not impossible, the road map is a long one, with a staggered implementation horizon that allows employees to get acquainted with the new demands step by step. Showing successes in mirroring techniques can also increase the speed of adaptation.

Scenario 4: From shared meaning to ideology

Most top managers love the shared meaning paradigm, where the typical traits depict an organization in perfect alignment. Employees are enthusiastic about the leadership vision, and the CEO is seen as the charismatic main driver and protector of this new vision. However, when a leader starts believing that he or she is irreplaceable, and direct reports remain uncritically silent, a highly dangerous situation can develop. An organization that's working well under the shared meaning model is about to be dragged into the ideology model.

This can happen, for example, in smaller consultancy firms, where the founder and rainmaker is cherished as the driver of success, even as only good news gets emphasis, while negative signals are ignored. The same can happen in family-owned companies with long-lasting personal leadership by one family member. In such cases, the leader begins to exhibit increasingly megalomaniac behaviour. Consequently, the shift from a shared meaning towards an ideology paradigm is often made implicitly, and hardly ever explicitly. However, the dangers of overvaluing one person and their ideas are obvious and highly threatening to an organization's continuity.

Ideology works for Greenpeace, but does not serve most business well.

So, should employees resist the gradual transition? The communication director, serving in the role of court jester, might be able to stimulate some hard thinking among other members of the firm's dominant coalition, at least with regard to reining in the leader's behaviour. Awareness of this shift – and the dangers involved with it – will hopefully come when intelligence is gathered in line with the steps suggested in this chapter.

However, as with all other companies, management with an ideology-focused perspective will present its new strategic objectives as brilliant plans for a broader product portfolio, or a more sophisticated offering in existing markets. Testing the fit between this new strategic objective and the company's identity and employee behaviour will most probably show a weak fit with the perceived identity – *if* employees are honest about their situation. Hopefully, this will stimulate self-reflection at top management level and a reassessment of the organization's internal direction.

Notes

1 D. Dell, Y. Tsaplina and R. Kramer, *Forging strategic business alignment*, New York: The Conference Board, (2003).
2 C.B.M. van Riel, G.A.J.M. Berens and M. Dijkstra, 'Stimulating strategically aligned behaviour among employees', *Journal of Management Studies*, (2009), vol. 46(7), pp. 1197–1227.
3 A. Smidts, A.Th.H. Pruyn and C.B.M. van Riel, 'The impact of employee communication and perceived external prestige on organizational identification', *Academy of Management Journal*, (2001), vol. 49(5), pp. 1051–62.
4 Ibid.
5 E.W. Morrison and F.J. Milliken, 'Organizational silence: a barrier to change and development in a pluralistic world', *Academy of Management Review*, (2000), vol. 25, pp. 706–25.
6 F.J. Milliken, E.W. Morrison and P.F. Hewlin, 'An exploratory study of employee silence: issues that employees don't communicate upward and why', *Journal of Management Studies*, (2003), vol. 40, pp. 1453–76.
7 A. Bandura, *Self-efficacy: the exercise of control*, New York: Freeman, (1997), p. 604.
8 J.D. Johnson, W.A. Donohue, C.K. Atkin and S. Johnson, 'Differences between formal and informal communication channels', *Journal of Business Communication*, (1994), vol. 31, pp. 111–22.
9 J. Dutton and J.W. Penner, 'The importance of organizational identity for strategic agenda building', in J. Hendry and G. Johnson (eds), *Strategic thinking: leadership and the management of change*, New York: Wiley, (1993).
10 J.J. Trombetta and D.P. Rogers, 'Communication climate, job satisfaction, and organizational commitment', *Management Communication Quarterly*, (1988), vol. 4(1), pp. 494–514.
11 S. Zimmermann, S.B. Davenport and J.W. Haas, 'Communication meta myths in the workplace: the assumption that more is better', *Journal of Business Communication*, (1996), vol. 33(2), pp. 185–203.
12 P.G. Clampitt and C.W. Downs, 'Employee perceptions of the relationship between communication and productivity: a field study', *Journal of Business Communications*, (1993), vol. 30(1), pp. 5–28.

13 F. Varona, 'Relationship between communication satisfactions and organizational commitment in three Guatemalan organizations', *Journal of Business Communications*, (1996), vol. 33(2), pp. 111–40.

14 Clampitt and Downs, 'Employee perceptions of the relationship between communication and productivity: a field study', pp. 5–28.

15 W.C. Redding, *Communication within the organization: an interpretive review of theory and research*, New York: Industrial Communication Council, (1972).

16 D.P. McCauley and K.W. Kuhnert, 'A theoretical review and empirical investigation of employee trust in management', *Public Administration Quarterly*, (1992), vol. 16(2), pp. 265–84.

17 R.D. Rosenberg and E. Rosenstein, 'Participation and productivity: an empirical study', *Industrial and Labor Relations Review*, (1980), vol. 33(3), 355–67.

18 J. Collins and J. Porras, *Built to last: successful habits of visionary companies*, New York: Harper Business, (1994).

19 M. Weber, *Economy and society. An outline of interpretive sociology* (1922/1968), vols. 1–3, eds G. Roth and C. Wittich, New York: Bedminster Press.

PART II

Building external alignment

5

GATHERING INTELLIGENCE AIMED AT CREATING EXTERNAL ALIGNMENT

Organizations, and especially large corporations, are affected by the environment in which they operate, and by forces over which they may have little or no control. Because they touch so many segments of society, such companies are particularly vulnerable to the impact of external turbulence, be it from government regulations or investigations, activist groups, rivals bent on a hostile takeover, angry consumers or media that portray the organization in a poor light. The ability to manage the potential negative consequences of external pressures is predicated on understanding the beliefs of those external stakeholders upon whom a firm depends.

External intelligence can be distinguished by three focal points: first, organizations have to be at least aware of developments in beliefs about *issues* that might impact the firm now and in the future. Some issues earn such a prominent position in public debate that they evolve into a public-opinion problem. In such a case, a large number of people know about the issue, express an opinion about it and urge governments to take actions to reduce an assumed negative impact. However, not all issues become visible to large masses and media, but remain within the territories of specialized non-governmental organizations or other lobby groups; while their size might be limited, that does not mean that their influence is restricted.

Second, organizations should also be focused on gathering intelligence about larger and more visible audiences regarding beliefs that are not directly linked to a specific issue. This can either be *public opinion* or *reputation* research.

A third focal point is the collection of ad hoc information that is needed to stimulate alignment around a specific strategic objective. This includes a variety of research avenues, such as an analysis of competitors, researching into specific consumer behaviour or studying the impact of publicity in either the traditional or the new media.

TABLE 5.1 Focus points in external intelligence

External intelligence	Focus points
Issue scanning	• Early-warning systems
Stakeholder beliefs	• Public opinion
	• Reputation
Additional ad hoc intelligence	• Competitor analyses
	• Tailor-made market research

Issue scanning

An issue becomes relevant when it stimulates concrete actions by crucial stakeholders that might result in organizational damage. Quite recently, the Wikileaks scandal and widespread anger about bonuses paid to financial executives triggered steps that could affect governments and the banking industry. *Early-warning systems* can at least help by creating awareness about an issue, enabling organizations to prepare an appropriate reaction in advance of a crisis, and possibly averting one. Although infrequent scanning is often conducted as a crisis-management response, an annual or continuous research programme will usually inform ongoing strategic decision-making.

Information about issues must be assessed in two dimensions, including its *potential impact* on the company and the *likeliness* of its occurrence. Multiplying the potential impact by the likeliness gives us a good indication of its importance to the firm. Perrott[1] describes a different typology, distinguishing issues as highly important if they impact both the organization and society, as against less significant issues that have only an operational and internal affect.

Issues appear to evolve in more or less predictable life cycles, an idea illustrated in academic literature by Buchholz,[2] whose model describes an issue life cycle in four stages:

- *Entering the agenda* reflects changing public expectations of an industry and its companies, creating pressure to solve the problem with regulation.
- *Political disputes* then arise in the media and among key interest groups, resulting in the start of a formal public-policy process.
- *Legislation* essentially institutionalizes the issue in a set of formal rules.
- *Litigation* follows when there is a breakdown in negotiations between companies, governments and interest groups about enforcement standards and timetables.

Scanning should not only focus on these stages in the political arena, but also on the impact of opinion formation within interest groups. In examining the development of an issue over time, a researcher might ask: What is the gap in

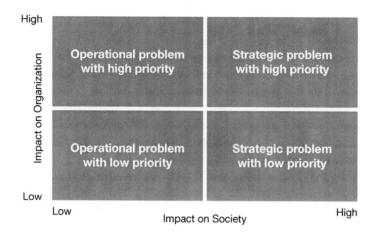

FIGURE 5.1 Issue scanning[3]

mutual expectations between the organization and external interest groups? To what degree does this create a controversy? And, what would be the organizational impact of such? The earlier a company can identify a potential threat, the earlier it can develop an adequate response that may even short-circuit the threat's development.

In turn, the nature of the response depends upon the cause of each gap. For example, an issue that arises over a dispute about facts requires a factual reaction, through trustworthy research that reveals well-supported qualitative points. This is what Shell tried to do during the infamous Brent Spar crisis, disclosing all internal studies behind its decision to sink the floating oil-production platform to the bottom of the ocean. Obviously, a pragmatic and practical response does not always work, as, when emotions are inflamed, facts bounce uselessly off deaf ears.

A different reaction is required when the gap is more normative in nature, such as a disagreement over what ought to be standard practice. In the case of the Brent Spar, Shell's critics in Greenpeace stated that it was simply not acceptable to pollute the sea. At the time, the environmental impact of hauling the platform to shore and disposing of it on land didn't really register with the public imagination, even though the process was ultimately worse than disposal at sea. As the conflict grew, Greenpeace took command of the argument with the compelling fear of an oceanic disposal that fouled the Atlantic and killed fish, turtles and marine mammals.

Finally, a gap might be based on completely different ideals. In the case of the Brent Spar, it came down to a debate between Greenpeace idealists fighting for a cleaner environment and the engineers and business types at Shell who viewed oil production as a vital factor in economic development. The latter two gaps are difficult and practically impossible to bridge.

In summary, issue scanning should result in intelligence based on answering three practical questions, stated in Figure 5.2.

Box 5.1 BRENT SPAR CASE[4]

Just like cars and ships, offshore oil-production platforms do not have an eternal life and, as a consequence, need to be retired and removed. Some are taken ashore and cut into pieces. Others, particularly in the Gulf of Mexico, are cut loose from their legs or moorings and purposely sunk, with government permission and encouragement, as cleaned-up old rigs make excellent artificial reefs that host flourishing populations of sea life. Not all production platforms, however, are created equal.

During the 1990s, a Shell-owned floating oil-production storage and tanker-loading buoy in the North Sea, offshore from Scotland, called the Brent Spar, outlived its usefulness, having been replaced by a pipeline that brought oil to an onshore terminal. Shell started an extensive study on the best solution for the Brent Spar's removal. Several salvage companies, engineering firms and institutes delivered over thirty reports on the project. The final conclusion was clear: after cleaning and removing as much of the waste and loose materials as possible, sinking the Brent Spar in the deep Atlantic was the safest, cheapest and least environmentally damaging method of disposal. Several Scottish institutions, including the Scottish Association for Marine Science, agreed to the Spar's sinking in the North Fenni Ridge area, west of the Shetland Islands. Following discussions with British authorities and governments of all countries bordering the North Sea and the East Atlantic Ocean, no objections were submitted.

The leaders of Greenpeace, one of the world's best-known environmental activist groups, felt differently. About two months after learning of the plan to sink the Brent Spar, four Greenpeace activists boarded and occupied the buoy in the spring of 1995. Over the next three weeks, some twenty-five activists, photographers and journalists converged on the Spar, while Greenpeace waged an intense media campaign on the environmental dangers of deep-ocean disposal. According to Greenpeace, the Brent Spar contained more than 5,500 tons of oil sediment and additional tons of low-level radioactive deposits, a mixture that included poisonous, non-degradable chemicals and heavy metals. Greenpeace suggested that sinking the Brent Spar platform in the North Sea would establish a precedent for the 416 fixed oil platforms in the North Sea, and that the permission given by the British government to sink the Brent Spar in the sea had been given on the basis of limited, one-sided information provided by Shell.

The debate escalated and led to a boycott of Shell service stations in northern Europe, an arson attack on one, and severe damage to the firm's reputation around the world. Shell produced facts that showed the Bent Spar contained less than 50 tons of sediment. But the numbers meant little in a clash that spun totally out of control for two reasons. First, the political context in which

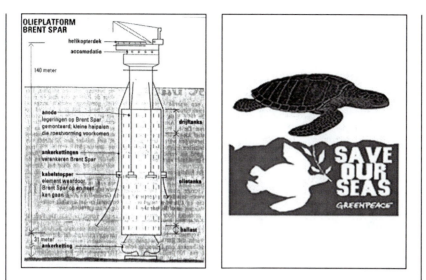

the debate evolved blocked any chance of a rational discussion between opinion leaders. Left-leaning politicians in Germany and Denmark used Brent Spar as a convenient symbol of unacceptable corporate behaviour towards the environment, while others throughout Europe publicly supported the consumer boycott. Second, Greenpeace used highly expressive messaging in making their case, including a simple drawing of a dead turtle that accompanied the slogan 'Save our seas'. In response, Shell published an advocacy advertisement clearly expressing the view of a company insider, full of details only relevant to engineers.[5] The public pressure on Shell intensified so strongly that sinking the Brent Spar was no longer an option. Eventually towed to a port in Norway, it was partly dismantled and recycled.

Following the decision, Shell asked a leading verification organization to conduct independent research into Brent Spar, which indicated that the vessel possessed far less poisonous material than suggested by Greenpeace. The activist organization accepted the outcome of this study and apologized to Shell, and even came under criticism for its posturing, tactics and misrepresentations of the truth. And yet, in the case of the Brent Spar and public opinion, the idealistic Greenpeace message clearly prevailed over the pragmatic response by Shell.

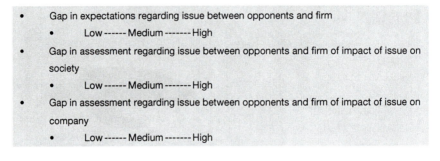

- Gap in expectations regarding issue between opponents and firm
  - Low ------ Medium ------- High
- Gap in assessment regarding issue between opponents and firm of impact of issue on society
  - Low ------ Medium ------- High
- Gap in assessment regarding issue between opponents and firm of impact of issue on company
  - Low ------ Medium ------- High

FIGURE 5.2 Fit between strategic objectives and issues

Tracking beliefs of crucial external stakeholders

Creating alignment with selected external stakeholders requires a basic understanding of their beliefs about the organization. This can be achieved by tracking perceptions of those relevant stakeholders, which is essentially the firm's reputation. However, we know from research that the assessment of an individual organization is also coloured by other sets of beliefs, such as product evaluations, industry reputation and public opinion.

In contrast with reputation, public-opinion research is not specifically focused on one organization, but on individuals and organizations that dominate a public-opinion debate, such as media and leaders of advocacy groups. To deal better with external stakeholders, it is useful to explore the theoretical and methodological backgrounds of public opinion and reputation.

Public opinion

The foundations of reputation research are rooted in public-opinion literature. Publications about this topic go back to the eighteenth century, when demographic analyses were used to predict future behaviour. Johan Graunt's book,[6] called *Observations on the bills of morality*, showed that, with the help of census data – including mortality, marriages, births and citizenship – one could understand the 'physics of society' and make fairly accurate forecasts of impending behavioural patterns.

A boost in public-opinion research took place in the middle of the nineteenth century with the launch of the representative-survey technique. This quantification of public-opinion trends was used in debates about what a government should do or should not do. The next accelerator in the field came in the 1930s, with the creation of the academic journal *Public Opinion Quarterly*, stimulating academics to contribute to the further development of public-opinion research. In the opening article of this journal, Allport[7] defined public opinion as, 'interpretations of topics of national interest that can be expressed freely by individuals outside the government, intended to influence decision making by the dominant powers in a specific society'.

FIGURE 5.3 *Public Opinion Quarterly*[8]

According to Allport, people express an opinion because they expect others will confirm their point of view: e.g., 'You start cleaning the snow in front of your door because you expect others to do the same'.[9] Another reason people express opinions publicly is their fear of isolation, a punishment for not joining the dominant stream of social thought. In addition to these individual needs, public opinion is also affected by context factors, more precisely by the influence of a social group on opinion formation, such as family, school, church, work environment and, last but not least, the media.[10]

Originally, most authors writing about the effects of mass media on public opinion typified the impact of the press as 'a giant hypodermic needle influencing the masses quite easily'. However, the assumed power of newspapers, magazines, radio and television was overestimated, as later studies showed. The dominant belief today is that media are only effective in confirming existing public trends, and are not able to change them radically. According to Brouwer,[11] the creation of public opinion works like a mycelium: one sees the mushrooms standing up – the media – and not the network of roots below the ground. In reputation circles, we call what moves through that network 'informal communication', but it is the most important element of the mycelium's survival.

Brouwer stresses that mass media are the most visible and spectacular part of opinion creation. The real drivers of opinion creation, though, are informal communication and the negotiations between members of the public that lead to a dominant opinion. Research by McCombs and Caroll[12] showed that a medium's impact is larger when it devotes time and space to an issue. This is the media's so-called 'agenda-setting' function. That is, the more attention is paid to an issue, the higher the likelihood it will become relevant in the minds of the medium's readers or viewers.

Recent research into the impact social media hold over public opinion indicates that such avenues are more powerful than we've assumed in the past.[13] A key characteristic of social media is that interest groups that want something specific to happen drive the issues. In the past, pressure groups were forced to depend upon attention from conventional media. Now they communicate directly, and the impact of their interventions increases tremendously when their messages make their way into, and are echoed by, old-style media such as television or newspapers, which still carry influence. Old media give third-party validation to what's appearing in the new media.

The basic principles of the creation and development of public opinion can be found in the so-called 'spiral of silence' theory of Noelle-Neumann.[14] The basic notions of her theory can be summarized as follows:

- Individuals have a strong need to be accepted by the group of which they want to be part, and they greatly fear isolation over expressing a point of view that is not aligned with the (perceived) dominant opinion. That is why most people are opinion followers, instead of opinion leaders.
- People who consider their opinion to be part of the dominant logic in society tend to express it loud and clear, whereas people who consider their personal view to be a minority point of view have a tendency to stay silent.
- Choosing to be part of the silent majority is driven by individual characteristics – the fear of isolation – combined with group pressure, resulting from repeated messaging by the media and peer groups stressing the same dominant opinions, while avoiding the minority views.
- This mixture of personal and group characteristics results in the 'bandwagon effect' and the spiral-of-silence mechanism that reduces public discussion of minority topics; as the majority point of view gets more attention, the number of its supporters increase.
- Dominance in public opinion, however, is never for ever. If an opponent group is excluded from public debate over a period of time, it will strengthen and sharpen its opinions, and its repression will be eventually followed by a larger degree of popularity, owing to the underdog effect. If it perseveres, its vision might become the new dominant public opinion. After that, the opinion formation and control process described here repeats again.

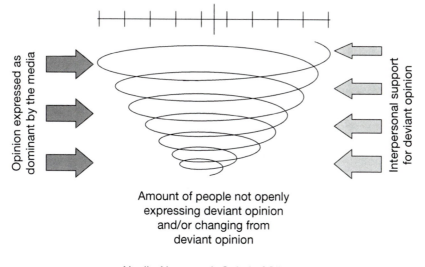

Noelle-Neumann's Spiral of Silence

FIGURE 5.4 Spiral of silence[15]

Public-opinion research has a long tradition, is rooted in solid philosophical foundations and methodologies, and is expressed in interesting theoretical explanations. Nearly all the above-mentioned notions can also be used to explain the creation and development of reputation. A key point of differentiation from reputation research is that, in public-opinion studies, the emphasis lies on the impact of issues upon the political decision-making process, including legislation and, later, litigation. Discussions about public opinion are nearly always focused in the end on governmental decisions. In contrast, discussions about reputations result in a variety of stakeholder demands either granting – or limiting – a licence to operate to a specific organization. Still, the practical consequences of public opinion are twofold:

1   Organizations should scan carefully those issues that might impact them when crucial groups in society consider a topic in the firm's domain as highly important and push for actions by a governmental institution aimed at 'solving' the perceived problem through legislation.
2   Awareness of the issue is one thing, but taking the right actions is totally different and more important. A key point for organizations to understand and accept about public opinion is to avoid, as much as possible, becoming the public's object of irritation. Consider the negative sentiments about obesity in the Western world as a dominant issue of public opinion. Pressure groups purposely selected McDonald's as the epitome of the problem, a smart choice from their point of view – for McDonald's, not so much. The US government now

- Might the issue evolve into a public opinion topic?
  - Low ------ Medium ------- High possibility
- What is the risk of being blamed solely as a firm for a public opinion topic?
  - Low ------ Medium ------- High possibility
- Will government be supportive when the firm comes under attack?
  - Low ------ Medium ------- High possibility

FIGURE 5.5 Fit between a strategic objective and public opinion

requires restaurants to publish calorie counts in foods, and, although this may not deter anyone from eating two Big Macs and a large serving of French fries, it does reflect negatively on all companies that serve high-calorie meals, broadening the accusations to an industry level.

Figure 5.5 summarizes the key points that have to be addressed in gathering relevant intelligence about public opinion in the context of a specific strategic objective.

Reputation

Reputation derives from the Latin words *re*, which means over and over, and *putare*, which is to calculate. Reputation literally means calculating over and over again the pros and cons of a subject, a person, an organization or its products. This is a rational process that also holds an emotional component. Reputation is a perception about the degree of admiration, positive feelings and trust an individual has for another person, an organization, an industry or even a country.

Reputation is rooted in an assessment of the performance of an organization over time, including in the past and with expectations about the future. For companies, it means a comparison with similar organizations. However, no concrete, immutable or permanent reputation ever exists. An organizational reputation is an aggregation of individual opinions measured *at a specific moment in time*, among a sample of the audience it is intended to represent.

Some well-known rankings – *Fortune* magazine's 'Most admired companies' and the *Financial Times*/PwC European ranking – all see reputation as equal to an attitude. An attitude is an evaluation of an object, idea or person, with a cognitive and rational component, an affective and more emotional piece, and a behavioural tendency, as it often predicts what people will most probably do. The dominant paradigm in this line of research assumes that reputation is a summation of a set of attributes, measuring the performance and social responsibility of organizations.

For example, *Fortune* measures companies looking at eight attributes, including the quality of management; products and services; financial soundness; ability to attract and keep talented people; use of corporate assets; value as a long-term investment; innovativeness; and community and environmental responsibility. They calculate the average scores for each attribute and then divide the sum by eight, to determine the company's 'most admired' ranking. A critical review of this research states that *Fortune* ratings are overly coloured by financial performance and media coverage, therefore suggesting that respondents unconsciously factor financial viewpoints in their judgements, as has been shown by Fryxell and Wang.[16] That does not mean at all that this attitude approach – or the *Fortune* ranking – is useless. It can add value, especially when the approach combines the evaluations with expectations, resulting in more relevant information. This is especially relevant when expectations appear to be high, as we have found frequently in reputation studies for the Dutch police. Most people in the Netherlands appear to make a modestly positive evaluation of the police, with a rating between 59 and 63 on a 100-point scale. However, when the same respondents are asked to reveal their expectations about the core task of the police – taking care of public safety in a professional and socially responsible way – the average scores range between 80 and 90 points. In other words, the gap between evaluations and expectations is more interesting than the evaluations alone.

My personal view is that reputation can better be analysed using the 'Gestalt' approach as the starting point in measurement. 'Gestalt' is a term developed in

FIGURE 5.6 Reputation rankings

German psychology that refers to the 'wholeness' in information processing. The underlying theory assumes that the mind of an individual works holistically. So, in the case of reputations, people who are confronted with a company name tend to form an instant judgement, identifying it with a simple assessment of being *good*, *bad* or *ugly*.[17]

In this view, reputation can be measured directly by asking respondents to describe their overall judgement of an organization. The Reputation Institute used this approach to develop a new scale to measure reputation, which is called the 'Pulse score'.[18] It is derived through the following four concepts: *positive feeling*, *high esteem*, *trust* and *admiration*. The scores for reputation are based on global research, and, in each country, the data are corrected for cultural bias. Judgements on these four concepts are driven by perceptions of quality, broken down into seven key drivers: product and services, innovation, role as employer, social responsibility, governance, leadership and performance.[19] Positive or negative evaluations of each of the drivers impact the Pulse score. In addition to the *drivers* or antecedents of reputation, we also have to distinguish the *consequences* of reputation, which can include the intention to invest in a firm, a desire to work for it, a willingness to buy its products and services, or speaking positively about the organization in general. This line of argument is used by the Reputation Institute in developing its RepTrak model; see Figure 5.7. Simply summarized, this model measures 'do you love me' (Pulse score = reputation), 'why do you love me?'(dimensions that form the drivers of reputation) and, finally, 'what are the consequences in behaviour of this expression of love (or lack of it)?' (supportive behaviour).

The RepTrak model is used in global research and, up until now, has been the only source in the world where one can find reputation data on companies operating on all continents. More than a decade of research with this instrument has revealed the following trends:

- Reputation can be expressed quantitatively on a scale from 0 to 100. Empirical data show that companies with a score above 80 are seen as world-class reputation leaders, whereas firms that score below 45 are in the extreme-danger zone.
- Reputation differs tremendously between types of stakeholder. Each group tends to assess an organization on those aspects that matter most to that specific group. Evaluations by financial analysts are coloured by their assessments of the financial performance, whereas people at idealistic non-governmental organizations (NGOs) tend to overemphasize corporate social responsibility.
- Reputation scores stay within a bandwidth that is typical for a specific industry. Some industries are bound to higher ranges, such as retail and food, whereas telecommunication firms and railways fall into a lower category of scores.
- Strong reputations are stable, even in crisis situations. Weaker reputations are more vulnerable, but can be restored as well when the right set of actions is implemented.

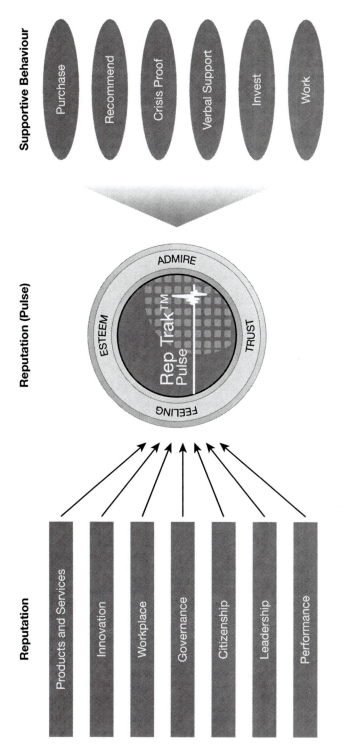

FIGURE 5.7 RepTrak™ model, Reputation Institute

TABLE 5.2 Global ranking, Reputation Institute, 2011

Rank	Company	RepTrak™ Pulse	Rank	Company	RepTrak™ Pulse
1	Google	79.99	16	Nestlé	76.01
2	Apple	79.77	17	Hewlett-Packard	75.90
3	The Walt Disney Co.	79.51	18	Michelin	75.75
4	BMW	79.42	19	L'Oréal	75.72
5	LEGO	79.26	20	Kellogg's	75.2
6	Sony	79.05	21	Goodyear	75.09
7	Daimler	79.03	22	Ferrero	75.01
8	Canon	78.07	23	Philips Electronics	74.84
9	Intel	77.56	24	3M	74.68
10	Volkswagen	77.33	25	Nintendo	74.66
11	Microsoft	77.29	26	Colgate-Palmolive	74.62
12	Nike	76.92	27	IBM	74.41
13	Panasonic	76.84	28	The Coca-Cola Co.	74.27
14	Johnson & Johnson	76.75	29	Honda Motor	73.99
15	Nokia	76.17	30	Danone	73.92

The Reputation Institute annually publishes the results of its Global Pulse Study, taken from the general public with regard to about 2,500 of the largest companies in forty countries (see: www.reputationinstitute.com and www.forbes.com). Table 5.2 shows the results of the 2011 measurement, in which Google's scores made it the most admired company in the world.

Reputations matter, but antecedents differ per stakeholder group

A positive reputation matters greatly, if only because it substantially reduces an organization's costs. There are piles of studies showing that a solid reputation decreases costs in the labour market, as it is easier to attract and retain new employees; that it decreases the costs of attracting capital and simplifies finding potential joint-venture partners; and, last but not least, it lowers litigation costs, simply because these types of organization are trusted more and sued less. An excellent reputation also gives a firm certain advantages with specific stakeholder groups, as follows, for example:

Financial audiences

A good reputation with these stakeholders mitigates financial damage in a stock-market crisis. Moreover, having a good corporate reputation positively impacts securities analysts' earnings forecasts.[20] Future profitability is associated with higher reputation, as evidence has shown that corporate reputation has beneficial implications for future profitability, by helping organizations attain superior performance outcomes.[21]

Two types of financial audience are especially important in reputation-building activities: securities analysts and institutional investors.[22] Analysts who study stocks have shown a certain 'herd mentality', meaning they are influenced by opinion leaders within their own field of work. Reputation appears to affect investment decisions made by institutional and individual investors too. From an organizational perspective, maintaining a good corporate reputation with institutional shareholders is most critical, given the financial power they can wield.

A recent study by Wang *et al.*[23] provides evidence on the reputation–equity–performance relationship. By comparing firms with high and low rankings in a reputation ranking list, as well as firms not mentioned in a reputation list, Wang *et al.* found that its simply being listed in a reputation ranking increases investors' appreciation of a firm, and a high reputation ranking appears to have an even more positive effect and gives a competitive advantage.[24]

Governments

Building favourable relations with government institutions has a positive pay-off, as it allows the organization to achieve, maintain or enhance cooperation with public-sector institutions.[25] However, data providing 'evidence' of the degree to which a sound reputation makes a difference in the public sector are hard to find and mainly anecdotal. The explanation is obvious: civil servants and politicians never admit that they are influenced by excellent reputations, just as they claim to be immune to the whispers and contributions of lobbyists.[26,27]

Customers

A good reputation among consumers increases the likelihood of favourable purchase decisions. Advertising claims about being best in class are credible only if the organization has a good reputation.[28] A good reputation pays off, especially in high-risk purchase situations. In these risk assessments, corporate reputation associations with, especially, innovation and trustworthiness become more prevalent when the product is evaluated, thereby tipping the scale in favour of purchasing goods from a high-reputation organization.[29,30]

Companies with a good reputation are also able to charge higher prices and build a customer base that is more loyal and that buys a broader range of products and services.[31] When faced with a new product, the customer will take into account the reputation of the parent behind the brand: if an organization has built a good reputation based on its abilities, this will spill over into positive perceptions of new products offered by that organization.[32] It must be noted that these effects are likely to be most prevalent when the organization uses a monolithic branding strategy.[33]

Labour market

A company's reputation as an employer is based on its past actions and jobseekers' expectations of the organization's future behaviour.[34] An organization with a good workplace reputation is seen as having an increased ability to attract the most talented employees efficiently.[35,36,37] In times when there is full employment and ample opportunities for people with high-potential talent, they are more willing to react to recruitment ads from admired organizations.[38] Research has also shown that jobseekers are more willing to pursue jobs with organizations that have a reputation for social responsibility.[39] Coldwell et al.[40] posit that a jobseeker builds an opinion of an ethical fit with an organization based on perceptions of the organization's corporate social responsibility-derived reputation. Not only is an organization with a good reputation able to attract a larger number of applicants: under certain circumstances, it can even select higher-quality jobseekers.[41] Having a good reputation increases the influx of executives from other blue-chip companies.

Hence, companies should safeguard their reputation around employment, because it is likely that a negative reputation will bring trouble with hiring employees in the future.[42] Formulated more positively, having a reputation as a preferred employer will not only positively impact the organization's hiring process, but it will also have a positive effect on the organization's stock-market valuation.[43]

Non-governmental organizations

A favourable reputation with NGOs is critical for organizations, especially for those of substance and international scale. Mostly self-appointed watchdog or advocacy groups, NGOs typically operate on charitable donations from foundations and individuals and focus on issues such as human rights, the environment, certain diseases, child development and corporate behaviour. Although a cynic might suggest that a good protest issue is a fine way to raise more funds, these groups play an increasingly important and needed role in both local and global societies, often addressing issues that governments overlook and that hold no interest for business. Because their motives appear ethical, NGOs can make life difficult for corporations in their sights. Building cooperative alignments therefore reduces the chance of contentious or hostile interactions.

For example, when Starbucks received criticism from an NGO regarding its coffee-purchasing activities, the Seattle-based firm decided to switch to Fair Trade coffee[44] rather than fight. As an NGO can attack an organization's network of customers, financers, insurers and suppliers, such non-profit organizations often have surprising power. In some ways, their very existence depends on how frequently and effectively they apply that power.[45]

Reputations matters, but organizations have to be known first

A positive reputation can have many advantages, but an organization has to be known first by its relevant audiences. This is called the 'top of mind awareness' of the corporate brand. Most studies on name awareness present a list of company names and then simply ask to what degree a respondent feels familiar with each. This so-called 'aided awareness' test is occasionally replaced by an open-ended question, such as 'Which corporate names can you mention in banking and automotive?'. Presenting the list simplifies life for the respondent, but too often exaggerates name awareness. Top of mind awareness can be increased substantially by using a highly distinguishing symbol, such as the logo of the Spanish bank La Caixa, which was created by the famous artist Miró.

Outcomes from open-ended questions reveal that most large corporate brands remain below 35 per cent in terms of name awareness, and only a few prestigious and popular firms routinely exceed 70 per cent.[46] Nevertheless, name awareness of corporate brands is much lower than the familiarity of product brands. This is partly caused by differences in advertising budgets, where more money is typically

Box 5.2 THE CREATION OF LA CAIXA'S LOGO[47]

✕ "la Caixa"

The visual identity of La Caixa marks a turning point in the world of communication and design, setting trends in the field of corporate communication. The top of mind awareness of La Caixa increased substantially owing to the quality of the logo. For the first time, a corporate identity was based on an artistic creation.

The La Caixa logo is very distinctive in comparison with those of the other financial entities, easily recognizable, without reference to a specific geographical area or industry activity. The symbol is able to combine the dual economic and social dimension of La Caixa (savings bank) as a differentiating factor.

Of the different options, the one selected seems to be the most appropriate and innovative: Joan Miró created the logo from a tapestry.

spent on product advertising than in shaping a corporate image. The inverse exceptions to this rule are multinational oil companies, who compete against each other to win concession contracts from national governments and are always under pressure from a variety of NGOs. As oil production generates the greatest earnings by far for these firms, the majority of petroleum advertising dollars are spent on corporate reputation, with marketing petrol a distant second. Gaining concessions offshore from West Africa, Brazil or Thailand means winning a licence and permission to operate, the core goal of reputation management.[48]

People appear to have a limited memory-storage capability for brand names, especially when the involvement with the object is low. Research into product branding has shown that most people can only memorize about seven brand names in a product category, even though the individuals' involvement with the items is often medium to high. Involvement with the company behind the brands is even more limited, which is why corporate name awareness lags behind that of products.

However, it is remarkable that some business-to-business corporate brands are highly familiar in their country of origin. Take, for example, the business-to-business corporate brands of Maersk and Novo Nordisk in Denmark, AkzoNobel in the Netherlands and Vale in Brazil. All appear to be well known by the general public in their home nations. Awareness comes in part from how often these firms are mentioned in the national press, as well as in advertising, but that is only a part of the explanation.

In general, at least seven other factors appear to be relevant in building strong name awareness for a corporate brand, which is measured in a top-of-mind awareness score, or ToMAC:

- Firms with well-known product brands, whose products are purchased frequently by a large and diverse group of consumers, have a higher degree of ToMAC of the corporate brand.
- Firms with a high degree of visibility related to the location and architecture of their outlets have a higher degree of ToMAC.
- Firms who are mentioned in the media frequently have a higher degree of ToMAC.
- Size matters: the larger the firm, the higher the ToMAC.
- Being listed on the national stock exchange increases the degree of ToMAC.
- The more a company links itself to a social cause, the higher the degree of ToMAC.
- National firms are well known in their own country and are seen as part of the national heritage.
- Recently privatized firms have a higher, but negative, degree of ToMAC, primarily because of intense media during the privatization phase.

The most crucial drivers of name awareness at the corporate level are media coverage, stock listing and, above all, being perceived as a national-heritage icon.

FIGURE 5.8 Global advertisment for Itaú

Companies with global operations are especially famous within their own national boundaries. Firms that have not been rooted in a country for a long period of time must score highly on the other drivers to match the familiarity of national icons. Some firms succeed in doing this on a global scale, such as Google, Ikea, Shell and Nokia. An interesting example of trying to achieve more name awareness outside the country of origin is the Brazilian bank Itaú. It used Brazil's famous actress Alice Braga to attract attention among potential foreign investors in Brazil to the existence of Itaú as the leading bank in Brazil that could help them enter this fast-growing BRIC country. This advertisement has been used in *The Economist*, *Wall Street Journal* and many other internal outlets that are read by financial specialists.

Reputation matters and is impacted by 'economic' and 'responsibility' drivers

While name awareness of a corporate brand is evoked by a set of specific visibility-type drivers, the same logic applies to reputation. Antecedents of a corporate reputation can be distinguished by drivers clustered around an evaluation of economic performance and drivers clustered around corporate social responsibility. Economic performance is measured by the quality of products and services, degree of innovation and financial achievements. Evaluation of social responsibility is measured by indicators that include the firm's quality as an employer and its citizenship and governance attributes. Longitudinal studies by the Reputation Institute, using the RepTrak methodology (see Figure 5.6), have shown that economic drivers of reputation have, on average, more impact on a company reputation than those of social responsibility. Of course, this differs greatly by firm and industry.

This is why reputation research should be carried out on a continuous basis, enabling a firm to get elaborated answers to questions such as: How do we compare with the rest of the industry? What is the difference compared with last year? What are the differences between the key stakeholders we depend upon? Which attributes matter most, can we change them, and, if so, how can we transform this into actions?

An interesting example of an in-depth analysis of the reputation drivers that most impact behaviour is shown in Figure 5.9. The example is based on the RepTrak analysis of a hypothetical company, showing the impact of the economic and responsibility clusters of reputation drivers (divided into twenty-three attributes) on behavioural intentions. As can be seen in Figure 5.9, this creates clarity about which buttons to press in the next communication effort, as it shows exactly which attributes are positively contributing and which appear to be lagging or outright failures.

Positive scores can be found for the evaluation and the impact on behaviour for 'product and services' (01) and 'future growth' (23). The opposite is found in the quadrant labelled 'danger zone'. The attributes plotted in this quadrant – mostly responsibility attributes – are evaluated as very low and have a high impact on behaviour. All reputation attributes that have a negative impact on behaviour must be given the highest priority by corporate communication and senior management.

Reputation matters and is impacted by industry characteristics

The reputation of an individual organization is affected by the nature of the industry in which it operates. Corporations in the pharmaceutical business are, for example, more or less automatically placed in a bandwidth between 60 and 65 points on the Reputation Institute's 100-point scale. However, if the same pharmaceutical company redefines its portfolio and presents itself to the world as a life-sciences

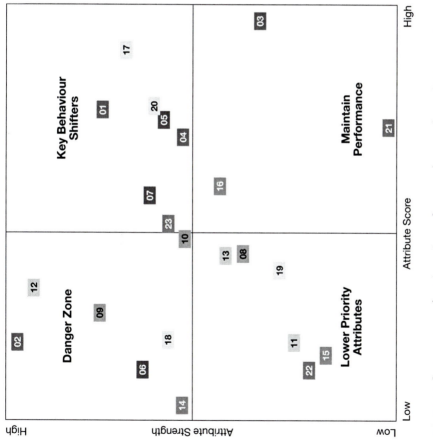

	Products and Services
01	High quality
02	Value for money
03	Stands behind
04	Customer needs
	Innovation
05	Innovative
06	First to market
07	Adapts quickly
	Workplace
08	Rewards fairly
09	Concern for employees
10	Equal opportunities
	Governance
11	Open and transparent
12	Ethical
13	Is fair
	Citizenship
14	Environmentally responsible
15	Supports good causes
16	Positive influence on society
	Leadership
17	Well-organized
18	Strong and appealing leader
19	Excellent managers
20	Clear vision
	Performance
21	Profitable
22	Better results
23	Future growth

FIGURE 5.9 Impact on purchase intentions of twenty-three attributes driving reputation

company, it will likely move up to a 65–70-point bandwidth. Recent studies show that the assessment of a firm is not only determined by its own actions, but also by those of other firms within the industry. These spillover effects have the greatest impact when the firm is prominent and frequently interacts with the public through advertising, sponsorships and other avenues that boost awareness.

Reputation matters: gathering relevant intelligence with four questions

Summarizing the key points regarding the gathering of intelligence about reputation, the four questions in Figure 5.10 have to be answered, enabling an organization to be well prepared for external-alignment efforts in the context of reputation management.

Integration of all gathered external intelligence

Gathering intelligence about the issues and beliefs of external stakeholders prepares an organization to build sustainable relationships with key external audiences. A precondition for doing this in an effective way is consistency. This requires organizations regularly to track and integrate the information in a way that simplifies decisions on the what, why and when with regard to aligning external stakeholders. The key points addressed in this chapter regarding the gathering of external intelligence are summarized in Figure 5.11.

This 'External-context fact sheet' enables managers to set clear priorities from a strategic communication viewpoint, to create a road map for actions aimed at building external alignment. The fact sheet, however, represents just a first step in

- What is the overall reputation and how does this compare with rivals?
  - Low ----- Medium ------- High
- Which drivers impact reputation most?
  - Attributes X, Y, Z have a positive impact .....
  - Attributes A, B, C have a negative impact ......
- Which drivers impact behaviour most?
  - Attributes X, Y, Z have a positive impact ......
  - Attributes A, B, C have a negative impact ....
- To what degree is the firm impacted by industry reputation?
  - Low ----- Medium ------- High

FIGURE 5.10 Fit between strategic objectives and reputation

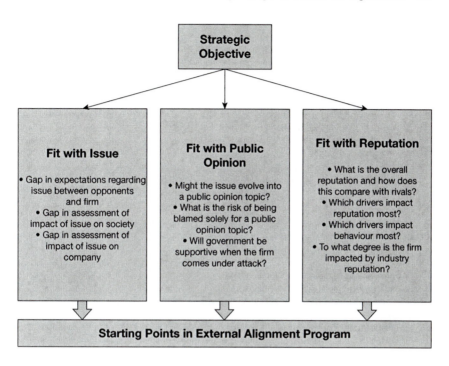

FIGURE 5.11 External-context fact sheet

what can be a long and significant journey. The next step involves *applying* the information to that external world, be it winning over adversarial stakeholders or even creating brand-new entities to advocate on your industry's behalf. The techniques used in this environment can be as soft and seductive as adverts featuring fuzzy animals and soothing music – or litigation that is as blunt as a hammer blow to a nail. In the real world of governments, non-governmental advocacy groups and individuals aching to film and spread damning images that go viral, your business today is everyone's business. How it's managed is the core of building external alignment.

Notes

1 B. Perrott, 'Strategic issue management: an integrated framework', *Journal of General Management*, (1995), vol. 21(2), pp. 52–63.
2 Ibid.
3 R.A. Buchholz, *Essentials of public policy for management* (2nd edn), Englewood Cliffs, NJ: Prentice Hall, (1990).
4 F.A.J. van den Bosch and C.B.M. van Riel, 'Buffering and bridging as environmental strategies of firms', *Business Strategy and the Environment*, (1998), vol. 7(1), pp. 24–31.
5 Shell Nederland BV, archive 1995.
6 J. Graunt, 'Natural and political observations made upon the Bills of Mortality', in Charles Henry Hull (ed.), *The economic writings of Sir William Petty*, vol. 2, (1899), pp. 321, 370, 379.

7 G.W. Allport, *Personality: a psychological interpretation*, New York: Holt, Rinehart, & Winston, (1937).

8 *Public Opinion Quarterly*: Summer 2011, vol. 75(2), Oxford: Oxford University Press.

9 Allport, *Personality: a psychological interpretation*, New York: Holt, Rinehart, & Winston, (1937).

10 H.L. Childs, *Public opinion: nature, formation, and role*, Princeton, NJ: D. van Nostrand, (1965).

11 M. Brouwer, 'Mass communication and the social sciences: some neglected areas', *International Social Science Journal*, (1962), vol. 14(2), pp. 303–19. (Reprinted as pp. 547–67 in A.L. Dexter and D.M. White (eds) *People, society and mass communications*, New York: The Free Press/Collier-Macmillan, (1964).)

12 C.E. Carroll and M. McCombs, 'Agenda-setting effects of business news on the public's images and opinions about major corporations', *Corporate Reputation Review*, (2003), vol. 6(1), pp. 36–46.

13 M.L. Hunter, L.N. van Wassenhove and M. Besiou, 'Stakeholder media: the Trojan horse of corporate responsibility', *Working Paper*, INSEAD, (2009).

14 E. Noelle-Neumann, 'Turbulences in the climate of opinion: methodological applications of the spiral of silence theory', *Public Opinion Quarterly*, (1977), vol. 41(2), pp. 143–58.

15 Ibid.

16 G.E. Fryxell and J. Wang, '*Fortune*'s corporate "reputation" index: reputation of what?', *Journal of Management*, (1994), vol. 20(1), pp. 1–14.

17 Wikipedia website, http://en.wikipedia.org/wiki/Gestalt_psychology (accessed 19 January 2010).

18 L.J. Ponzi, C.J. Fombrun and N.A. Gardberg, 'RepTrak™ Pulse: conceptualizing and validating a short-form measure of corporate reputation', *Corporate Reputation Review*, (2011), vol. 14(1).

19 Ibid.

20 J. Cordeiro and R. Sambharya, 'Do corporate reputations influence security analyst earnings forecasts?', *Corporate Reputation Review*, (1997), vol. 1, pp. 94–8.

21 P.W. Roberts and G.R. Dowling, 'The value of a firm's corporate reputation: how reputation helps attain and sustain superior profitability', *Corporate Reputation Review*, (1997), vol. 1, pp. 72–6.

22 Ibid.

23 Y. Wang, G. Berens and C.B.M. van Riel, 'Managing reputation rankings: a crucial step for attracting equity investors?', ERIM: *Working paper*, (2011).

24 Ibid.

25 J.E. Grunig (ed.), *Excellence in public relations and communication management*, Hillsdale, NJ: Lawrence Erlbaum Associates, (1992).

26 J.E. Grunig and T. Hunt, *Managing public relations*, New York: Holt, Rinehart and Winston, (1984).

27 C.J. Fombrun and C.B.M. van Riel, *Fame and fortune. How the world's top companies develop winning reputations*, New York: Pearson Publishing and the *Financial Times*, (2004).

28 M. Goldberg and J. Hartwick, 'The effects of advertising reputation and extremity of advertising claim on advertising effectiveness', *Journal of Consumer Research*, (1990), vol. 17(2), pp. 172–9.

29 J.B. Thompson (ed.), *Political scandal: power and visibility in the media age*, Cambridge: Polity, (2000).

30 Z. Gürhan-Canli and R. Batra, 'When corporate image affects product evaluations: the moderating role of perceived risk,' *Journal of Marketing Research*, (2004), vol. 41(May), pp. 197–205.

31 R.G. Eccles, R.M. Grant and C.B.M. van Riel, 'Reputation and transparency: lessons from a painful period in public disclosure', *Long Range Planning*, (2007), vol. 69(4), pp. 353–9.

32 T.J. Brown and P.A. Dacin, 'The company and the product: corporate associations and consumer product responses', *Journal of Marketing*, (1997), vol. 61(1), pp. 68–84.

33 G.A.J.M. Berens, C.B.M. van Riel and G.H. van Bruggen, 'Corporate associations and consumer product responses: the moderating role of corporate brand dominance', *Journal of Marketing*, (2005), vol. 69(3), pp. 35–48.

34 H.L. Carmichael, 'Reputations in the labor market,' *American Economic Review*, American Economic Association, (1984), vol. 74(4), pp. 713–25.

35 K.W. Chauvin and J.P. Guthrie, 'Labor market reputation and the value of the firm', *Managerial and Decision Economics*, (1994), vol. 15, pp. 543–52.

36 T.A. Judge and D.M. Cable, 'Applicant personality, organizational culture and organizational attraction', (1997), *Personnel Psychology*, 50, pp. 359–94.

37 D.M. Cable and D.B. Turban, 'The value of organizational image in the recruitment context: a brand equity perspective', *Journal of Applied Social Psychology*, (2003), vol. 33, 2244–66.

38 R.D. Gatewood, M.A. Gowan and G.J. Lautenschlager, 'Corporate image, recruitment image, and initial job choice decisions', *Academy of Management Journal*, (1993), vol. 36(2), pp. 414–27.

39 D.W. Greening and D.B. Turban, 'Corporate social performance as a competitive advantage in attracting a quality workforce', *Business and Society*, (2000), vol. 39, pp. 254–80.

40 D.A. Coldwell, J. Billsberry, N. van Meurs and P.J.G. Marsh, 'The effects of person–organisation ethical fit on employee attraction and retention: towards a testable explanatory model', *Journal of Business Ethics*, (2008), vol. 78, pp. 611–22.

41 Cable and Turban, 'The value of organizational image in the recruitment context: a brand equity perspective', pp. 2244–66.

42 Carmichael, 'Reputations in the labor market', pp. 713–25.

43 Chauvin and Guthrie, 'Labor market reputation and the value of the firm', pp. 543–52.

44 P.A. Argenti, 'Collaborating with activists: how Starbucks works with NGOs', *California Management Review*, (2004), vol. 47, pp. 91–116.

45 Greening and Turban, 'Corporate social performance as a competitive advantage in attracting a quality workforce', pp. 254–80.

46 C.B.M. van Riel, 'Top of mind awareness of corporate brands among the Dutch public', *Corporate Reputation Review*, (2002), vol. 4(4), pp. 362–73.

47 La Caixa website, www.lacaixa.com/informacioncorporativa/historia_en.html (accessed July 2011).

48 Coldwell, Billsberry, van Meurs and Marsh, 'The effects of person–organisation ethical fit on employee attraction and retention: towards a testable explanatory model', pp. 611–22.

6

A ROAD MAP AIMED AT CREATING EXTERNAL ALIGNMENT

Organizations depend on a range of external stakeholders either to support, or at least not to oppose, the company's business operations. At the minimum, a company must build awareness of the firm's ambitions and intended actions, the first step towards building a willingness to engage in dialogue. Ultimately, if there is a mutual understanding and mutual benefits in a company's relationship with those stakeholders, we have alignment – and the organization can proceed to implement its plans fully.

As with building internal alignment, this can be done through the same basic techniques of *negotiation* or *confrontation*. Within each, two variants can be distinguished. Negotiation consists of *consultation* and *consensus*, whereas confrontation contains *mirroring* and *power play*.

Negotiations clearly present the lowest business risk, whereas confrontation can have its downsides in both the short and long term. By the nature of negotiations, an organization has more control over the process and outcome. Confronting an opposing stakeholder with legal action, for example, brings others into the situation – in this case a judge or jury, and with them a greater risk of unpredictable and potentially damaging results. Thus, most organizations focus on negotiation and turn to confrontation only when the former fails to create sufficient external alignment.

Although confrontation can produce alignment, it is usually at the expense of trust. Therefore, confrontational strategies are often followed by negotiations aimed at regaining some measure of stakeholder faith. However, no matter which strategy is applied, doing so successfully requires an orchestrated approach by experts from inside, and sometimes outside, an organization. The emphasis here, in this book, is on corporate communication. As that function is first and foremost corporate, and only then communication, a professional communicator must fully understand the roles of executives and experts in other departments and areas of skill.

A summary of the range of techniques a company can choose from is shown in Table 6.1.

TABLE 6.1 Building blocks in a road map to external alignment

Negotiation	Confrontation
Consulting	**Mirroring**
• Interlocking directorates	• Lobbying
• Informal consultations	• Advocacy
Consensus	**Power play**
• Ad hoc platforms	• Legal actions
• Buffering	• Competitive pressure (smoking out competitors)
• Joint ventures	

Negotiation

Companies do not act in isolation. Decisions are critically observed and at times condemned by a large variety of groups, driving adaptations, changes and compromises in policy. Nearly all major companies within industries of note face what are known as 'external dependencies', the threat or promise of actions a government, a competitor or a pressure group might take, and which can hinder an organization's success. In this age of social media and activist citizenry, companies are increasingly vulnerable to whatever claim a pressure group makes.

These vulnerabilities are reduced when organizations forge links and communicate routinely with critical constituencies. Such links can be one-to-one relationships between a firm and the most influential and important stakeholders. Many stakeholder engagement maps are constructed this way, with the firm the hub of a wheel and stakeholders positioned at various points along the spokes.[1] The concept suffices so long as a firm can identify and isolate the most important stakeholders.

More common, however, is an environment in which firms must interact with several stakeholders, who in turn interact with each other. This creates a network of influences. Dealing with such complexity can distract an operation from its core, most important business focus. This is why many companies rely on trade organizations such as the American Petroleum Institute, the Alliance for Better Foods or the National Manufacturers Association, to lobby, wage advocacy campaigns and deal with disparate, multilateral influences. This is called *buffering* and is done by creating structures that signal a commitment to institutionalized beliefs and that represent the organization favourably to valued stakeholders. In addition to formal buffering organizations, other, less formal buffering activities can be applied too. This might include financing a philanthropic company foundation, funding an independent academic research institution or sponsoring a charity. External

Box 6.1 TELEFONICA'S CORPORATE SOCIAL RESPONSIBILTY PROGRAMME 'PRONINO'

Proniño is a social action programme, founded in 1998, carried out by the Telefónica Group and managed by the Foundation alongside Telefónica Móviles operators in its thirteen Latin-American offices, and it contributes significantly to reducing child labour in the region. The programme is aligned with the regional goals of the International Labour Organization (ILO), which seeks to eradicate the worst forms of child labour before 2015, and all child labour before 2020.

Areas for intervention by Proniño

These three areas were developed in line with recommendations from the ILO:

- the comprehensive protection of working children;
- ongoing, high-quality education for these minors;

- strengthening of the social and institutional framework, guaranteeing sustainability of the intervention in the medium/long term.

Proniño results, 2008

Proniño has directly helped 107,602 children and adolescents in Latin America. The programme has intervened on an ongoing basis in 2,596 educational centres (2,177 schools and 419 assistance centres) in the thirteen countries in the region.

Its key foundations are the 105 prestigious NGOs with which it works directly, as well as the schools and public and private institutions with which it collaborates in each of the countries it operates in.

stakeholders who observe these formal structures may consequently see the organization as valuable and worthy of support.

An often-applied example of negotiation techniques is *interlocking directorates*, which include respected representatives from relevant stakeholders in a formal position in the company. This can be an appointment as a board of management member or another influential advice role in the organization. These appointments provide company leadership access to, and involvement with, groups it depends upon. Although interlocking directorates can be effective, they are also limited, owing to the relatively small number of people on any given board.

Not all strategies for managing external-stakeholder relations rely on such structured actions. Organizations can also respond on a more informal basis to pressure from specific centres of community power. For example, allowing a city council to influence a corporation's policy on a local issue recognizes the resources it commands as permission giver. This is labelled *informal consultation*. Small, ad hoc examples of collaboration with potential adversaries can at times have a greater business impact than the largest formal corporate programme. In some circumstances, this type of negotiation is extended to *ad hoc platforms*, which are aimed at creating consensus with a specific stakeholder group. The most advanced mode of negotiation – and, as a logical consequence, the most risky – is creating a *joint venture*, a formally legalized form of cooperation with one or more organizations.

Confrontation

Confrontational strategies can involve common and widely accepted practices such as lobbying to influence the political environment, or advocacy campaigns to move public opinion. I call these techniques *mirroring*. It literally means showing others what your intentions are based on reflections of reality as perceived by the organization.

**WWF position on forests and
climate change mitigation**

Executive summary

A strong post-2012 climate regime is essential to keep the rise in global temperature well below 2 degrees Celsius. Reducing emissions from deforestation and forest degradation in developing countries (REDD) is a critical component of the overall greenhouse gas emission reductions required to achieve this climate goal. The following strategies are needed to ensure REDD supports a successful global climate regime.

Phased approach

REDD will require significant preparation and planning to produce measurable, reportable and verifiable reductions. This is best achieved through national-level REDD programs with national-level baselines and monitoring. These programs should be developed in three rigorous phases: Planning (Phase 1), Preparing (Phase 2) and Executing (Phase 3). Graduation from one phase to the next should be based on clear, internationally approved standards within a United Nations Framework Convention on Climate Change (UNFCCC) defined framework. The post-2012 treaty will need mechanisms to oversee countries' passage through these phases at their own pace, and to determine and periodically review national baselines.

Financing REDD

REDD will need substantial and predictable amounts of funding starting immediately. There is an urgent need for capacity building and early action now. Developed countries should commit to provide such funding as part of the agreements reached at the 15ᵗ Conference of the Parties (COP15) in Copenhagen. **High levels of predictable funding from sources such as Assigned Amount Units (AAU) auctioning**, as well as other possible mechanisms including levies on international transport, **will be needed to secure the fast movement of countries through REDD development phases and as an incentive for emissions reductions and should be urgently pursued.** Additional funding from other public and private funding sources and voluntary carbon markets will also be needed.

Over time, **compliance carbon markets**[1] can also play an increasing role in securing adequate funding for REDD. This must happen in a way that maintains the integrity and overall functioning of the market, ensures developed countries have sufficient incentives to transform their domestic economies, maximizes funding for REDD and is perceived as fair in terms of the effort for emissions reductions demanded of different countries.

As a group, developed countries must commit to a 40% reduction by 2020 as compared to 1990 levels, with the vast majority (emissions reductions of 30%-35%) achieved domestically through transforming critical sectors such as energy. Simultaneously, developing countries must be supported to achieve at least 30% emissions reduction below business-as-usual (BAU) scenarios. **Annex 1 countries should assist developing countries to achieve this deviation by funding REDD and other emission reductions efforts with public or market-linked funding such as AAU auctioning.**

Compliance market is defined here as one where a credit can count against a UNFCCC commitment

FIGURE 6.1 WWF position paper on forests and climate change (page 1 of 12 pages) (copyright © WWF)[2]

Lobbying is the practice of influencing decisions made by government, more specifically aimed at influencing legislation or regulatory decisions on behalf of various groups. The job of the lobbyist is to communicate the organization's view to government, including a proposition's impact on a company or industry, consumers, the environment and – a legislator's most important audience – the voters. In addition, lobbyists provide government employees with information that helps them craft bills and regulations, and they inform their firm of the decisions of officials. Elected and appointed government officials typically receive a great deal of input on important issues from representatives in the public and private sectors, lobbyists from activist organizations such as Greenpeace and a myriad of other interests.

The professional lobbyist, often a representative of the large, international law firms, typically submits that information in a detailed policy report that explains, justifies or recommends a particular course of action. Most often fully disclosed on the website of a public institution, the report's impact is greatest when it is research-based and replete with factual knowledge, statistical inferences and informed opinion. Cleverly written papers include a pros and cons list that adds an opponent's claims – thereby co-opting a piece of the argument – with the weight of the argument obviously on one side. No one is ever fooled. Lobbyists sometimes even draft legislation, which is surprising to the public but a common practice that saves civil servants from an overwhelming volume of work.

Another technique applied by organizations that can be labelled as a mirroring type of activity is *advocacy*. This is a range of activities in which a company publicly exposes its point of view about a major issue by advocacy advertising or a range of publicity initiatives using interviews, press releases or public speeches. The ultimate goal of these investments is to evoke a two-step-flow effect. The hope is that the arguments will persuade the general public and, in turn, convince the decision-makers in government, who answer to voters. The goal is to decrease resistance or increase support.

Confrontation also includes a far more risky set of interventions that I label *power play*. For example, direct *legal action* literally compels other organizations to act in a desired way, if only because of the costs of defending against litigation or a potentially devastating courtroom defeat. Litigation typically resolves a conflict between parties before a judge or a jury. Although mediation and arbitration are comparable actions initiated by parties looking for an outsider's intervention, the courtroom is truly the arena of last resort. Fear is the reason many cases are settled right before attorneys open their brief-cases and start their opening arguments.

At first glance, litigation strikes one as a strange technique for creating alignment. However, organizations do apply it when further negotiations are hopelessly ineffective. Relations with the defendant are invariably damaged for a long period of time. Realignment is unlikely to happen soon. However, when the litigation process works out as intended, it can open avenues for alignment with yet other stakeholders who previously were unwilling to negotiate. Litigation can also communicate a company's belief in its values to a wide range of publics, its conviction in the legality of its position and a willingness to defend itself aggressively.

Another sensitive technique applied within the domain of power play can be labelled *competitive pressure*. This could include a major acquisition that increases market share, the hiring of a competitor's talent, or superior operational excellence – think Exxon Mobil – that simply forces others to align with the organization's goals. Another interesting example of competitive pressure is the way Japanese steel manufacturers operated in the United States in the 1970s, when they dumped their products on US markets at a loss, essentially destroying some of their American competitors. However, power play in general is a risky affair. It can destroy relationships, just as litigation does. However, it can also create a new starting point that enables the organization to link up with others more effectively. This can be illustrated by the cooperation between Nokia and Microsoft, starting in 2011, aimed at reducing the power of Apple and Google.

Two case studies: negotiation and confrontation road maps applied by Unilever and Monsanto around GM food

The practical use of negotiation and confrontation road maps is illustrated in the following pair of case studies. Both deal with the introduction of GM food plants. One shows the road map applied by the American company, Monsanto; another one is employed by the Anglo-Dutch company Unilever. Genetic modification of food is a complicated topic, especially for people who (like me) do not have a background in chemistry or biology. That is why I will explain first what GM food is, how it was developed, what kinds of debate took place and its current place in the global food chain.

The end of starvation or Frankenfood?

The introduction of GM food during the 1990s trigged intense debates that continue to this day, with supporters and opponents who have totally different world-views. As with other high-tech innovations, some see the crops as a solution to a world problem. Governments, companies and individuals who support the innovation believe biotechnology helps farmers meet the needs of a growing global population. Only special GM crops, they argue, can enable the Earth's limited supply of arable land to yield enough sustenance to fend off hunger, malnutrition and starvation.

Opponents denounced it as 'Frankenfood', a term that stems from author Mary Shelley's Dr Frankenstein and the monster he created. Coined in 1992 by a Boston College English professor, Paul Lewis, in a letter to *The New York Times*,[3] Frankenfood is a succinct and suggestive word and is still employed as a pejorative term for GM crops and a battle-cry for those who fear them. A loose collective that includes social activists and scientists with sincere reservations about the technology, these adversaries insist that altered organisms let loose into the environment hold great potential for unintended and harmful consequences to human health and the well-being of nature.

However, GM foods are now commonly found on tables in Europe, the United States and elsewhere, with fairly limited concerns from the majority of consumers and government regulators. Although government agencies have yet to approve genetically altered animals for human consumption, experiments on several species hint at enhancements comparable to those made to crops. Most pertinent to this discussion, though, is the current health of the GM food industry. Its very existence, in fact, is a testament to the trust-building effectiveness of both negotiation-based and confrontational communication strategies.

From Mendel to Monsanto

Ever since our hunter–gatherer ancestors began planting wild seeds and harvesting the domesticated output some 10,000 years ago, humans have looked for grains, legumes, beans and other plants that were the most bountiful, robust and resistant to pests, weeds, disease and drought. Don't doubt that those Neolithic forebears knew the difference between a weak and fruitful seed plant and sowed fields accordingly. However, the concept of heredity and the ability to manipulate plant genetics were not understood until the mid-1880s, with the experiments and writings of Augustinian monk and schoolteacher Gregor Mendel, and his famous garden peas.

Horticultural science quickly flourished, thanks to individuals such as the American botanist Luther Burbank. In a career spanning more than five decades, he used grafting, cross-breeding and hybrids to create more than 800 strains and varieties of fruits, vegetables, grasses and other plants, including the legendary Russet Burbank potato, reputedly still the world's most processed variety and mainstay of McDonald's French fry output. Moreover, Burbank's work encouraged US Congress to pass the Plant Patent Act in 1930, legislation that underpins the ongoing and often expensive research and development of new crop strains.[4]

During the middle of the twentieth century, agronomist and Nobel laureate Norman Borlaug led the development of high-yield, disease-resistant varieties of wheat and other basic crops. He also helped introduce modern agricultural practices in Mexico, Pakistan and India, enabling the nations to feed burgeoning populations. Proclaimed the 'father of the Green Revolution', Borlaug also drew criticism from environmentalists, who considered genetic cross-breeding unnatural, and the intensive use of herbicides and fertilizer harmful to nature, if not also profitable for agrochemical corporations. In his later years, Borlaug acknowledged these concerns, but remained convinced that the approximately 1 billion lives he is widely credited with saving trumped the critical viewpoints.[5]

The genetics game changed radically and forever when, at a 1972 conference in Hawaii on bacterial plasmids, a Stanford University associate professor of medicine named Stanley Cohen met Herbert Boyer, a University of California, San Francisco biochemist and genetic engineer. They decided to join forces. Cohen had been studying ways to isolate specific genes in plasmids that carry antibiotics; Boyer had discovered an enzyme that cut strands of DNA at specific points, which opened the way to splice different genes into a strand. The two agreed to collaborate and, within months, successfully spliced foreign DNA into a plasmid and put it into a piece of bacterium, whereupon it reproduced in the new form. That ability to combine genes from entirely different species sparked a revolution that has since transformed science, medicine and the business of food.

Shortly thereafter, genetic engineers developed numerous GM crops, including soybeans, canola and corn. This breakthrough promised astonishing improvements in yield and resistance to pests, diseases and weeds and to the herbicides used to control the weeds that compete with plants for nutrients.

The first commercially grown GM food was the FlavrSavr tomato. Developed by California-based Calgene, this tomato was modified to ripen without softening. Although not required, the company obtained US Food and Drug Administration (FDA) approval of the product in 1994. Although the tomato was a genetic success and seemed to be welcomed by consumers, Calgene had little experience in growing and shipping products. FlavrSavr never became profitable and, within a few years, disappeared from stores, and Calgene was acquired by Monsanto.

Meanwhile, a similar GM tomato was produced by the UK firm Zeneca, which turned it into tomato paste and labelled it as genetically altered. In a move attractive to consumers, it was priced below most competitors. The product was as much a marketing experiment as anything, to see if Europeans would accept genetically engineered food. Against this backdrop, businesses, governments and activists began preparing for a debate that promised to determine the very future of biotechnology.

The Frankenfood assertion certainly gave traction to its opponents. So did a statement by Britain's Prince Charles, who said that, 'companies are currently on a territory that belongs to God and to God alone'. Although the European Commission seemed initially enthusiastic about the potential good that might come from GM crops, its members grew suspicious when activist and public resistance towards the new technology increased.

FIGURE 6.2 Label used by Safeway for their tomato puree product in 1994

FIGURE 6.3 Greenpeace and other NGOs protest against genetic modification

In the United States, Monsanto assumed the role of spokesperson for the promoters of GM food technology, while Greenpeace took the role of key challenger. More and more institutions became involved, making bold statements about whether or not such foods should be legally approved by formal government organizations. With the backing of Nestlé, Unilever issued a statement that said, 'We support the use of biotechnology in food production with the necessary rules in place'. Deutsche Bank, however, advised its investors to divest themselves of shares in companies involved in the development of genetically altered foods, even before those rules could be adopted.

On both sides of the Atlantic, the companies that planned to develop GM food products faced an enormous challenge. They had to convince a broad spectrum of influential stakeholders – including regulators, farmers and consumers – that GM foods were something in which they could place complete trust. The US

FDA took a positive attitude towards the innovations. By 1990, it had approved a genetically engineered form of rennet, used to curdle milk, and, two years later, it stated that GM foods had to meet only the same standards as ordinary foods, eliminating any need for product labels to include a GM indication.

The first GM ingredient to be exported from the United States to Europe were seeds for Monsanto's Roundup Ready soybeans, which were genetically modified to resist the Monsanto-manufactured herbicide Roundup, a potent killer of weeds and grasses and a billion-dollar product that the Union of Concerned Scientists claims generates about 40 per cent of Monsanto's revenues. Monsanto argued that the use of these beans would allow farmers to stop using a popular herbicide containing atrazine, which has an active ingredient that persists in the environment. Roundup, which contains glyphosate, is less toxic.[6]

However, as fears and criticism of GM food increased gradually worldwide, activists in North America asked consumers to boycott certain food products that contained soy or corn. In response, Monsanto and Cargill actively promoted this new technology in food production. Moreover, Monsanto formed a joint venture

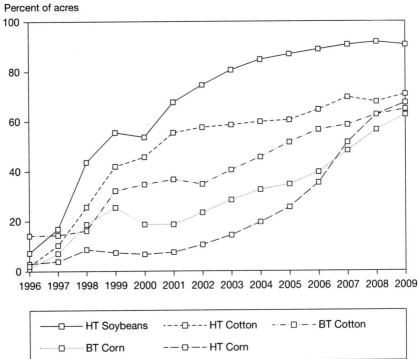

Rapid growth in adoption of genetically engineered crops continues in the US

FIGURE 6.4 Adoption curve of genetically engineered crops in the United States (United States Department of Agriculture, retrieved from www.usda.gov).

with Cargill, in 1998, to apply biotechnology to improved feed products for animals raised for human consumption.

In 2000, a study by the US National Academy of Sciences produced no evidence that gene-spliced crops were unsafe to eat, although certain variants have been confirmed to cause severe allergic reactions in humans. That same year, the Aventis company's Starlink corn – which does produce allergies and is used only in animal feed – accidentally showed up in tacos, corn chips, beer and muffin mix. Taco Bell announced a drop in sales after negative publicity about the link between tacos and Starlink corn, forcing the firm to replace their taco shells with food produced with other types of corn. Despite this cautionary incident, proponents of genetically engineered crops prevailed in US regulatory and scientific discussions. Farmers were obviously pleased, thanks to higher yields, lower pesticide use and greater profitability. The penetration rate of genetic modification in agriculture increased tremendously between 2000 and 2009, as can be seen in Figure 6.4.

Recent developments in GM food

Various outcomes of research in recent years provide evidence that GM food has more positive contributions than was suggested in previous publications from hard-line opponents. For example, in January 2008, the University of Queensland in Australia released a study saying that the risks of GM food were 'alarmist and exaggerated', and that Australian states should not ban commercial production of such foods. The study's author, an ethicist named Dr Lucy Carter, eloquently pointed

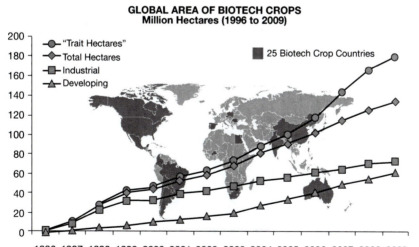

GLOBAL AREA OF BIOTECH CROPS
Million Hectares (1996 to 2009)

A record 14 million farmers, in 25 countries, planted 134 million hectares (330 million acres) in 2009, a sustained increase of 7% or 9 million hectares (22 million acres) over 2008.

FIGURE 6.5 Growth in application of GM technology in agriculture

Source: Clive James, 2009

out how genes isolated from cold-water fish and inserted into tomatoes created varieties resistant to frost damage in cold climates. She also explained that one variety of GM rice contained enough beta-keratin to help prevent blindness caused by vitamin A deficiency, a plague in the developing world.[7]

In 2010, 14 million farmers planted biotech crops on 134 million hectares (by comparison, the total land available for arable crops in the Netherlands is 820,000 hectares). The United States is by far the top producer of GM crops, followed by Brazil and Argentina. Europe still suffers from the Frankenfood fear syndrome. However, in the largest market of the world, China, GM food is seen as a necessity to guarantee continuity in food supply to their 1.5 billion inhabitants. Gradually, public opinion in Europe is also shifting to a more supportive attitude towards GM food. In a 2009 study by the National Centre for Social research and the Food Standards Agency (November 2009), the general public in the United Kingdom appeared to agree (17 per cent) or to show a neutral attitude (39 per cent), versus 31 per cent who did not believe that the 'advantages of GM foods outweigh the dangers' (don't know: 14 per cent). Despite this shift, one has to conclude that Europe in 2011 is still not whole-heartedly supportive of GM Food, whereas the rest of the world has accepted this new technology completely.[8]

The Unilever approach in launching GM food

Unilever is one of the world's leading manufacturers of foods and products for home and personal care, with a turnover of about US$60 billion (€44.3 billion) in 2010. The company is dominated by a strong belief in providing customer satisfaction to 2 billion people every day in 100 countries worldwide. Unilever is world market leader in the following food categories: savoury, spreads, dressings, tea and ice cream. Owing to its strong position in food, Unilever relies heavily on agriculture and forestry, resulting in strong dependency relations, not only with consumers but also with suppliers.

FIGURE 6.6 Unilever's logo

At the beginning of the 1990s, Unilever was aware of the negative trend in public opinion of GM food, especially in Europe. As a leader in marketing consumer goods, it understood that introducing GM technology in food would entail substantial reputation risks. Unilever decided to be very careful in deciding whether or not to work with GM ingredients in its product portfolio.

Unilever was not surprised when opposition to biotechnology from Greenpeace – as well as numerous academics and several governments – intensified. However, the company also saw the economic advantages of working with this new technology, which could lower the costs of the raw materials it purchased for food products. The benefits of genetically enhanced crops appeared compelling,

TABLE 6.2 Road map to external alignment applied by Unilever

Negotiation	*Confrontation*
Consultation	**Mirroring**

1 *Interlocking directorates*
  – Not applicable
	6 *Lobbying*
	  – Positioning papers aimed at EC and individual European governments (constraints on European companies in developing biotechnology in food)

2 *Informal consultations*
  – Meetings with related companies such as Ahold, Gist Brocades and Shell, governmental organizations, NGOs, academic world, consumer organizations, resulting in three informal and formal platforms
	7 *Advocacy*
	  – Educational campaign in the Netherlands about GM food
	  – Improved media relations with key journalists

Consensus	**Power play**

3 *Ad hoc platforms*
  – Informal consultations on biotechnology (1992–8)
  – Task force Product Board for Margarine, Fats and Oils (1995–8)
  – Project Team Biotechnology Product Boards (1998–2000)
	8 *Legal actions*
	  – Not applicable
	
	9 *Competitive pressure*
	  – Not applicable

4 *Buffering*
  – Product Board for Margarine, Fats and Oils, 2000–now
  – Broadening the scope of the Product Board to all other areas where GM is applicable (grain, seeds and legumes)	

5 *Joint ventures* – Cooperation with food industry (Nestlé, Nutricia etc.)	

financially attractive and practically inevitable to Europe's larger food companies. That is why Nestlé, Unilever and several other firms took the lead on the issue and began preparing for an expected, intense debate.

The main steps in building external alignment focusing on the role of Unilever, specifically in the Dutch context, are summarized in Table 6.2. Details about these steps will be provided in the next section of this chapter.

Negotiation: consultation

The company applied consultation techniques during the initial discussions on GM food by speaking with a broad range of relevant stakeholders in the Dutch food industry, including Royal Ahold (a retailer operating globally, with brands such as Albert Heijn, Stop & Shop etc.), Gist-Brocades (a biotech firm, now part of DSM), Shell (which has considerable experience working with critical opponents), the Dutch Consumer League, the University for Agriculture and the nation's Ministries of Economic Affairs and Agriculture. Over a period of six years, this group established three separate inter-organizational platforms intended to forge closer relationships with the most salient stakeholders.

Through these entities, Unilever created access to several of the stakeholders considered most crucial to the proposition, in particular the government agencies most likely to impose rules and directives on GM foods or, in the worst case, prohibition. It seemed clear that winning acceptance would be a public-opinion challenge. All of the organizations involved, especially those with retail customers, expected severe and damaging threats to company reputation. That same sense of expectation, however, compelled this collective to work with a series of organizations well in advance of the inevitable and more public reaction when the foods were actually introduced, thus creating links to institutions that could act as a buffer between the industry and public opinion.

Negotiation: consensus

In response to the rapid advancements in biotechnology, the European Union adopted two major directives on biotechnology (90/220/EEC and 90/221/EEC). The first focused on the deliberate release of transgenic organisms into the environment, and the second concentrated on their use in contained spaces such as laboratories and factories. The directives created a number of constraints on European companies developing biotechnologies. In contrast, United States-based Monsanto and Cargill were less hampered, after the US FDA decided in 1992 that altered foods had only to meet the same standards as all other foods, with no additional regulations. Although the European firms were clearly going to fall behind, cultural and political realities compelled them to build the foundations of alignment.

The informal consultations on biotechnology emerged out of a collective recognition that biotechnology and GM foods presented issues that transcended

FIGURE 6.7 Attacks on Unilever by Greenpeace

the boundaries of each individual firm in the industry. In a speech on the impact of biotechnology, Unilever's then-chairman Morris Tabaksblat, said:

> Whether you are buyers, traders, crushers, regulators, or [working] in another sector of the foods business, you represent an enormous range of products and sectors. It's impressive to see how diverse and yet how closely interdependent these different areas are. At the end of the day, however, we all share the same ultimate goal – serving the consumer better.[9]

Membership of the informal platform was not restricted to corporations. A number of NGOs were invited to participate, and a few, such as the Consumers League and Nature and Environment accepted. The consultations had two primary purposes: first, all of the participants wanted to collect and share information of mutual interest. Second, the meetings were intended to initiate an open dialogue between industry representatives and members of NGOs. Because these meetings started more than four years before the introduction of GM ingredients in the Netherlands, a communicative relationship between the parties developed long before the public debate over biotechnology grew heated. That did not guarantee lack of criticism, however, evident in the 1997 Greenpeace banner outside the headquarters of Unilever in Rotterdam.

After three years of discussions, industry members realized that the informal consultations were no longer sufficient, if only because the platform lacked staff, budget and a clear mandate. In the fall of 1995, the industry created the Product

Board for Margarine, Fats and Oils, a semi-public organization representing the interests of the food industry, which served as an official 'spokesperson'. The board employed a permanent staff of around thirty and was endowed with a sufficient budget, through compulsory contributions from industry members. Early in its existence, the board also created a task force to maintain close relationships with stakeholders during the introduction of GM foods.

As a Unilever manager explained, in response to the question of why his firm had conceded part of its autonomy in biotechnology affairs to the board:

> If you are serious about providing customer service, you need to use a central information point. A worried mother does not want to dial twenty different telephone numbers. From a consumer's point of view, centralization of responsibilities is the best alternative.

Recognizing the key role the media would eventually play, the task force organized press workshops to provide journalists covering biotechnology with factually correct information and informed perspectives. It initiated a national information campaign aimed at the general public, featuring toll-free telephone lines and brochures with background information. It also arranged a series of informal meetings for industry representatives and NGOs, where the parties could continue to develop their ongoing relationships.

Eventually, the group established more formal links with other government boards responsible for agricultural practices and food standards. Jointly, the agencies established a Project Team Biotechnology Product Board, which essentially 'absorbed' all the capabilities, resources and contacts of the task force, along with its funds and staff. The Dutch food industry then let the organization deal directly with critics, who now had a single source of information. As one of the network participants explained:

> What we have learned . . . is that it is important not to create a new platform for every new issue. Consumers do not distinguish between introductions. They are not interested in the differences between modified soy and modified corn, so it is better if they receive their information regarding the entire 'menu' of [modified] agricultural products from a single organization. You must respect existing channels, so to speak.

In addition to corporate and government participants, NGOs also joined the informal consultations on GM food. One of their policy directors explained why:

> We decided to join this platform because we do not think that informing the public is a task for the national government. And also because we think that the parties in the private sector are a little too eager to provide only that information that suits their interests best. Therefore, we have decided, in conjunction with the food industry, to inform the public at large for them. In return, we receive early access to new information.

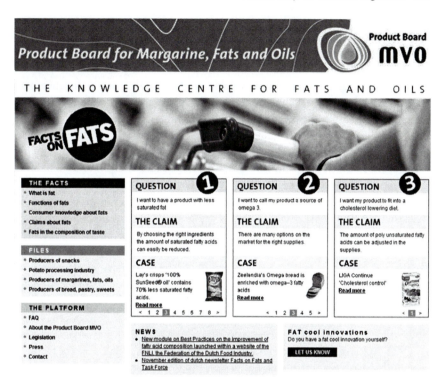

FIGURE 6.8 FACTS ON FATS is an initiative of the Product Board for Margarine, Fats and Oils (MVO)

The Dutch food industry's approach to GM foods is a classic case of consensus, creating networks that included links to consumers, universities and environmental groups likely to oppose such products. Most important was the proactive involvement with the national government, which essentially enabled the industry to preserve its autonomy in biotechnology-related affairs. A highly placed official working for the Ministry of Economic Affairs explained why the government essentially allowed the industry to regulate itself:

> We have decided not to intervene in the process because the industry informs us well. We often meet one another in a range of different settings, such as the Communicative Consultations on Biotechnology and the Regular Consultations of the Food and Drug Administration. That is how we keep a finger on the pulse.

By allowing government officials to exert (some) informal influence over their biotechnology policies, the Dutch food-producing organizations displayed their 'willingness' to relinquish some measure of authority to the affected audience.[10]

Confrontation: mirroring

The group of organizations around Unilever also decided to start a public information campaign explaining the nature of GM food to large audiences in Dutch
society. 'Fact packs' for every new product introduction were distributed to
affected or interested stakeholders. They continued an open dialogue between
scientists, the national government and NGOs. Additional press workshops were
held, and the Project Team conducted a public information campaign about Bt-
corn, featuring a toll-free telephone line and free brochures. These alignments,
evolving into a much more formal state, prepared the still nascent GM-food industry
for its next wave of challenges.

Another example of mirroring applied by Unilever was an improvement in its
media-relations function, owing to a smart application of a mutual-learning strategy.
By listening to critical journalists and changing its media policy accordingly,
Unilever fine-tuned and improved the relationship. Although the company
recognized that the press would most likely be a critical constituency of
biotechnology, it also represented a conduit to the public and permission-givers,
with professional needs that should be respected and met. As said by one of the
journalists involved in reporting on Unilever:

> They [have learned to] understand my profession. What matters to me is
> that I have a personal contact person inside the organization. I don't want
> to speak to some kind of Public Relations official, because they are only a
> burden. Unilever lets me speak to people that are of interest to me.

Confrontation: power play

Unilever purposely did not apply confrontation techniques such as litigation
or the application of competitive pressure around the issue of GM foods. The
European context, especially the dominant political view that GM foods would
be bad for consumers, did not create enough degrees of freedom to intensify pressure
on organizations in and around governments to stimulate the launch of this new
technology. The political climate in the United States was quite the opposite
compared with Europe. That is one of the reasons Monsanto applied different
methods in its road map for getting its external stakeholders aligned on GM
technology.

The Monsanto approach in launching GM foods

Monsanto is a United States-based company active in agricultural and vegetable
seeds, crop-protection chemicals and biotechnology. The company employs about
21,000 people, is active in sixty-six countries and had revenues of US$10.5 billion
in 2010. According to the company's website, the firm is 'one of the world's leading
companies focused on sustainable agriculture. We discover and deliver innovative

MONSANTO

FIGURE 6.9 Monsanto's logo

products that support the farmers who feed, fuel and clothe our world'. Monsanto stresses three advantages of working with technology including GM:

> helping to enable farmers to provide food, fuel, and fiber for the world; limiting the use of resources such as land, water and energy and in the context of the expected growth of the global population by 40 per cent in the next few decades; helping to increase food production exponentially aimed at meeting the needs related to the future population growth.

Monsanto typically states that the high-tech developments in modern culture and biotechnology have facilitated an increase in agricultural output in developed and developing countries, enabling farm operations of all sizes to be more economically sustainable. The result is food supply that keeps pace with demand growth, without increasing the use of precious resources such as water, land and energy. They label this 'sustainable agriculture', where farmers produce more food, conserve natural resources and improve the lives of people in their country.

There are substantial differences between Unilever and Monsanto. Three points are relevant in the context of how both companies acted in promoting the new technology in GM food. First, Monsanto is a business-to-business company, highly specialized in seeds and herbicides. As a consequence, customer satisfaction for Monsanto is increasing benefits for farmers, not end consumers. Second, market-place attitudes and support in its home country of the United States appeared to

Sustainable Agriculture
Producing More. Conserving More. Improving Lives.

FIGURE 6.10 Monsanto website, 2011

be more positive towards GM food for Monsanto, than they were for Unilever in Europe. Pressure from activists was intense for European food companies developing GM food. Activists were less hostile in the United States, where the public also had a more open-minded attitude towards high-tech food. Third, Monsanto had a long history of conflicts with critics who held a negative view of the company's ethics, around its sales of chemicals such as insecticides and especially the Agent Orange defoliant, a product manufactured by Monsanto for the US government during the Vietnam War.

Given this context, it is not a surprise that Monsanto applied a rather different approach in promoting GM seeds for soy, grains and legumes, and it has apparently worked. Two decades after the commercial launch of GM foods, the majority of the world has accepted the technology. In other words, from a commercial point of view, Monsanto succeeded in getting external alignment around their strategic objective to push for GM technology in agricultural production. According to Jerry Steiner, director of corporate communication at Monsanto, this can be explained as follows: 'We saw adoption rise steadily and then rapidly as farmers became more aware and confident of the value the products could bring them, either by experience on their own farm or by seeing their neighbor's.' In fact, in some cases, those neighbours were miles away, actually in neighbouring countries (including in Brazil and India), where regulatory approvals took five to six years longer than other countries, and some (thousands of) farmers did not wait and instead bought them across borders illegally before Monsanto could ever sell them. Steiner explains:

> The momentum was possible not through a push from Monsanto but through a strong pull from the farmers. Today 15 million farm families have adopted the GM technology and in almost every case where farmers have had the choice, they have overwhelmingly chosen biotech. Why? Because they work.

However, that does not mean that Monsanto did not face severe opposition. Activists still aggressively attack Monsanto on the GM food issues, which can easily be traced on the Internet on dozens of anti- Monsanto websites. This robust and continued resistance against Monsanto probably explains why their road map to creating external alignment emphasized what I have labelled in this book a *confrontation intervention strategy*, more than a *negotiation* approach. Steiner adds that:

> Our fundamental belief is that multiple forms of agriculture can and in fact have a proven record of coexisting (and competing), providing different choices for different consumers. GM products are an additional choice for farmers. If the crops have economic advantage, economics tell you that benefits will be shared with the chain via competition. Because of this, not everyone has to 'agree' to introduce a new technology.

TABLE 6.3 Road map to external alignment applied by Monsanto

Negotiation	*Confrontation*
Consultation	**Mirroring**
1 *Interlocking directorates* – Appointing BoD members from 'relevant' industries	6 *Lobbying* – Lobbying for support with FDA in USA
2 *Informal consultations* – Not identifiable from public sources	7 *Advocacy advertising* – Advocacy advertising in Europe, promoting GM food (done by British and French agency 1997–8. Campaign created huge irritation among NGOs and general public
Consensus	**Power play**
3 *Ad hoc platforms* – Not identifiable from public sources	8 *Legal actions* – Litigation with individual farmer Percy Schmeiser versus Monsanto about ownership using Monsanto seed
4 *Buffering* – Directly: relying on trade organizations: National Biotechnology Industry Organization, American Chemistry Council (creations that stand between their member organizations and their critics) – Indirectly: creating a formal structure that signals a commitment to institutional beliefs and that represents the organization favourably to valued stakeholders (philanthropic foundation, funding academic research, sponsorship)	9 *Competitive pressure* – Smoking out competitors: Monsanto versus Dupont
5 *Joint ventures* – Cooperation with companies in BRIC countries	

The main steps taken by Monsanto are shown in Table 6.3, in the same format as was applied earlier for Unilever. Striking differences become clear by only comparing the two road maps. The European giant did not apply 'power play' techniques, as Monsanto did. Unilever's main worry was consumer reaction to GM food and the consequences that this might have on the rest of the product portfolio of the company. Monsanto's focus was to gain government support for a science-based approval processes for its agricultural products, like several other multinational and multiple smaller competitors developing GM products and technology.

TABLE 6.4 Monsanto Board of Directors

Name	Job title/company
Frank V. AtLee III	Retired president of the former American Cyanamid Company and chairman of the former Cyanamid International
John W. Bachmann	Senior partner of Edward Jones
David L. Chicoine	President of South Dakota State University
Janice L. Fields	President of McDonald's USA
Hugh Grant	Chairman of the board, president and chief executive officer of Monsanto
Arthur H. Harper	Managing partner of GenNx360 Capital Partners
Gwendolyn S. King	President of Podium Prose
C. Steven McMillan	Retired chairman of the board and chief executive officer of Sara Lee Corporation
William U. Parfet	Chairman of the board and chief executive officer of MPI Research Inc.
George H. Poste	Chief executive of Health Technology Networks
Robert J. Stevens	Chairman of the board and chief executive officer of Lockheed Martin Corporation

Source: Monsanto, www.monsanto.com/investors/Pages/archived-annual-reports.aspx, accessed 2 July 2011.

Negotiation: consultation

Monsanto seems fully aware of the dependency position on key stakeholders and its effect on commercial successes. Crucial for Monsanto are board of directors members who, owing to their previous experience elsewhere, provided insight to the company about the market, the social context in which the company operates and the newest developments in technology. As is shown in Table 6.4, Monsanto's leading governance body has a proven and collective track record in food, technology, finance and politics.

Negotiation: consensus

Based on relationships with various industry organizations, Monsanto stimulated support for science-based regulations that were introduced in the United States by the FDA in 1990. Groups such as the National Biotechnology Industry Organization (BIO) and the American Chemistry Council are good examples of creations that stand between their member companies and critics, while lobbying governments and buffering criticism at higher and general levels. Member companies attempt to secure stability by outsourcing part of their information and communication functions. BIO offers an interesting example of how *buffering* works in practice (see Box 6.2).

Box 6.2 EXAMPLE OF A BUFFERING STRATEGY

BIO is the world's largest biotechnology organization, providing advocacy, business development and communications services for more than 1,200 members worldwide. Our mission is to be the champion of biotechnology and the advocate for our member organizations – both large and small.

BIO members are involved in the research and development of innovative healthcare, agricultural, industrial and environmental biotechnology technologies. Corporate members range from entrepreneurial companies developing a first product to Fortune 100 multinationals. We also represent state and regional biotech associations, service providers to the industry and academic centres.

Member services include:

- federal and state advocacy on issues affecting the industry;
- a dozen or more investor and partnering meetings throughout the year, with discounts for members;
- communications services that disseminate information about the benefits of biotechnology;
- BIO Business Solutions discounts for a variety of goods and services.

Brief history

BIO was created in 1993 through the merger of the Association of Biotechnology Companies and the Industrial Biotechnology Association. The goal was for the entire industry – from young start-ups to established companies – to speak with one voice for the industry on such issues as FDA reform, reimbursement policy, national healthcare policy, regulation of biotech crops, and small business and economic development issues.

Box 6.2—*continued*

Over the last 12 years, we have made progress on many fronts:

- Enactment of FDA reform in the 1997 food and Drug Administration Modernization Act.
- From the first significant commercial plantings in 1996, double-digit growth in each subsequent year has led to more than 252 million acres of biotech crops planted in 2006 in twenty-two countries.
- At least forty states have programmes in place to promote bioscience-related economic development.
- The US government has established aggressive, but realistic, targets for bio-fuels production, including key incentives for continued development of biotech-based fuels.
- Agricultural biotechnology has helped enable large shifts in agronomic practices that have led to significant and widespread environmental benefits, such as improved soil makeup and water, reduced runoff, and reduced greenhouse gas emissions from agriculture.
- Since their introduction in 1996, biotech crops have increased global farm income by $27 billion.
- Cloning can be used to protect endangered species. In Southeast Asia, both the banteng and the guar, which are meat-type bovines, have been cloned in conservation efforts to increase populations of species threatened by extinction.

BIO supports strong regulatory oversight for agricultural biotechnology from three federal agencies.

Source: BIO. www.bio.org, accessed 22 March 2011

As a stakeholder integration mechanism, buffering comes down to forging close links with representative organizations to avoid having to deal with many dispersed, sometimes anonymous and therefore less controllable, individual stakeholders. To some degree, these links shield the organization from environmental uncertainty by stabilizing external influences and making them more predictable. In essence, buffering mechanisms raise the height of organizational boundaries by joining together a group of organizations that have a similar interest in promoting a specific goal, sometimes shutting out unwanted influences on corporate policy and operations owing to the power of the collectivity.

Confrontation: mirroring

During the 1990s, US-based companies were disappointed with the relatively slow speed with which European regulators approached the approval of GM crops compared with other world areas and also compared with the timelines set by

Europe's own regulatory system. Early in this timeframe, Monsanto started an advocacy campaign aimed at informing the European public about the added value of such food, including for farmers and hungry populations. In 1997, Monsanto hired Bartle Bogle Hegarty, a British advertising agency, and Euro RSCG, a French one, to mount an advocacy campaign to reduce public perceptions of the dangers of GM food. Its message was that the production of traditional crops will be insufficient to feed a more populated world, and that organic food will become too expensive.

One Monsanto advertisement claimed that, 'Food technology is a matter of opinions. Monsanto believes you should hear them all'. Another stated that: 'More biotechnology plants means less industrial ones'.

The messages were not well received. In turn, Monsanto pointed out that the adverts featured contact numbers for environmental groups, including Friends of the Earth and Greenpeace, overtly encouraging consumers to hear both sides of the debate. Few critics cared. In 1999, the head of communications at Monsanto appeared on a BBC television programme to defend the company's stance, but his performance was also heavily criticized. The media stated that he gave an 'arrogant' impression and that he 'failed to read the rule book on how to behave in a crisis'.

As the Monsanto example demonstrates, adopting the advocacy advertising technique requires sophisticated communication skills from advertising agencies, managers and senior executives. In addition to an elaborated understanding of the cultural and political context in which an advocacy campaign is implemented, managers need to be active in discussions with supportive and opposing stakeholder groups at the same time. To avoid surprises and nudge public opinion in a desired direction require a level of planning and allocation of resources that is almost military in its demanding precision.

According to Monsanto's Steiner:

> Despite attempts having a dialogue with various stakeholder groups, the campaign failed to understand the fears of the public following several instances where government agencies were criticized for not handling food safety issues effectively. The lack of trust in government to protect food safety was not well understood at the time. Secondly, it was poorly understood that demand for food globally would grow as quickly as it is evident 15 years later. At this time, that reason seemed to be a made up industry answer for why the technology was needed.

Confrontation: power play

Monsanto has a long track record in litigation. Many of the legal fights focus on commercial entities, but some claims have been made against individuals too. An interesting example of such a case was between Monsanto and a Canadian farmer, Percy Schmeiser. In 1997, Schmeiser claimed to discover that the edge and portions of one of his fields contained canola that was resistant to Roundup. As Schmeiser had never purchased Roundup Ready canola seeds from Monsanto, he said this was a case of contamination. The plants that were resistant to Roundup were harvested and stored separately. The following year, Schmeiser followed his usual practice of sowing his land with seeds saved from the previous crop. In his stockpile were seeds that had demonstrated a resistance to Roundup. His 1998 canola crop was more than 1,000 acres.

In 1998, Monsanto sued Schmeiser for patent infringement, asserting that he had cultivated crops containing the patented genes and cells without a licence. Based on samples that were taken as part of the case, it was found that more than 95 per cent of Schmeiser's 1998 canola crop comprised the Roundup Ready variety. The trial judge found that Schmeiser knew, or ought to have known, that the seeds he harvested in 1997 and planted in 1998 were Roundup tolerant. The trial judge also found that Monsanto's patent was valid and had been infringed by Schmeiser.

This case drew, and continues to draw, widespread public attention and media coverage. The contest was portrayed as a David and Goliath struggle, with Schmeiser cast as the small farmer fighting a major corporation. Schmeiser maintained that it was a farmer's right to use the proceeds of his field and, hence, keep and sow the seeds again in the next season. Ultimately, the issue of patent infringement versus 'farmer's rights' was settled before the highest legal institution in Canada, the Supreme Court.

The Supreme Court ruled that the issue in the case was patent protection, not property rights, and that ownership was no defence to patent infringement. The main purpose of a patent, the court explained, is the ability of the patent owner to prevent others from duplication or use of a patented invention without permission. The Supreme Court upheld the decisions of the lower courts that Monsanto's patent was valid and had been infringed by Schmeiser. As the trial judge did not make a finding as to whether Schmeiser sprayed his crop with Roundup herbicide, the Supreme Court found that he did not earn additional profits as a consequence of using the patented invention. Monetary remedies were denied, and both parties had to pay their own legal bills.

Both sides, however, felt like winners, Monsanto because of the triumph of patent rights, and Schmeiser because he could return to his farm proudly, backed by several activists who would pay most of his legal bills. In response to criticism, Monsanto Canada's director of public affairs stated that:

> It is not, nor has it ever been Monsanto Canada's policy to enforce its patent on Roundup Ready crops when they are present on a farmer's field by accident. Only when there has been a knowing and deliberate violation of its patent rights will Monsanto act.

But this was not the end of the story. In 2005, Schmeiser brought a small claims court case against Monsanto for costs associated with the removal of 'volunteer' canola plants from a fallow field. The case settled in 2008. As part of the settlement, Monsanto agreed to pay $660 to pay for removal of the volunteer plants.

A less nuanced power play occurred in the GM food sector and was described in a *New York Times* article of 16 August 2006:

> Monsanto will acquire the Delta and Pine Land Company, the nation's leading supplier of cotton seeds, in a move that would add to Monsanto's commanding position in the business of biotechnology crops. Indeed, Monsanto tried to buy Delta and Pine Land in 1998, only to drop the deal the following year, saying it could not obtain approval from federal regulators. Delta and Pine Land, saying Monsanto did not try hard enough to win clearance, sued for $2 billion in damages and the companies have had a somewhat fractious relationship ever since. The new deal would end that litigation as well as an arbitration proceeding in which Monsanto is seeking the right to revoke Delta and Pine Land's licence to use Monsanto's genetically engineered technology to provide cotton with herbicide and insect resistance.

The announcement of this acquisition sparked fierce competition between Monsanto and its rival, DuPont. Following the announcement and the actual acquisition, both companies have engaged in a series of power-play activities, as described in Box 6.3.[11,12,13,14]

Lessons learned by Monsanto

At a conference in Brussels in 2002, Monsanto Public Policy Vice President Kate Fish made statements about the lessons learned by the corporation after the criticism the company encountered in Europe. Fish confirmed that, despite outreach efforts with stakeholders, Monsanto lacked insight into major issues people have with biotechnology, such as religious issues (Is bio-engineering tampering with the realm of God?); health issues (Does biotech food impact my health?); the power of multinationals (Are these crops forced upon nations by a handful of companies with too much control?); and the trust issue (Who exactly will ensure safety?). She concluded that companies should no longer directly market their products – especially those involving what's perceived as a new technology – to consumers without first understanding and dealing with broader public issues and concerns.

As a consequence, Monsanto introduced a more *negotiation*-type approach, starting with an intense, more systematic round of consultations with stakeholder groups, varying from food companies to Greenpeace. These consultations resulted in major conclusions such as: excellent science and regulatory approval are no longer sufficient and need to be introduced in ways that make the technological information and strategic intents more transparent. The latter evoked the need at Monsanto management to create the so-called Monsanto Pledge:

> The Pledge is our guide to how we behave within an industry and a world that depends on agriculture as a building block of global security. We will listen carefully to diverse points of view and engage in thoughtful dialogue

to broaden our understanding of issues in order to better address the needs and concerns of society.

The pledge is still in place today, and each year five to seven teams receive a pledge award for actions that best exemplify it.

Monsanto introduced an additional example of a *buffering technique* by creating an external *Biotechnology Advisory Council*, which invited a range of constituencies

---

Box 6.3 POWER PLAY BETWEEN MONSANTO AND DUPONT[15]

2006–7: DuPont unsuccessfully tries to block Monsanto from buying the nation's largest cotton-seed supplier, Delta and Pine Land Co. DuPont complains to government officials about Monsanto's acquisition of the cotton-seed giant. DuPont is concerned that Monsanto's business practices are reducing competition in agriculture.

May 2009: Monsanto files a lawsuit against DuPont for patent infringement, based on DuPont's Hi-Bred seed business developing a herbicide-resistant soybean that contains two genes, one of which was developed by Monsanto.

June 2009: DuPont countersues, accusing Monsanto of being anti-competitive. DuPont fires back that Monsanto's prohibition on combining its genes with those of other companies to form new seeds was neutralized in 2008, when the US Justice Department ordered Monsanto to abandon similar restrictions on cotton-seed breeders.

18 August 2009: The chairman of Monsanto sends a letter to the chairman of DuPont in which he accuses DuPont of using third parties to attack Monsanto, activities he says, which are 'misleading to the public and a serious breach of business ethics far beyond honest competitive behavior'. The letter asks that DuPont name a committee of independent directors to investigate the allegations.

An attorney for Monsanto says the tactics used against his company include forged letters to Congress, misinformation, attempts to improperly influence public officials and financial support to a special interest group that opposes Monsanto.

28 August 2009: The president and CEO of DuPont sends a letter to Monsanto's chairman that dismisses the allegations by Monsanto. The letter states that Monsanto tries to raise 'two-year-old accusations that were all proven false'. DuPont accuses Monsanto of unfairly attempting to distract attention from a public battle over competition in the crop biotechnology business.

with an interest in biotechnology to meet, discuss, advise and help the company make decisions. The changes in Monsanto's road map, as Kate Fish noted, are reflected in a quote from the academic journal *Nature Biotechnology*: 'Biotechnology's future ultimately relies on governing institutions listening and responding to the public, rather than discounting key stakeholders as irrational, scientifically illiterate, or technophobic.'

Differences and similarities in the external-alignment road maps of Unilever and Monsanto

In most situations, large companies apply the full range of external-alignment techniques. Emphasizing a soft or a hard approach is not a free choice, but depends greatly on the nature of the market in which a company operates, the intensity of confrontations with opponents, and the executive leadership's world-view of the legitimacy of external critics.

The above probably explains the differences in the road maps applied by Unilever and by Monsanto. Unilever is a consumer-focused company, selling products through the network of retailers around the world; their customers (retailers) will take the heat from unhappy consumers. The danger of a negative spillover on to other products in its portfolio is what probably pushed Unilever into a negotiation-focused style of stakeholder engagement. In contrast, Monsanto operates primarily in the business-to-business environment, which seldom causes consumer concern; consumer concern is voter concern, which invariably draws in governments.

Another explanation for the difference was the intensity of the confrontations with critical pressure groups. For Monsanto, these confrontations were very contentious, especially with NGOs, but the criticism did not prevent Monsanto from convincing the stakeholders who mattered most – governments and farmers – that GM foods were a good thing. Governments in the United States, Asia and South America were largely supportive, if only because governments are profoundly interested in the guaranteed production of food for their populations. Farmers agreed, as they experienced the clear commercial advantages of using the Monsanto products, through reduced herbicide use that lowered production costs and seeds that created a higher yield. With end consumers far from Monsanto's mindset, a confrontation style was a logical choice.

The third explanation involves the two world-views embedded in these companies. The American opinion of technological innovation and health issues is quite different from a European one. On the old continent, pressure from NGOs and other types of opponent seems to result more frequently in dialogues with these pressure groups than in the United States, and certainly more so than in China. The changes in Monsanto's world-view, expressed in its Monsanto Pledge of 2002, indicate that working globally makes a company more sensitive to government decision-makers, almost forcing it to show respect for diversity of opinion.

TABLE 6.5 Who does what in creating external alignment?

Strategic road map	Tactics	Board and business unit management	Staff support	Marketing and sales	Corporate communication
CONFRONTATION	**Consultation**	Appointing BoD	Input for BoM role	Providing input to BoM about the market	Providing information to board about issues, stakeholder beliefs
	Consensus	Linking pin in buffering roles	Representing firm in buffering and platform roles	Providing input to BoM about the market	Long term focused corporate communication actions
NEGOTIATION	**Mirroring**	Lobbying, speeches, interviews	Speeches, interviews	Adjusting marketing communication	Long term focused corporate communication actions
	Power play	Granting permission to start power play actions	Litigation, competitive pressure	Orchestrating commercial actions attuned with power-play actions	Short term focused corporate communication actions

However, there are also similarities in the two approaches. Both choose to seek some kind of external alignment. Both employed specialized and well-coordinated professional staff, including corporate communication, legal and lobbyists. Both used buffering techniques. And, depending on how individuals view the growth of crops from GM seeds, both companies are helping ease world hunger, while also unleashing Frankenfood into a world that ought to be much more vigilant.

A summary of the main managerial efforts and the allocation of tasks related to these actions is shown in Table 6.5.

Notes

1 P.P.M.A.R. Heugens, F.A.J. van den Bosch and C.B.M. van Riel, 'Stakeholder integration: building mutually enforcing relationships', *Business & Society*, (2002), vol. 41(1): 37–61.
2 WWF Global website, http://wwf.panda.org/what_we_do/footprint/climate_carbon_energy/climate_change/publications/position_papers/?173281/WWF-position-on-forests-and-climate-change-mitigation (accessed September 2011).
3 Letter to the editor regarding a 1 June op-ed entitled, 'Tomatoes may be dangerous to your health', *New York Times*, 16 June 1992.
4 Wikipedia website, http://en.wikipedia.org/wiki/Luther_Burbank (accessed 14 January 2010).
5 J. Tierney, 'Greens and hunger', *New York Times*, (2008), http://tierneylab.blogs.nytimes.com/2008/05/19/greens-and-hunger/?pagemode=print (accessed 23 March 2011).
6 'Roundup Ready soybeans', Union of Concerned Scientists website, Food and Agriculture section, 14 January 2010, www.ucsusa.org/food_and_agriculture/science_and_impacts/impacts_genetic_engineering/roundup-ready-soybeans.html (accessed 23 March 2011).
7 'GM benefits outweigh risk', ScienceAlert.com, 24 January 2008, www.sciencealert.com.au/news (accessed 23 March 2011).
8 National Centre for Social Research (NatCen) and the Food Standard Agency, United Kingdom, 2009, www.food.gov.uk/news/newsarchive/2009/nov/gmreport (accessed 23 March 2011).
9 P.P. Heugens, F.A. van den Bosch and C.B. van Riel, 'Stakeholder integration: building mutually enforcing relationships', *Business & Society*, (2002), vol. 41(1), pp. 36–60.
10 Facts on Fats website, www.factsonfats.nl/ (accessed 3 March 2010).
11 Scott Kilman, 'Monsanto sues Dupont over biotech patents', *Wall Street Journal*, 6 May 2009.
12 Scott Kilman, 'Monsanto, Dupont escalate patent fray', *Wall Street Journal*, 19 August 2009.
13 Chuck Neubauer, 'Monsanto chief accuses rival DuPont of deceit; seed business giant decries tactics as beyond competition', *Washington Times*, 18 August 2009.
14 Chuck Neubauer, 'DuPont, Monsanto trade barbs over competition', *Washington Times*, 28 August 2009.
15 Chuck Neubauer, 'Monsanto chief accuses rival DuPont of deceit; seed business giant decries tactics as beyond competition', *Washington Times*, 18 August 2009.

7

BENEFITING FROM CORPORATE COMMUNICATION SUPPORT IN CREATING EXTERNAL ALIGNMENT

Alignment is defined in this book as '*a mutually rewarding relationship between a company and its key stakeholders, enabling the firm to realize its purpose*'. Managers can select a road map that either stresses negotiation or confrontation. Implementing these road maps can be carried out in two different styles. One is called a *rational approach*, in which corporate leadership convinces stakeholders that they are receiving an offer so beneficial that it can't be refused, a tactic most pertinent for consumers. A second style of working is the *normative approach*, in which the organization stresses the advantages of alignment by showing how it serves a social purpose. This is more useful with a variety of stakeholders with different interests. Both approaches, however, rely greatly on corporate communication to articulate and project the mutually rewarding benefits of alignment. (See Figure 7.1.)

The same is true during *negotiations* with external audiences, through well-crafted messages that stimulate an *awareness* of the firm in general, while specifically demonstrating or proving its *legitimacy*, making it clear to stakeholders that the organization is a worthy and worthwhile dialogue partner. Stakeholders will also be more inclined to participate in dialogue and alignment if the company is *perceived as attractive*, thanks to content in communication about the financial and social benefits that could follow.

Likewise, corporate communication professionals also contribute to external alignment through *confrontation* techniques. While almost identical goals must be met, confrontation demands more intense messaging. Some stakeholders will be challenged with bold statements about their actions, suggesting that opposition to the company does not serve a higher purpose. However, confrontational messages should also be accompanied by others aimed at existing supporters, to reduce the risk of alienation that turns an aligned stakeholder into an opponent.

The need for a range of blunt and extremely nuanced messaging can be met only by a skilled communication staff, with leaders who fully understand the

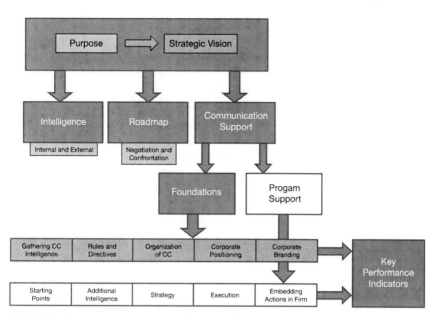

FIGURE 7.1 Two corporate communication roles in creating external alignment

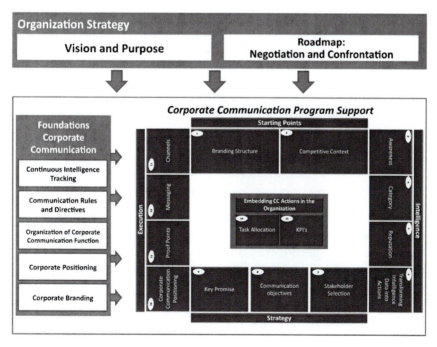

FIGURE 7.2 A detailed description of the two roles of corporate communication

corporation first and foremost, but also are masters of the creativity and discipline of their profession. We examined the basics of an effective corporate communication function earlier, including the creation of an infrastructure that supports programmes and strategic objectives. Here, we begin with an illustration of what creating those foundations entails.

Except for start-ups that use public relations agencies for communication support, few corporate executives have an opportunity to build this function from scratch. Most newly appointed leaders inherit a number of communication channels and traditions and a professional staff that's useful. However, I intend to describe the needed foundational building blocks – needed for external and internal communication – as if a company were starting with a blank organization chart. This allows for a critical emphasis on *corporate positioning*, which is essential to forging stakeholder alignment when a new strategy is being launched, be it the result of a merger, a major change in the product portfolio or in response to external critics whose assertions threaten the firm's reputation with governments, and thus its unrestricted licence to operate.

Organizations don't change basic strategy all that frequently. That's why corporate communication more routinely deals with increasing alignment around the strategic objectives of specific programmes. For example, Unilever has positioned itself with the following vision: *We work to create a better future every day. We help people feel good, look good and get more out of life with brands and services that are good for them and good for others.* This is the core of its corporate-branding efforts. However, Unilever has various programmes that address the subordinate goals of the strategy. For instance, one of its communication programmes, launched on 15 November 2010, is designed to generate external alignment. By 2020, Unilever will attempt to halve the environmental footprint of its products, help more than 1 billion people take action to improve their health and well-being, and source 100 per cent of its agricultural raw materials sustainably. See Figure 7.3 for the three broad areas of Unilever's ten-year Sustainable Living Plan.[1]

Let us first look at the foundations of corporate communication.

Foundations of corporate communication

There are four building blocks that comprise the foundations for all corporate communication. They form a structure that also includes bandwidth for specialized programmes around specific strategic objectives that are implemented by communication professionals in areas such as government relations, policy development and investor relations, and others supporting management and the company's negotiation or confrontation strategies. These foundations provide clarity about nomenclature, rules and directives that guide corporate social-responsibility programmes, sponsorships, donations and media relations, and they streamline potentially time-consuming discussions of ad hoc requests from internal or external audiences. They provide clarity about the visual, rational and emotional carriers

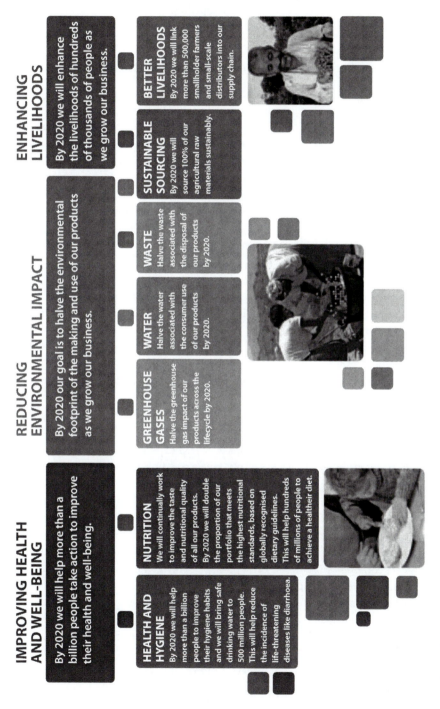

IMPROVING HEALTH AND WELL-BEING

By 2020 we will help more than a billion people take action to improve their health and well-being.

HEALTH AND HYGIENE

By 2020 we will help more than a billion people to improve their hygiene habits and we will bring safe drinking water to 500 million people. This will help reduce the incidence of life-threatening diseases like diarrhoea.

NUTRITION

We will continually work to improve the taste and nutritional quality of all our products. By 2020 we will double the proportion of our portfolio that meets the highest nutritional standards, based on globally recognised dietary guidelines. This will help hundreds of millions of people to achieve a healthier diet.

REDUCING ENVIRONMENTAL IMPACT

By 2020 our goal is to halve the environmental footprint of the making and use of our products as we grow our business.

GREENHOUSE GASES

Halve the greenhouse gas impact of our products across the lifecycle by 2020.

WATER

Halve the water associated with the consumer use of our products by 2020.

WASTE

Halve the waste associated with the disposal of our products by 2020.

ENHANCING LIVELIHOODS

By 2020 we will enhance the livelihoods of hundreds of thousands of people as we grow our business.

SUSTAINABLE SOURCING

By 2020 we will source 100% of our agricultural raw materials sustainably.

BETTER LIVELIHOODS

By 2020 we will link more than 500,000 smallholder farmers and small-scale distributors into our supply chain.

FIGURE 7.3 Three main targets in the Unilever Sustainable Living Plan

of the corporate brand. Most importantly, solid foundations enable corporate communication to create a solid and compelling *corporate story*, so that the organization can build and maintain a positive reputation.

Gathering continuous corporate communication intelligence

The ability to manage stakeholder demands is predicated on an understanding of the belief systems underlying each and every stakeholder group. Any response – be it proactive, defensive or the passive–aggressive technique of simply ignoring the source of discord – depends upon the organization's relationship with that external entity and the sensitivity of the issue to the company's strategy. Tracking the dominant trends in public opinion is one step towards developing a comprehensive grasp of the external context. A corporation also needs to track the status of its reputation at several levels, including its relative position within an industry and in each of the countries where it does business.

As was explained in Chapter 5, the gathering of external intelligence can be divided into three layers:

(a) systematically scanning issues that might threaten the firm in the short or the long run, resulting in shifts in public opinion that might have a negative impact on the firm;
(b) tracking external beliefs such as trends in public opinion and developments in reputation; and
(c) gathering additional intelligence on specific alignment-building programmes.

Rules and directives

A uniform nomenclature, be it words or a preferred expression of a visual identity, and the standards for using it are usually articulated in a house-style handbook. When an organization develops stand-alone products or communication items, these should use the preferred nomenclature. Although uniformity isn't always a goal in itself, this resource at least provides clarity for the starting point.

Handbooks are useful for managing brands, corporate social-responsibility programmes and sponsorships, and in creating documents and visual broadcast media that reflect consistency of the corporate purpose. A brand-value book, for example, can be used as a reference manual to describe the mission, vision and brand values, and to describe how to use the brand values in communication. Most branding handbooks or manuals also contain a piece on the meaningfulness, uniqueness and credibility of the values; a description of the positioning of the values; ideas of how employees can live the brand values in their day-to-day activities; and a description of how employees at all levels can contribute to those values. Along with describing how the visual identity of the brand values should be expressed, the book provides a standard for product and service delivery.

FIGURE 7.4 Example of a corporate handbook

Organization of the corporate communication function

Excellent communication departments have a clear idea of how to organize and coordinate the activities between their people, as well as the executives and managers responsible for the organization's daily business. The desired and actual forms the communication function takes correspond strongly with the kind of company of which it is a part. Some businesses are simply less affected by external turbulence than others. The world's largest paperclip manufacturer will probably never get a rise out of Greenpeace. However, for airlines, banks and oil companies, external turbulence is a way of life, forcing them to organize communication in a corresponding manner.

A standard, ideal organizational chart for a corporate communication department simply does not exist. The roles, skills and tasks required of a specific group totally depend upon the type of organization it serves and the strategy being deployed. There are, however, several basic competencies communication managers need in order to become successful:

- *communication* skills, including an ability to obtain information, critique, edit and write and speak effectively;
- *business* skills, including an understanding of external and internal customers, products and markets;
- *leadership* skills, including knowledge of business complexities and an ability to act as strategic partner with executives and managers;
- *context-awareness* skills, which involve knowledge of the corporate environment and related legal, regulatory and policy requirements;

- *stakeholder-integration* skills, or the ability to build public trust and enhance the reputation of the business;
- *sales-support* skills, or an understanding of how to integrate diverse media channels to help promote products, services and organizations.

A well-run communication function ultimately comes down to the abilities of the people within it. Equally, and perhaps even more, important is whether senior line executives respect and trust that talent, make good use of communication counsel and allow these professionals to do their best work.

Corporate positioning

Creating a clear and robust infrastructure for all communication activities – including the communication roles initiated by managers – will increase consistency in the look and feel of corporate messaging. Consistency in messaging avoids fragmentation and increases the degree of recognition and predictability. In my opinion, *corporate positioning* should start with the development of a *corporate story* that describes the firm's key identity traits and its strategic intents. This story is the core and essence of what has to be communicated, and in variations that match various media, be it in print, in advertisements, on the Internet, broadcast or delivered in live individual presentations. As soon as there is clarity about the corporate story, decisions on *corporate branding* can focus on three points: what will be the visual carrier, the emotional carrier and the rational carrier of the corporate brand?

A *corporate story* is a structured description that communicates the essence of the company to all stakeholders. It helps strengthen the bonds that bind employees to the company, successfully positions the company against rivals and frames corporate communication. The entire statement or document is not necessarily appropriate for widespread distribution. But the story and its proof points provide a useful briefing tool, not only for internal audiences, but also external vendors such as advertisers and consultants. An ideal corporate story is built up by identifying unique elements of the company, creating a narrative that weaves them together, and presenting it in an appealing fashion. These unique building blocks should be based on a combination of desired and perceived identity traits and, of course, external expectations and evaluations.

There are various *narrative structures* an organization can use to plot the story in a specific way. One rational approach is structuring the facts in what's called the 'triple-A model', or *activities, accomplishments* and *abilities*. With this narrative structure, one should start with a description of the core activities, including the nature of the business and its industry, the product portfolio and the company's regional, national or global scale. The second piece includes the organization's accomplishments, such as facts and figures on market share, customer satisfaction, reputation and return on investment. Only then should the narrative move into its third chapter, which describes the organization's ability to accomplish a given

BBVA BBVA is a global group that offers individual and corporate customers the most complete range of financial and non-financial products and services. It enjoys a solid leadership position in the Spanish market, where it first began its activities over 150 years ago. It also has a leading franchise in South America; it is the largest financial institution in Mexico; one of the fifteenth largest US commercial banks; and one of the few large international groups operating in China and Turkey. BBVA employs 104,000 people in over thirty countries around the world, has more than 47 million customers and 900,000 shareholders. BBVA recently introduced a new positioning rooted in a corporate story that was developed in conjunction with employees. The key points of the story can be summarized with the following corporate principles: *Customer* as the centre of our business; *Creation of shareholder value* through business activity; *Teamwork* as the key to generating value; *Management* style that generates enthusiasm; *Ethical conduct* and personal and professional integrity as a way of understanding and conducting business; *Innovation* as the engine for progress; *Corporate social responsibility* as an intrinsic part of development.

FIGURE 7.5 Visual story-telling workshop at BBVA

set of objectives.[2] Preparing a corporate story requires substantial discussions among key internal managers, as has been done, for example, at BBVA; see Figure 7.5.

Certain questions can give clarity to this third piece of the corporate story. For example, why did a certain way of working produce successful results? What is different about the way the company operates, especially versus its competitors? What most determines organizational continuity? What is the most pertinent and consistent factor that links the company's past success to its future? The answers

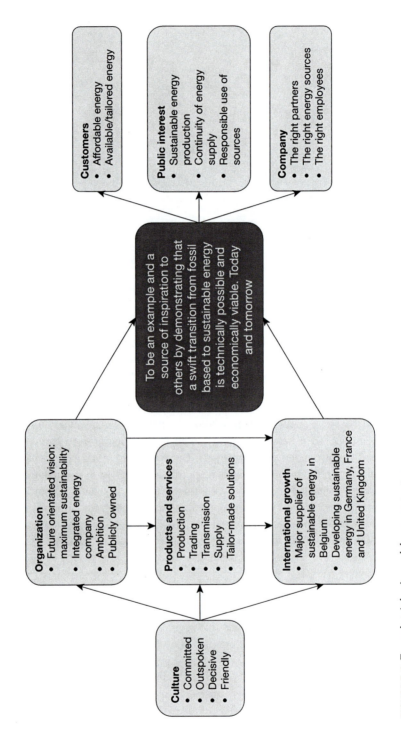

FIGURE 7.6 Eneco's triple-A-model corporate story

to these triple-A questions are well illustrated by Eneco, a Dutch energy company (see Figure 7.6).

Based on the triple-A model, Eneco developed text for its corporate story: see Box 7.1.[3]

The world of energy companies is changing rapidly. In the past, a few firms produced energy, which was distributed by a larger number of energy providers that delivered electricity and gas to millions of customers. This may have been typical in the past; the future requires a totally different style of working. Now we will be able to decentralize in the production of sustainable energy. The CEO of Eneco, Jeroen de Haas, is convinced that:

> The energy infrastructure will be fully reorganized, from production to delivery to the client. Production is no longer the monopoly of a limited group of producers. Cities, corporations and individual households all can become energy producers. Of course, this has huge consequences for the function and role of an energy firm. They will grow into a different role where they are no longer solely producers or distributors of energy, but increasingly transforming into a linking pin role. That is: providing advice about how to reduce energy and stimulating others to become producers of energy themselves. This implies the necessity for centralized mass production of energy to be attuned with decentralized production on smaller scale. This will force the energy company of the future to become and act as an allocator of energy, instead of a pure producer or distributor of energy.

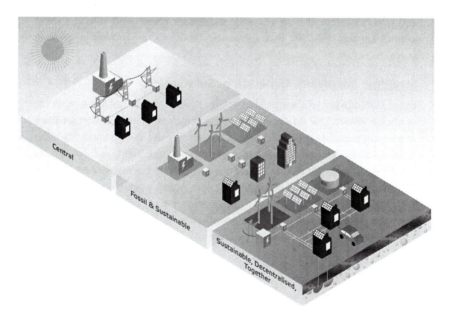

FIGURE 7.7 Eneco: old–transition–new

Box 7.1
ENECO'S CORPORATE STORY

SUSTAINABLE ENERGY FOR EVERYONE

Vision: sustainable energy holds the future

We are standing at the threshold of a new era of energy. Fossil fuel sources are running out. Growing oil and coal consumption is creating increased dependence on non-European, sometimes unstable countries. Global warming is moreover challenging us to find clean and smart solutions for future generations. Sustainable energy provides the best guarantee for the continuity of our energy supply from an economic, social and ecological perspective.

Mission: sustainable energy for everyone

Eneco is a sustainable energy company. Our core activities are producing and supplying sustainable energy and conceiving smart sustainable energy solutions. We are one of Europe's cleanest energy companies and are committed to retaining this position. Our mission is: sustainable energy for everyone. We are consequently dedicated to supplying energy that is reliable, affordable and clean. For today and tomorrow. For customers, shareholders, employees, partners, government officials and citizens alike. And their children and grandchildren. This passion stems from our connection with the world around us and the fact that sustainable strategy generates the greatest economic value.

Strategy: Supplying. Generating. Solutions.

Eneco is dedicated to a sustainable energy supply. We do not have coal-fired or nuclear plants. Our economies of scale and independence furthermore give us a strong foundation that furnishes the necessary decisiveness and flexibility. These qualities are both vital for spurring new development, reacting rapidly when opportunities arise and sometimes rising above the rest. Eneco operates at the heart of society and the economy: committed, outspoken and decisive. With business units that work with and reinforce each other. And that think from the perspective of customers' needs relating to supplying, generating and solutions:

- We are committed to supplying the daily energy our customers need to live and work.
- Eneco consequently invests in energy sources in the Netherlands, Germany, Belgium, France and the United Kingdom that combine sustainability and healthy returns with acceptable risks.

- We tap into our expertise and experience to find solutions to everything from global energy issues to local energy generation in neighbourhoods and installing equipment in buildings. Focused on the future, but never forgetting our past. We are proud of the fact that we are an independent Dutch company. We opened our first gas plant in Rotterdam back in 1827. It was the bedrock from which we have grown into the company we are today. A company that is owned by 60 Dutch municipalities and supplies energy to more than two million private and business customers.

Supplying

A financially healthy supply and trading company forms the core of Eneco. Our customers rely on our supply of energy day in and day out. It is consequently Eneco's responsibility to live up to this trust by supplying ever-cleaner energy. And by calculating reasonable prices stated in easy-to-understand invoices. Our customers view this as the most natural thing in the world, and it should stay that way. Eneco does everything in its power to structure processes and systems so that our customers do not have to pay any attention to them. We invite them to join us in using clean energy as smartly and efficiently as possible.

Generating

In order to achieve our ambitions, we invest extensively in clean energy generation such as at onshore and offshore wind farms and based on thermal and cooling, solar, biomass and water power. We have chosen to use natural gas en route to a completely sustainable energy supply. We utilize this cleanest source of fossil fuel flexibly in order to guarantee the continuity of supply when there is not enough wind or insufficient sunlight. We build up stocks of natural gas in order to ensure stable prices, making Eneco less sensitive to natural gas price fluctuations in the energy market. We make our investments in new sustainable generation both independently and in partnership with others. Besides building new plants, we also acquire existing plants. We have sustainable production activities outside the Netherlands in Germany, the United Kingdom, France and Belgium. This international diversification enables us to gain broad experience in the production of new energy sources and allows us to spread our risks.

Solutions

Companies and consumers increasingly produce their own energy via geothermal heat, biogas, high-efficiency e-boilers, heat pumps, solar panels, stakes in wind turbines and other means. We couple this with other innovations, such as electrical transportation. As a result the energy supply is becoming more and more of a joint effort: users can be a customer today if the wind is blowing and a supplier for us or their neighbour tomorrow if the sun is shining.

Box 7.1—*continued*

Eneco actively seeks out this co-operation and ensures flexible and continuous availability of clean and affordable energy. This requires high-quality expertise and the application of practical local solutions for generating power and saving costs and energy. It also demands top consultants and professional technicians. All with the aim of facilitating internal and external co-operation that is mutually reinforcing. We are pleased to share the knowledge and experience we gain through this process with our community.

All for sustainability: committed, outspoken and decisive

Energy is a primary necessity of life. It is also invisible and intangible. It might seem difficult for us to develop a real connection with our community based on sustainable electrons and gas molecules. But Eneco's strength lies in our relevant and distinctive position. In fulfilling our promises, not in the packaging of our products. We are a down-to-earth Dutch company that follows an unconventional course: sustainable energy for everyone. This conscious choice naturally ensues from our involvement in the community, which in turn inspires us to pursue co-operation and to enter into alliances.

It forms the basis for healthy business operations. With result-focused leadership that never loses sight of the human dimension and that encourages partnership. Our employees make an individual contribution every day towards achieving our mission together. They form the foundation for our success as a company. Employees are proud of our organisation – and Eneco is proud of its employees. Our values of committed, outspoken and decisive are reflected in everything our employees do and how they do it.

Another approach to building an appealing story is the so-called *epos narrative structure*.[4] Taken from the Greek word for an epic poem, *epos* is a most venerable way of telling a heroic story. In fact, the eight steps shown in Figure 7.8 are embedded in just about every saga involving a hero ever written or told.

In the standard hero story, a strong young man – and in a growing number of cases a female, with Wonder Woman leading to Buffy the Vampire Slayer and still others[5] – has the outstanding skills and drive to act as the protector of a specific community. In a real-life example, Nelson Mandela's life fits perfectly into this structure. Smart and charismatic, Mandela worked to end racial discrimination in South Africa, but he endured years of struggle and suffering, especially during his twenty-seven years of imprisonment, much of it on the notorious Robben Island. Mandela fought for a noble cause, the end of apartheid, against obstacles posed by segregation-defending opponents in South Africa's white minority-controlled government. Upon his release from prison, however, he led the nation into its post-apartheid era, providing hope for black South Africans and inspiration to

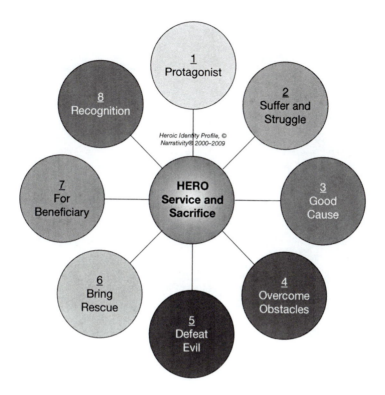

FIGURE 7.8 The eight building blocks of a hero story

hundreds of millions of people around the world. His reward was not millions of dollars and other material items, but to receive eternal respect on a global scale.

This *epos* structure is found in stories from many cultures, from Homers' Odyssey to Beowulf and tales of legendary characters from Indian, African and South American history, including mythological and real-life figures. The basic ingredients in hero stories can be applied to corporations. Although the tone of voice is somewhat different, the steps and structure are exactly the same. Should an organization choose to use this formula, it should pay attention to at least three elements of the *epos* structure.

First, people are emotionally inspired by an individual, or a group, who holds a dream and realizes that dream, especially when it involves a struggle. And many corporate stories fit well into the *epos* structure, especially when they begin with the company's modest history as a proof point. Indeed, the small garage on Addison Avenue in Palo Alto, California, is more than an iconic structure. It is where young Dave Packard and William Hewlett built their first product in the late 1930s, an audio oscillator. The two founded Hewlett Packard, a partnership that very much gave birth to Silicon Valley. Their tale is one that goes from the very modest to an absolutely epic scale.

FIGURE 7.9 The Garage, Palo Alto, CA. In 1938, William Hewlett (25) and David Packard (26) flipped a coin to see whose name would come first and started the company that started Silicon Valley.

A second lesson to be learned from the *epos* format is to position the corporate activities as fighting for a good cause. Although it is difficult to imagine a company doing anything comparable to the life and achievements of Nelson Mandela, many companies and advocacy organizations do very good work. Producing drugs that cure diseases plaguing the developing world is a strong story for a pharmaceutical firm. The first company to produce durable and affordable thin-film solar materials that, without government subsidies, generate electricity more cheaply than any utility-company power plant – overcoming barriers that for decades have held back the technology – will have a ripping yarn to tell its stakeholders.

The third lesson for organizations that apply the *epos* structure in story-telling involves being certain that their claims to fame are substantiated with hard evidence. Truth and ethics are exceptionally important, especially with a storyline that follows the *epos* structure. When a company represents itself with such a tale, it stakes its reputation on positive internal behaviour and values. If greed and misbehaviour are made public, the projected image is then seen as extremely hypocritical, and the company's reputation takes a brutal hit, much more so than if the company had not pretended it was heroic. The financial institutions on Wall Street should never use an *epos* narrative, at least not while their executives continue to pay themselves enormous bonuses that appear wholly unrelated to performance.

Yet another excellent example of the dangers of misusing this narrative concerns Accenture and its relationship with Tiger Woods. The consultancy's advertising,

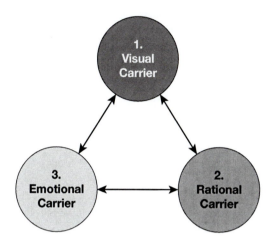

FIGURE 7.10 Three building blocks of corporate branding

based on the golfer's heroic on-course performance, communicated well for several years. But, when Woods' personal escapades became public late in 2009, the logic of Accenture's *epos* structure shattered, right along with the image of Woods as a good husband and disciplined ascetic. And, even though the company dropped its relationship with Woods, the reputation capital that Accenture had built through monstrously expensive advertising and sponsorships was diminished.

Corporate branding

In addition to establishing a consistent infrastructure for corporate communication, with clear rules for house style, media relations, sponsorship and an overarching corporate story, a vital last step in guaranteeing clarity in all corporate positioning lies in describing the key choices in corporate branding. Corporate branding can be described as, 'a set of activities undertaken by an organization to build favourable associations and a positive reputation with both internal and external stakeholders'. These activities can be grouped in three clusters: actions aimed at creating a consistent visual expression of the corporate brand, or a *visual carrier*; actions aimed at creating a promise and proof points expressed by the corporate brand, which is a *rational carrier*; and the feelings or reaction the corporate brand likes to evoke, which is an *emotional carrier*.

The visual carrier

An essential problem with corporate branding is when to use it and when to avoid the visualization of the parent behind the brand. Some organizations have a corporate name that is the same as their most well-known product brands, such as Heineken and Siemens. Still others have a corporate name that's not reflected in any projects or brand. Procter & Gamble, for example, has nearly one hundred brands, twenty-two of which generate more than $1 billion in annual revenues. Many of those brands are better known than P&G itself. The portfolio problem in corporate branding, however, is solved in different ways around the globe.

In Asia and the United States, most companies make branding and corporate-naming decisions based on who is in charge. A good example is General Electric, which automatically applies the GE name to any business it acquires. In Europe, acquiring companies tend to be more careful, sometimes too careful, about forcing a company name upon all businesses that are part of a conglomerate. Although there are exceptions on all continents, the general – monolithic – trend seems to be dominant.

In situations where an organization has to make a decision about its corporate-branding portfolio, two main questions need to be answered. First, is it logical and commercially attractive to create a uniform branding policy? Second, how do we convince internal audiences that a uniform approach will work best? The answers to these questions are complex. In general, a strong emphasis on the corporate brand will add value when market research shows the corporate name has stronger recognition and preference with consumers than does the business unit name.

Although the market is vital when deciding upon a uniform branding policy, so is the need for internal support. Support, and especially compliance, can be acquired through changing the decision-making structure, as uniformity in corporate branding only works when decision-making is centralized. Nevertheless, serious work is needed to convince employees that a different brand name has added value for them, even when market research reveals that their business operations will have more value under a corporate name such as, for example, ING.

The rational carrier

Changes in the visual expression of a corporate brand evoke deeply rooted emotions among managers and their employees. Strangely enough, this is less the case when companies define the rational carrier of a corporate brand. The rational carrier in corporate branding is the explanation of the key promise made by the corporate brand, substantiated with proof points.

When Nokia claims to be the world leader in *mobility, driving the transformation and growth of the converging Internet and industries*, it has to substantiate the claim, explaining how its specific fusions of mobile communication devices with the Internet and computers create an enriched consumer service. Nokia claims to do this in part because of its crack research centre, which is exploring an activity tracker that automatically stores information such as speed, distance and time in an athlete's training diary. Another proof point is the Nokia Booklet 3G, a device that connects people at any time and virtually anywhere, which is in many ways a crossroads of mobility and a personal computer.

Many companies seem to select comparable rational carriers for a corporate brand, such as being innovative, having a strong customer focus, operating worldwide

Box 7.2 ING VISUAL CARRIER

Until recently, ING was a multi-branded organization, with stand-alone brands, all fully responsible for their own operations. After many acquisitions, the brand portfolio listed forty-seven different brands. Although, initially, the company was intended as a multi-branded organization with low visibility of the parent, the holding brand 'ING' received much pressure to revise

its multi-branded approach. With the take-over of Barings Bank, the corporate name increasingly had global recognition. The challenge for ING was whether or not to create a monolithic brand for all forty-seven subsidiaries and, if so, at what pace. Many of the smaller brands were in favour of leveraging the strength of the parent brand in order to create competitive advantage in their home countries. Research showed that ING would benefit from a stronger endorsement by the corporate brand for nearly all subsidiaries. The financial conglomerate started an internal process aimed at creating simi-

larity between the business units, centralized decision-making in four lines of business, including asset management, corporate banking, and retail banking and insurance. They also started an intensive corporate campaign *internally* to increase support for the ING values, in combination with an intensive campaign *externally*, to increase the recognition of ING and those values. Corporate communication helped define and clarify those brand values, while functional management began negotiations with all forty-seven business units on the transition to ING. The process wasn't automatic but step by step. Business units had to provide evidence that their local market share was decreased, and that moving to the ING brand would enable them to recover the share and add value.

services and being socially and environmentally responsible. Although they often use similar, almost meaningless terms, the organizations do differ, mainly through an emphasis on one of the attributes in the context of a specific set of organizational associations. Brown & Dacin[6] distinguish *ability* and *responsibility* types of organizational association, which can be stressed in the key promise in corporate branding. Their groundbreaking 1997 study and article, confirmed in many others, concluded that, in the end, ability associations have more impact on supportive behaviour of external stakeholders than responsibility associations.

So, does this mean that companies that have stressed social-responsibility associations in their corporate brand have made a fundamental mistake? I don't think so. The only problem is that, despite many attempts by academics all over the word to prove it, no hard evidence can be found that there is a *direct* causal relationship between responsibility associations and supportive behaviour of commercial audiences. There is evidence of an *indirect* relationship between the two, as has been shown by Orlitzky *et al.*[7] This study showed that responsibility associations impact internal learning mechanisms, as managers learn new things while involved with corporate social-responsibility projects and reputation efforts. As responsibility might indirectly be positive, perhaps the best course is to apply a mix of both associations.

Finally, selecting a rational carrier in corporate branding should be based on selecting either a so-called *product-dominated* set of associations, or a set of *organization-dominated* associations. Carlsberg is a typical product-dominated corporate brand, whereas General Electric is a typical organization-dominated corporate brand.[8] Organization-dominated brands allow much more freedom in adding business unit names, evident at General Electric, where plastics, aircraft engines, transportation and financial services are linked to one and the same corporate name. Product brands such as Carlsberg are more limited. Although it is probable that Carlsberg can successfully add only other beer brands, it does have an advantage of a good position in a clearly recognized category. Defining the rational carrier in corporate branding means combining the ability versus responsibility choices with a selection of either a product- or organization-dominated branding strategy, as is explained in the matrix in Figure 7.11.

The emotional carrier

The power of communication is not in conveying facts but in evoking emotions, which is as true for an organization as it is for novels and movies. Many US companies are masters of this. They apply the basic principles of the *epos* hero narrative, aimed at evoking human emotions that will implicitly be linked to the own organization. Accenture was tapping into a *very powerful* gestalt with Tiger Woods. From an academic point of view, the golfer's fall from grace should not colour judgements about the worthiness of the intellect and emotion conveyed by the Accenture advertising words and images.

FIGURE 7.11 Decision-making about the rational carrier in corporate branding

Corporate communication programmes supporting specific strategic objectives

Starting from a sound foundation providing a clear communication infrastructure, specialized communication programmes can be developed around strategic objectives. The role of corporate communication managers can be distinguished in decision points clustered around five phases:

1   defining the starting points of a corporate communication programme;
2   gathering additional intelligence;
3   developing a specific communication strategy for the programme;
4   executing communication actions; and finally
5   embedding the communication programme into the overall organizational context.

These phases can be divided into fifteen decisions, summarized in Figure 7.12, which looks much like the venerable board game *Monopoly*. Simply said, it is a reputation-management implementation scheme (RMI scheme).

Phase 1: Starting points

Implementing programmes as extensions of the overall corporate strategy requires a sophisticated orchestration into the broader context of the *overall corporate-branding strategy*. The first question to be asked is what starting point has to be used, as a logical consequence of the *overall corporate-branding promise*. Which branding structure is dominant: monolithic, branded or endorsed? The second step here is simply determining which *competitors* have to be taken into consideration, and identifying their strongest characteristics compared with the firm developing the programme.

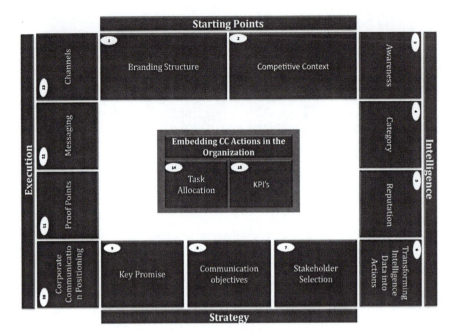

FIGURE 7.12 Reputation-management implementation scheme

Phase 2: Gathering additional intelligence

The first question to be answered in this phase concerns the degree of external *awareness* about the firm in general, and about the programme's specific strategic objective. Also important is the top-of-mind awareness (ToMA) of the firm in general and of the specific activities of the company where the programme is focused. Moreover, when other companies are doing similar things, we should know their degree of familiarity with external audiences, too.

The second point to focus on is the degree of familiarity among key stakeholders regarding the specific *category* in which the company is involved. The third step is using existing knowledge about the *reputation* of the company. What is the overall reputation score, and how does this score compare with key competitors? What drives the reputation and behaviour of key stakeholders most? For specific programmes around strategic objectives, additional reputation intelligence may be required.

When all the intelligence is gathered conclusions have to be drawn using the following framework.

• Is the firm sufficiently known by key stakeholders? Who are these stakeholders?
• Is the firm correctly linked with the desired categories the firm likes to be positioned in?
• What is the impression of the firm looking at publicly available intelligence?

	Own Firm	Top-3 peers in your country		
		Peer 1	Peer 2	Peer 3
Familiarity *(high/medium/low)*	High	High	Medium	Medium
Reputation *(good/moderate/low)*	Moderate	High	High	Low
Category fit *(high/medium/low)*	High	High	Medium	Medium
Key reputation shifters	• High quality products • Good value for money	• Stands behind its products • Meets customer needs	• Good value for money • Adapts quickly to change	• Meets customer needs • Positive influence on society
Key reputation barriers	• Is generally first to market • Open and transparent	• Open and transparent • Is an innovative company	• Fair in business • Meets customers needs	• Well-organized company • Good value for money
Key behaviour shifters	• High quality products • Good value for money	• Meets customer needs • Is a profitable company	• Adapts quickly to change • Strong prospects for growth	• Supports good causes • Meets customer needs
Key behaviour barriers	• Open and transparent • Positive influence on society	• Open and transparent • Is an innovative company	• Behaves ethically • Open and transparent	• Excellent managers • Good value for money

FIGURE 7.13 Phase 2: Gathering additional intelligence

- What does the quantitative data show about the firm? Which attributes impact reputation and supportive behaviour most? And what is the degree to which they impact the implementation of the strategic objective?

Phase 3: Corporate communication strategy around a specific programme

Based on the answers to these questions in phase 2 managers can start developing a communication strategy, starting with selecting the *key stakeholders* the programme should focus on. This is done by answering the following questions:

- Which stakeholders (SH's) are most crucial to build relationships with?
- What is their degree of awareness, understanding and to what degree might they perceive the firm's promise as conflicting with their own interests?
- What is their power to influence the organization?

The next step in the strategy formulation phase focuses on the prioritization of the *communication objectives*. What should be stressed most, an increase in knowledge, attitude or behaviour?

5 key focus points for action	Communication objective		
	Creating awareness/ knowledge	Creating a positive attitude	Behaviour (purchase, verbally support, etc.)
1. Is generally first to market	V		
2. Good value for money		V	V
3. High quality products		V	V
4. Open and transparent	V		
5. Positive influence on society	V	V	

FIGURE 7.14 Phase 3: Corporate communication strategy around a specific programme

This is followed by a crucial fourth step in which communication managers have to decide what the *key promise* of the programme will be. In most situations this requires communicators to select an idea that is focused on what the firm intends to do, and which stresses the collective benefits that can be gained from the programme.

Phase 4: Execution

Executing a corporate communication programme focused around a concrete strategic objective starts with selecting one of the four positioning strategies for the program about a specific strategic objective:

1   Increase the delivery aspects of the key promise: **We can do it**.
2   Emphasize the uniqueness of the key promise: **Only we can do this**.
3   Increase the importance of the key promise: **You can't continue without it**.
4   Attack a competitor by stressing the differences the firm can offer compared to the other firm: **We can do it better**.

FIGURE 7.15 Four positioning strategies

The second step in the execution phase is looking for proof points using practical examples of facts and figures proving the claims of the firm. A method to find these proof points is searching internally and externally for 'pearl projects' that provide facts and figures as illustrations of the appealing and realistic nature of the claims. This can be illustrated as follows with Unilever examples (see Figure 7.16).

Creating a better future every day *We meet everyday needs for nutrition, hygiene and personal care with brands that help people feel good, look good and get more out of life.*	
	Pearl Projects in Business Performance
Products and services	Dove (increasing self esteem of women)
Innovation	Becel (decreasing cholesterol levels)
Workplace	Employing many people all over the world
Governance	Being open
Citizenship	Reducing the CO_2 footprint
Leadership	Taking leadership in developing countries in building sustainable production processes
Performance	Double digit growth

FIGURE 7.16 Unilever's pearl projects

The third step implies focusing more in-depth on the message. Here the following choices have to be made:

- Emphasizing the *core activities* that the firm will implement around the strategic objective, primarily reporting facts and figures; Dove soap cleans your skin perfectly well;
- Emphasizing the *individual benefits* that the actions around a strategic objective will evoke, such as increasing the self-esteem of a woman who uses Dove soap: 'YOU will feel better';
- Emphasizing the *benefits that society* will have at a more holistic level, including the consequences of better self-esteem for women in general, which contributes to a more positive minded society.

The last decision to be made in the execution phase is which *channel* will be used. Every piece of an organization's communications must have a set of key messages, each of which is based on those several easily understood proof points. The headlines need to be identical for all target groups, but different points can be accentuated quite differently.

Communication themes (five key focus points)	Core activities	Benefits for individual stakeholders	Benefits for society at large
1. Is generally first to market	V		
2. Good value for money		V	
3. High quality products	V		
4. Open and transparent	V		
5. Positive influence on society			V

FIGURE 7.17 Phase 4: Execution

Nevertheless, the messages must contain basic truths, not just for reasons of principle, but because of the increased demands for corporate transparency. Today, transparency is fundamental to earning trust, especially in an age of the Internet, Twitter and other social media that expose lies and spread truth worldwide in a matter of minutes. Social media have become more important in creating and maintaining alignment. What is most interesting about social media is the absence of a hierarchy, or gate-keeping editors. Literally anyone can decide to join a public debate, which is both the strength and weakness of social media. Nevertheless, if traditional and social media are largely aligned on a specific viewpoint, it comprises an audience with vast power, however temporary.

The technologies and culture of social media potentially comprise the greatest disruptive force ever hit corporation communication. Out on the so-called edges of an organization, non-professional communicators from marketing, product development and any other department are now interacting with the greater outside world through Facebook, Twitter and the like. By their nature, these conversations are frank and direct. What's more, an ill-considered comment made in haste or an incident captured on a mobile-phone camera has the capacity to leak and go viral, with a carefully constructed reputation going up in YouTube flames.

Social media together are a beast that's beyond the control of communication managers and senior executives. However, most large companies have embraced social media for both internal and external uses, finding them exceptionally beneficial. Communication departments now have sections devoted to writing Twitter posts about company developments, setting up Facebook fan pages for the firm or its products and services, and engaging in a dialogue with internal and external stakeholders who want to be included in 'the discussion'.

Social media have certainly worked for Dell Computers. Once widely criticized for its poor and often unobtainable customer service, Dell opened a two-way dialogue with those critics. It now has a website called IdeaStorm, on which customers vote on future products and features, and collaborate directly with Dell employees. In December of 2009, it added 'Storm Sessions' to the site, where Dell posts a specific topic and asks customers to submit observations over a limited time, making the discussion targeted and relevant. In three years, about 10,000 ideas have been kicked around on IdeaStorm, while Dell has implemented more than 400 of them.

Phase 5: Embedding the programme in the overall organization context

In the last phase of the RMI scheme, attention has to be paid to two points. First, one needs to create clarity about who does what while implementing the steps to make the programme achieve its objectives; see Figure 7.18. Although a large chunk of this work falls to communication professionals, there are chores that can be done more effectively by line executives, both at headquarters and at a business-unit level.

The final action to be implemented is defining key success factors, expressed in quantitative terms showing the success or failure of the work on the programme objectives. Gathering feedback about communication efforts around a specific strategic topic can improve the next steps of a communication programme. Programme managers will have to look for indicators of success and failure of a programme in data gathered continuously at corporate level around issues and reputation. In addition, they can look for intelligence that is relevant for the communications efforts around the specific strategic issue. The evaluation of a programme during its implementation phase can result in the necessity of making

Key Promise		
Who does what?	**Execution**	
	Internal	**External**
CEO		
Top Management		
CC Manager		
CC Department		
Investor Relations		
Media Relations		
Business Unit Managers		
Human Resource Managers		
IT		
Finance		
Marketing		
Other...		

FIGURE 7.18 Task allocation

improvements suggested in monitoring. This not only increases the impact of communication efforts, but also reduces costs, as a more effective approach can be applied when one knows in time what to do and what to avoid.

Differences in programme support depending on selected road map

Basically, most programme support provided by communication managers is typified by the five phases described in the previous sections of this chapter. However, different accents can be necessary when the emphasis in programme support is coloured by a negotiation or confrontation type of road map; see Figure 7.19. In negotiation-focused road maps, corporate communication managers are supposed to provide relevant intelligence in which the outside-in point of view particularly is shown to top management. In addition, communicators are supposed to be sensitive about who can or should act as spokesman in this phase and, above all, who should not take on this role. Attuning programme messages carefully to the overall corporate positioning, especially when a crisis pops up, is a crucial role for communication managers too.

The confrontational road map requires similar efforts by corporate communication managers, but also different ones; see Figure 7.20. This becomes especially clear when the power-play technique is applied. In that case, close cooperation with the legal department becomes a necessity, just as it will be highly relevant to anticipate, in good time, reactions of stakeholders who might turn into opponents, by interacting with them simultaneously when the attack on a clear opponent is made.

Wrap-up

Building and maintaining external alignment demands professional efforts from corporate communication managers. However, they can't do this on their own. Building relationships is surely not the sole responsibility of the communication department, but rests on the shoulders of all managers who are responsible for a specific strategic objective. Jointly taking responsibility in building bridges with external stakeholders is not only the duty but also the right of other managers outside the communication discipline. Corporate communication specialists are the ones who should contribute with intelligence, maintaining consistency and developing appealing messages, while other managers are supposed to contribute with more specialized – often content-driven – building blocks in creating external alignment. Creating mutual benefits with groups outside the firm often starts with healthy mutual respect and cooperation *inside* the organization.

Respect for the role of corporate communication increases when this department can clearly show its added value by showing positive figures in KPIs. Which indicators can be used and how this works in practice will be discussed in the next chapter.

Additional Intelligence	Positioning	Execution	Evaluation and Adaptation
• Using input from specialized departments	• What is the overall claim of the firm?	• To what degree are the meetings public? Who will attend?	• When will the process be evaluated?
• Crucial Role for CC if topic can't be attributed to one section of the firm solely and/or might impact the firm as a totality	• What might become the promise of the firm in the context of a specific strategic objective?	• When will the firm reveal the existence of the meetings?	• By whom?
• Specific Stakeholder studies	• What is the logical link between the overall claim and the promise to be made in the program?	• Who will act as spokesman on behalf of the firm?	• Using which criteria?
• Specific Issue scanning	• What is the room to maneuver for the firm in the context of the consensus oriented negotiations?	• What will be shared at those meetings in writing?	
	• To what degree will buffering organizations be free to make statements about the strategic objective?	• What will be shared solely confidentially and in one-to-one dialogues?	
		• What are the exact rules of engagement in buffering and joint ventures?	
		• When does a buffering or joint venture cooperation start and more important when does it end?	

FIGURE 7.19 Contributions of corporate communication in a negotiation road map

Additional Intelligence	Positioning	Execution	Evaluation and Adaptation
• Using input from specialized departments	• What is the overall claim of the firm?	• What will be the 'frame'? Script, rhetorical, themed?	• When will the process be evaluated?
• Crucial Role for CC if topic can't be attributed to one section of the firm solely and/or might impact the firm as a totality	• What is the exact promise of the firm in the context of a specific strategic objective?	• How will the social media be used?	• By whom?
• Specific Stakeholder studies	• What is the logical link between the overall claim and the promise to be made in the program?	• How to attune attacks on an opponent simultaneously with diplomatic gestures in the direction of existing neutrals or supporters?	• Using which criteria?
• Specific Issue scanning	• When does mirroring and power play about a specific strategic objective start and when does it end?		
• Input from LEGAL in order to avoid litigation			

FIGURE 7.20 Role of corporate communication in a confrontation road map

Notes

1   Unilever website, www.sustainable-living.unilever.com/ (accessed 23 March 2011).
2   C.B.M. van Riel and C.J. Fombrun, *Essentials of corporate communication*, Abingdon: Routledge, (2007).
3   Eneco website, http://corporateuk.eneco.nl/ABOUT_ENECO/Pages/Default.aspx (accessed 18 July 2011).
4   A. Ramzy, *Heroic identity profile*, (2000) www.narrativity-group.com (accessed 23 March 2011).
5   J.K. Stuller, *Ink-stained Amazons and cinematic warriors: superwomen in modern mythology*, London: I.B. Tauris & Co. Ltd, (2010).
6   T.J. Brown and P.A. Dacin, 'The company and the product: corporate associations and consumer product responses', *Journal of Marketing*, (1997), vol. 61(1), pp. 68–84.
7   M. Orlitzky, F.L. Schmidt and S.L. Reynes, 'Corporate social and financial performance: a meta-analysis', *Organization Studies*, (2003), vol. 24(3), pp. 403–41.
8   O.J.M. Maathuis, C.B.M. van Riel and G.H. van Bruggen, 'Using the corporate brand to communicate identity: the value of corporate associations to customers', *Abstract Conference on Corporate Reputation, Identity and Competitiveness*, Amsterdam, (1998).

PART III

Key performance indicators in establishing alignment with corporate communication

8

MEASURING THE SUCCESS OF ALIGNMENT EFFORTS

Key performance indicators are the last building block in the central model of this book to building an organizational alignment with key internal and external stakeholders (see Figure 8.1). The performance measures are no more nor less than indicators of success or lack therefore. As a consequence, KPIs are often used as metrics to determine financial compensation – and perhaps promotions – for those managers responsible for implementing specific communication actions.

However, bonus programmes are not the only reason for using indicators. More important is their added value in improving organizational success. If applied in a correct way, KPIs will force organization members to focus on those efforts that matter most in achieving the company's objectives.

Indicators and bonuses notwithstanding, it's important to consider what can and cannot be expected from corporate communication. Let us focus now on what can be expected from corporate communication managers in general.

Expectations about corporate communication in general

All professions need clarity on the value a job adds to both departmental and corporate performance and, hopefully, its meaning to other people, institutions and society, however indirectly. A job, after all, is a large piece of one's life. In certain professions, the non-financial rewards are immediate and profound. A teacher, for example, plays an essential role in broadening children's cognitive and affective skills; a doctor contributes to improving a patient's health; and a police officer contributes to security.

In practice, there can be a much more nuanced discussion of specific contributions. A teacher's insensitive criticism can demotivate more students than are inspired; a doctor's reluctance to order discretionary tests that are painful to patients might inadvertently lead to a poor long-term mortality rate; police officers might do a great job of patrolling one favoured street, while criminals know they

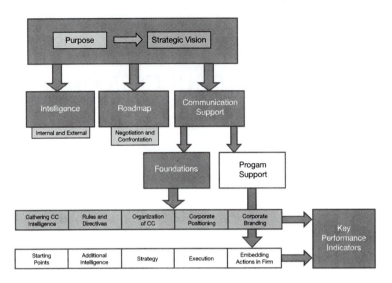

FIGURE 8.1 Overall model, the alignment factor book

have free rein three blocks away. Nothing is ever completely obvious, and the same is true for communication managers. However, they deal with issues that are often easily labelled, especially in the eyes of outsiders.

Communication professionals are expected to increase *awareness* of, and *appreciation* for, the organization and, as a logical consequence, increase and maintain the organization's *support*. The daily reality is much more complex. Again, consider the value of police. By definition, society holds law-enforcement officers most responsible for many elements of public safety, including the apprehension of criminals, response to accidents and enforcement of traffic and other laws. However, it is impossible for officers to do this alone.

One example involves the hooligans who plague so many European football stadiums. In the past, at many high-risk games, platoons of officers would stand ready to tackle troublemakers. Today, football clubs have an explicit responsibility to take actions that minimize the possibility of hooligans interrupting games, confronting fans of a different club or creating utter devastation. Supporters of visiting clubs are now led through enclosed access bridges to a separate zone in the stadium, shielded with large gates and netting, where they are watched, row by row, by stewards from their own club, assigned to suppress conflict before it starts. Access for supporters of the home team is through separate gates. The fans of the two sides are kept in well-divided sections that limit contact, and they may well be separated by an electrified fence, a measure that's also been used to protect the pitch. It is draconian, yes, but necessary and effective. The point is that stadium safety is no longer solely a police responsibility, but one also shared by both the home and visiting clubs.

FIGURE 8.2 Antecedents of licence to operate

Just as safety is often a shared responsibility, so is increasing awareness and appreciation, which improves organizational support. Again, in times past, the responsibility was assumed to rest mainly with communication, just as police were most responsible for handling hooligans. Today, it is clear that many elements within an organization have a role in enhancing reputation and building trust with stakeholders, even if communication retains a distinctive and leading role.

Earlier, we looked at how excellence in performance multiplied by excellence in communication and divided by the social context in which a company operates is the formula that leads to an unrestricted licence to operate. It is a hypothetical licence, to be sure. However, when an organization can function without the distraction and hurdles of punishing legislation, regulation and customer discontent, the importance of that restriction-free licence cannot be underestimated. It is the result of an aligned set of stakeholders, who, together, enable a company continually to meet strategic objectives, including the well established and the new. Hence, once more, an organization obtains its licence through the formula shown in Figure 8.2.

In practice, there are three groups that do most to determine the extent of the licence, the extent to which it will be retained, and the restrictions that may limit peak performance. The first is the communication function. The second group is comprised of general managers largely responsible for the organization's performance in customer satisfaction, innovation and finance. 'Society at large' is the third group: external stakeholders who can have both a positive and a negative influence on the social context in which the organization operates.

The greatest challenge organizations face in the twenty-first century is the need to anticipate social developments that now, or in the future, could have a negative impact on operational licence. In turn, perhaps the greatest contribution of communication managers is to discover and monitor these developments, and to convince executive management to develop policies that protect the firm from the external threats. With the policies implemented, communication managers can start communicating about the actions, hopefully generating recognition for the firm's efforts. This process continues over and over again.

Good performance supported by exceptional communication is the start of building a sustainable licence to operate. However, no matter how carefully and

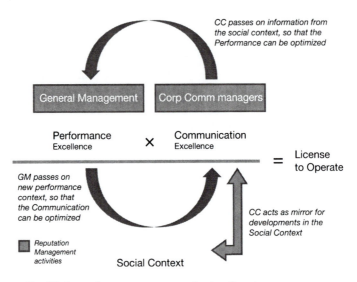

FIGURE 8.3 Equilibrium of corporate communication function

industriously a company goes about its business, broader and more powerful developments can undermine the best-laid plans. That's why the social context is a critical denominator in the formula of trust.

Take the American fast-food chain McDonald's, which, for decades, has been a favoured dining establishment for parents with young children. There does not seem to be any great problem with the quality and taste of McDonald's products. The company's communications and adverts appeal to a large population, measured by the firm's worldwide success. For McDonald's, there seems to be nothing wrong with the formula's numerator.

Problems, however, now lie with the denominator. In recent years, McDonald's and other fast-food chains have come to be blamed for serving hamburgers, fries and other foods that contain far too many unhealthy calories and are a leading cause of America's obesity epidemic. An increasing awareness of the need to eat healthier fare has changed the social context in which McDonald's operates. The company has put more salads and other low-calorie items on its menu. However, in the eyes of opponents who see only the 'super-size' nature of the company's operation, McDonald's response is too little and too late. Consequently, the corporation's figurative 'licence to operate' has been put under pressure, from cities that may no longer easily give permits for new franchises or allow them to add child-appealing toys to meals, to school districts unwilling to serve McDonald's in cafeterias, to parents who no longer cave into their children's pleas for Chicken McNuggets.

A more positive story can be told about the American firm Johnson & Johnson (J&J). One of the leading suppliers of pharmaceutical products, medical devices and diagnostic equipment and household-care products in the world, J&J has a well-established reputation for innovative, quality products[1] and has maintained a

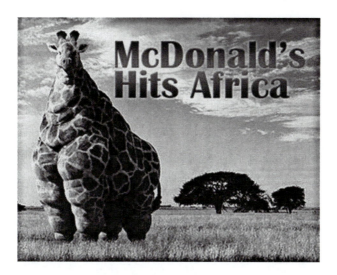

FIGURE 8.4 McDonald's under fire

healthy financial standing by funding major acquisitions primarily through accumulated cash reserves, rather than burdensome levels of debt. It is currently one of the few global companies to hold a triple-A credit rating.[2] Furthermore, J&J has an outstanding track record of performance, including seventy-six consecutive years of sales increases, twenty-five consecutive years of adjusted earnings increases, and forty-six consecutive years of dividend increases.[3]

J&J's excellent reputation has been captured in numerous rankings throughout the years. Key drivers for this sound reputation are the ability and desire to anticipate social developments, address them through business actions and embed messages about these in appealing communications. All actions are rooted in the famous J&J Credo, a corporate belief system that embodies social responsibility and that was written in 1943 by then-chairman and CEO Robert Wood Johnson, son of one of the company's founders, long before anyone ever heard of the term. The credo challenges employees to put the needs and well-being of the people they serve *first*.

A recent example of J&J's capability to anticipate in the social context of emerging and potentially threatening issues was the company's 'nursing campaign', in which J&J addressed a looming shortage in the profession. The aim of the campaign was not only to bring more people into nursing, but also to develop more nurse educators and to retain the talent already working. The campaign appeared to be a great success, in that the US market does now have enough nurses. The remaining problem – still being addressed by J&J – is the lack of nurse educators.

Although the precise genesis of this campaign is unknown, I suspect that the company's communication people were key supporters, recognizing the value of an initiative in which the company could take leadership and serve as a social protagonist. The ability to see the need to take responsibility for such an issue,

FIGURE 8.5 Images used in the Campaign for Nursing's Future by Johnson & Johnson

mobilize internal forces to work on a solution and then communicate in a way that puts the company in a thought-leadership position in the public perception is a perfect example of excellence in corporate communication.

Expectations communication specialists have to deliver

Corporate communication managers are expected to create awareness, understanding and appreciation for the firm in a range of audiences. The leaders in the profession have a holistic, outside–in view of their organization, carefully monitor for potentially threatening external issues, and convince executive management to adopt policies that prevent limitations in the firm s future licence to operate. As has been explained in the previous sections, this is not a task that communicators implement on their own. Communication managers need to join forces with executives in other disciplines, as well as colleagues in fields within the communication profession. Table 8.1 shows the expectations of those specialists.

Labour market

Skilled individuals can remain safely in one place for a long while, or are able to freely move from one company to another, without negative career consequences. However, no organization can long survive or be successful unless it can attract

TABLE 8.1 KPIs per stakeholder group

Stakeholder	KPIs
Labour market	Attracting and retaining key employees
Investors	Attracting and retaining shareholders
Regulators	Appreciated member of society
Employees	Supportive behaviour in line with strategy
Customers	Purchase intention and market share
Media	Fact-based and positive articles

and retain people who are suited to the firm, its business and mission. It's why a major KPI for communication managers is the attraction and retention of talented employees, mainly by creating awareness, appreciation and trust, and imparting a broad knowledge of what the organization stands for and aims for.

Awareness is just a start. Communication must next use measurements to determine if prospective employees hold a positive opinion of the firm. The real success, however, may only reside in the number of candidates that actually apply. That's because many studies have shown there is no absolute certainty about the relationship between what potential employees think about a company and their inclination to seek employment there. We do know that most youngsters coming of age today would love to work for Google, but whether the firm purposely communicates in ways that created this attraction – or just organically became popular – is not well understood. In any event, employee-satisfaction studies are useful with people already working for the organization, addressing such issues as whether employees feel at ease while at work or in their relationship with their direct supervisor or, among other concerns, are satisfied with their position.

Investors

Investing capital in stock may well be the greatest expression of trust an individual can show a corporation. Whether for purely speculative reasons or a long-term buy and hold plan, investment in shares of public companies is the ultimate commitment from individuals and institutions. These are wagers, with real money put at risk, on a company's future. In turn, an organization's success or failure is greatly determined by the opinions of investors who provide the company with capital. It is for these reasons that the legal dictates of corporate governance require board members and executives to put the interests of shareholders above all else – no matter what is expressed in mission statements.

It therefore stands to reason that a corporation must keep stakeholders in the financial world well informed and continuously updated on the organization's strategic direction. In line with the labour market, the KPI that many publicly traded companies can employ is summarized as 'attracting and retaining investors'.

FIGURE 8.6 Google headquarters in Zurich, Switzerland. *Left*: moving around: a slide allows quick access from different floors; *Right*: innovation: large boards are available just about everywhere, because 'ideas don't always come when seated in the office', says one of Google's managers

Or, one might add, 'attracting and retaining of the most desired types of investor'. This last point is the result of various investor-relations studies that prove that institutional investors – such as those representing pension funds and broad mutual funds – not only are the most useful to corporations, but also cause management the least distraction and fewest difficulties.

Success is evident in studies that show investors already thinking about a company in a positive manner, even while considering a purchase. However, in light of the often-baffling fluctuations of stock-market trends and prices – which behave about as predictably as a stormy atmosphere – these types of KPI seem difficult to fulfil. As so many factors are in play governing a stock, communication professionals can't be expected to influence purchasing intents.

As a result, these types of KPI must be analysed indirectly, such as by breaking down analyst reports for their factual knowledge and establishing whether they recommend a buy, sell or neutral position on the company's stock, or whether they're using language that's been articulated by company executives and the communication department. The same is true for the contents of the financial press: if journalists begin repeating the company's message in their own voice, it means that the message is clearly getting across and taking hold. Yet another possible measure is whether the company wins awards for its annual report, or recognition for the quality of its investor-relations department, be it from a group of experts or publications that rate performances. Although terribly subjective and even borderline dubious, the awards are a form of third-party validation, and executives, who often privately say they don't care about such trifling matters, then publicly boast of the accomplishment.

Regulators

Regulating bodies are crucial for any type of organization, not just for the rules they institute, but, perhaps more importantly, for the regulations that are not put in place. Communication managers are expected to influence both outcomes. In most organizations, this is an activity labelled public affairs or government affairs and assigned to high-ranking executives who are not within a communication department's structure. Although it doesn't really matter who does what or where this function reports organizationally, the more important point is that the KPIs in this arena are achieved.

In Table 8.1, the KPI that relates to regulators is described as 'being an appreciated member of society'. For some businesses, it is good enough merely to be an 'accepted member of society', but, in both instances, it is necessary to monitor effectively what legislation is being prepared, or even may be prepared in the future. Communication managers are also expected actively to influence – through lobbying – the development of policies that result in regulations. This will only succeed when elected politicians, their staff and appointed government officials know and value the organization.

The impact of such efforts is hard to measure, as neither politicians nor officials will want to admit to being influenced by lobbyists. However, it's a fact that lobbyists often draft legislation that is given to an elected representative's or regulator's staff, usually with a few self-serving provisions that favour the lobbyist's employer. Although the staff may or may not use all of the provisions that go into the version presented to a legislative body or regulatory agency, the lobbyist will likely win a few points, if only for being helpful. Although the general public is largely unaware of this practice, it's fairly common and quite simple to measure.

In other cases, it is not uncommon to measure a KPI through *derived* forms of success. Are the arguments brought forward by a lobbyist actually being used, and, if so, are they seriously applied? Is the argument taken into account when the regulation is complete and being interpreted? Are the arguments, be they positive or negative, reflected in the media?

Employees

In the discussion of KPIs that measure labour-market communication, we have already touched on employee satisfaction. This KPI revolves around retaining the people crucial to the organization. Senior management may also reasonably ask that communication people contribute to a KPI that encourages and drives employees to display active support for the company's primary strategy in their daily behaviour. As the details of this were elaborated on in Chapter 2, the following is limited to the tasks of communication professionals.

Registering and *reacting* are the two most pertinent demands. Registering means sensing the right signals, at the right time, about what is occurring in the organization around support – or a lack of support – for the strategy. This is a continuous process. Reaction means bringing in senior management to reinforce points and fill in the gaps in compliance. Moreover, fulfilling the KPI depends upon awareness, appreciation and understanding of what exactly defines active support.

Support is proven by the successes of an organization in its chosen strategic direction. The more abstract the strategic goals are, the more difficult it will be to prove that one has been successful in mobilizing support. Once more, derivative issues can and should be investigated as proxies for success. Alignment and engagement studies are good examples, as well as analysis of endorsements that can be derived from web-based discussions focusing on the strategy.

Customer KPIs that express success in relationships

Customers are an essential group for any organization, be it a private enterprise that sells goods and services that please customers, or an NGO that, say, successfully harasses whaling vessels, thereby giving satisfaction to the donors who fund the organization's activities. Governments may not always have a clear supplier–customer type of relationship, but it is quite evident whom a government should serve. The degree to which groups support the organization determines its success. The majority of customer-satisfaction surveys consist in measuring the degree and nature of satisfaction among the client segments that matter most. Among the more popular methods used today are the so-called net promoter score (NPS) measurements.[4] An NPS score is an indication of loyalty to a brand. Although the scores differ according to the industry in question, scores exceeding 75 per cent are considered high.[5]

Media relations

No organization in the world is numb to what journalists write for print or the Internet or say on radio and television. Actors, athletes and executives often claim they neither pay attention to, nor are affected by, a negative critique or unflattering review. Most are not telling the truth. Because they are human and have feelings, harsh words hurt, and it's the same for organizations as it is for individuals.

Communication managers are still struggling to develop a process to measure the often vague and ever-shifting impact of social media. We know that negative incidents can go viral within hours, as when two employees from the Domino's Pizza chain pretended to adulterate a pizza before its delivery and put the offensive video on YouTube. Domino's responded vigorously, firing the two, filing charges against them and putting its own video up within a few days. Because smart companies have long held drills that prepare them for a defensive crisis response, handling a viral social-media attack is a natural evolution. KPIs on developing and winning a positive response – beyond getting lucky when something becomes instantly popular – are developing, through the use of company Facebook accounts, Twitter posts that gain followers and other methods of gaining attention in the ether of social media.

For traditional media and from the organizational perspective, the following KPI is succinct and fundamental: *publicity should be correct in content and preferably positive*. Lengthy debates on both issues may be needed to determine when this is

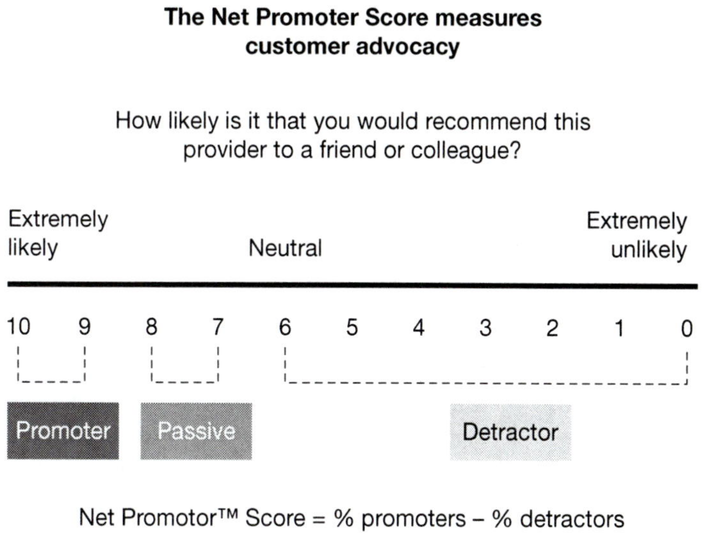

**The Net Promoter Score measures
customer advocacy**

How likely is it that you would recommend this
provider to a friend or colleague?

Extremely likely		Neutral								Extremely unlikely

10	9	8	7	6	5	4	3	2	1	0

Promoter	Passive		Detractor

Net Promotor™ Score = % promoters – % detractors

FIGURE 8.7 Net promoter score[6]

exactly being achieved. This is, and will always be, a subjective matter. In fact, it is so strongly subjective that a neutral-to-slightly-negative article can disrupt and even shatter a relationship between top executives and the communication manager.

Company spokespeople thus do not lead an easy life and are, in fact, often caught between that proverbial rock and a hard place. Although they clearly understand the needs of journalists, they are ultimately judged by their company's management and consequently can't please both equally. Interestingly, two new developments in the area of media relations have had a positive effect for spokespeople. The first development is themed messaging, and the second is 'educating' journalists.

Themed messaging involves crafting core messages within boilerplate stories and placing them on an Internet website, with headlines, pull-quotes, photographs, charts and all else that would go into a published piece. Access to the website is limited to a select group of journalists, who can download and adapt the articles with complete freedom from copyright.

The 'education' of journalists is a concept with roots in the United States. An organization selects a group of journalists, depending upon the size of the country, company or marketing intent. The selection is based on the medium or the characteristics of the journalists and their outlet. The group is invited to meetings held by the organization where, as objectively as possible, it is explained what the organization does, what problems exist, and how it intends to be successful. This pulls journalists deeper into an organization and its issues, without compromising their editorial integrity. Personal relationships may even develop.

In no way does this mean journalists will be less critical – these leopards seldom lose their spots – but they may give an organization the benefit of a doubt, or at least provide context when reporting on an event that deserves a critical slant. Nevertheless, this is perhaps the most difficult area for professional communication. Although media-tracking studies show that positive reports have reputational benefits, in executive minds, one negative article with an unflattering photograph can grossly overshadow a large body of positive publicity.

Showing accountability: a necessity for staff departments

Internal budget pressure is an ever-present corporate reality that forces managers to find ground truth on departmental performance. However, there is also curiosity and desire among modern executives to understand non-financial contributions, define them and work with managers and employees to make improvements. A culture of 'knowledge is measurement' is taking shape in more enlightened organizations. This trend is apparent through the increased use of KPIs and other *performance tracking tools* as integral parts of a *dashboard*. Not all disciplines are equally eager to be subjected to such instruments. A recent study of American chief marketing officers shows that 80 per cent of them are dissatisfied with their company's dashboard. And the attitudes are not much better with communication managers, who, as much as or more than any other profession, deal with the abstract.

According to Laura Patterson,[7] an ideal marketing dashboard should do the following: show the progress of marketing, help assess productive areas, and help in the decision-making. This way, marketers prove the value of their function and solidify their alignment with the remainder of the business. Patterson states that KPIs run parallel with an organization's hierarchy of goals. At the most basic level, the activity is about attracting attention. In decades past, this could be determined by the number of newspaper clippings a communication manager could show executives. These days, attention might be measured by the number of clicks on the organization's website. A second level deals with how well the group develops a campaign or organizes something such as a crucial trade show. Success here depends upon things such as staying within a budget, the number of visitors to a booth and whether sufficient staff have been on hand to speak with stakeholders and contribute to awareness.

Consequently, communication managers are wise to take into account the experiences of marketers when building, and especially managing, dashboards. Four issues seem to be particularly crucial at this point:

- A dashboard is the result of clear and measurable KPIs that have been determined and approved though dialogue with top management.
- The chosen KPIs need to be based – again in dialogue with top management – on methods of measurement that are seen as a relevant and a reliable quantification of each individual area.
- A dashboard needs to display clearly interpretable scale values – such as red is bad, green is good and yellow is neutral – that clarify the added value of communication and an obvious way forward for logical and necessary actions.

- A dashboard provides information at three levels: the most abstract is meant for top management; a second is aimed at business–unit management, on matters relevant to their business. The third provides information at a project level, such as a campaign or trade show, which in turn adds input to the first two levels.

How to use metrics in corporate communication?

Accountability has become an increasingly established notion for managers in almost any profession or industry. This literally means accounting and being responsible for the performance of both individuals and an entire department. The developments just described in the area of marketing are mostly applicable to corporate communication too.

However, while the willingness to measure performance exists, there does not yet seem to be a set of widely supported starting points. Fortunately, there are an increasing number of positive exceptions. One is the story that was related to me by Ron Wunderink, the former director of corporate communication of KLM, or Royal Dutch Airlines. During one of the several reorganizations the national airline underwent during the 1990s, a McKinsey consultant asked Wunderink to clarify what his department actually contributed to the performance of KLM. Ron asked the consultant to please leave and come back in thirty minutes.

Upon his return, the consultant looked in amazement at the large table on which Ron had spread national and international newspapers and magazines that had been published in the previous several weeks. Most of them had large, rectangular holes cut out. As Wunderink explained, the holes represented issues that would probably have featured KLM in a negative light, had not his department interacted with journalists and other stakeholders to explain why these issues were either trivial or untrue, but were instead clippings that shed a positive light on the airline. The consultant left the room, and the budget of the communication department remained intact.

Today, however, much more is needed to convince top management and cut-throat consultants of the added value of the corporate communication function. For years, the performance of communication departments at companies such as Philips, Cap Gemini and Chevron was measured by the opinion of internal customers who led all staff and operating departments. The chairman, vice chairmen, the head of human resources and the presidents of operating companies were asked to rate corporate communication on a numerical scale.

Consequently, performance reviews, salary treatment and career paths rested on whether an operating unit had been featured in the company magazine of late, or whether an executive had been bailed out of a potentially embarrassing media encounter. Personal opinions prevailed. Although useful to communicators in figuring out what certain executives liked or disliked, it was a terribly crude indicator of the department's real value in building and maintaining reputation and trust.

Smart companies today use results of quantitative research as denominators of the success or failure of the communication function. And yet, selecting the right hard indicators for the communication department's soft activities is difficult. This is especially true as more organizations release abstract visions and missions, with obtuse goals that have to be supported by communication.

Sometimes, it seems simple. Reaching, for example, a specific and predetermined goal such as 'improving earnings by 20 per cent over the next year' is quite apparent, especially as the measurement is concrete and easy to show. If, however, the chosen goals are abstract and intangible, recognizing success is terrifically difficult. When FedEx says that, 'When people are placed first they will provide the highest possible service, and profits will follow', how exactly do they know? The credo of J&J is to 'put the needs and well-being of people we serve *first*'. The concept is crystal clear, but collecting proof that every employee in the company is doing this consistently every day can be a daunting and amorphous challenge.

Both of these firms also set forth annual financial objectives, along with other hard targets that probably include market share and cost containment. The most direct stakeholders, including employees, shareholders and securities analysts, will critically track the degree to which these objectives have been met. Executives of publicly traded companies are acutely aware of being watched and thus, by custom and law, acknowledge accountability, taking responsibility for both success and failure. However, numbers don't always tell the complete story.

A more thorough definition of success is derived from the sum of the organization's integrated efforts, including the work of research and development, operation's productivity, the savvy of marketing and sales and all of the supporting expertise in human resources, IT, finance and communication. As each department has a specific task, it needs to demonstrate that the task has been executed, no matter whether it's measured on a profit and loss sheet or through some other metric. However, even when all of these pieces come together as expected, the performance picture is still not yet complete.

When analysing the performance of such independent departments, executives typically ask three questions. Has everyone in each group made a clear, quantifiable contribution? Is everyone clear on what those contributions mean to the organization's overall success? And, does an integrated picture exist so that it's clear how the collective contributions add up? An example of an integrated picture is the *balanced scorecard*, developed by Kaplan and Norton.[8] A widely used instrument, a balanced scorecard offers a coherent perspective on how multiple, quite different contributions help an organization reach its financial objectives.

A conventional, financially oriented scorecard does not account for a trend among the world's larger corporations, which is to set forth abstract concepts such as defining a place in society or contributing to peoples' well-being – whatever that might mean. In fact, there is a hierarchy of objectives in which the abstractions are placed at the top of the pyramid, with the more tangible objectives filling out the supportive and enabling base. A good example comes from the Novartis mission, seen in Box 8.1.

Box 8.1 NOVARTIS MISSION

ۍ NOVARTIS

We want to discover, develop and successfully market innovative products to prevent and cure diseases, to ease suffering and to enhance the quality of life. We also want to provide a shareholder return that reflects *outstanding performance* and to adequately reward those who invest *ideas and work* in our company.

The Novartis mission dictates clear and significant demands upon its communication group. Management wants to ensure that the most important stakeholders are aware of the value of the company's innovative approach and its intent to improve quality of life. Communication managers are asked to demonstrate the added value, as well as describe the company performance that provides shareholders with a solid return, either in dividends, an appreciation in stock price or both, which is known as total shareholder return. Although these issues might initially seem contradictory – a desire to mean something to people emotionally, versus concrete financial performance – both need to be highlighted.

The mission of the Swiss pharmaceutical company Novartis shows an appealing corporate goal. Their overall target of meaningfulness – to improve the quality of life for people with certain illnesses and to produce first-class medicines that can cure them – is a noble thing indeed. It shows socially responsible leadership. However, to remain in business, the company's employees must understand perfectly that *stockholder* satisfaction is a requirement. What's more, as organizing the chemicals that make up new medicines demands a talented group of researchers, this firm must also pay generous attention to its people. In other words, there is a hierarchy of goals, as shown in Figure 8.8.

For Novartis, one could then articulate several KPIs for each goal and sub-goal, an interpretation of which is shown in Figure 8.9.

The KPIs formulated here are no more than an academic concept. Without a doubt, there are people within Novartis who have much greater insight into the internal and external factors that influence the company's key performance agreements. Nevertheless, this reasoning represents several basic starting points that are, in fact, applicable to most organizations.

The next step to apply is being more concrete about each of the sub-points mentioned in Figure 8.9. This can be done by using the drivers of reputation explained in Chapter 5, with the RepTrak™ model. For the sub-goal 'being an attractive employer', the workplace attributes section of RepTrak™ asks: 'Does the

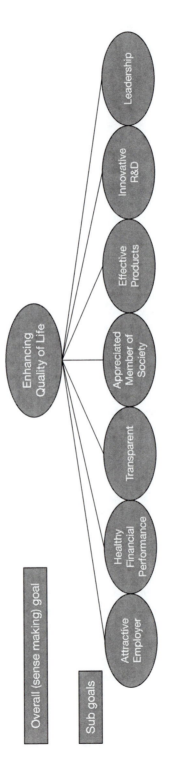

Overall (sense making) goal

Sub goals

FIGURE 8.8 Goals and sub-goals

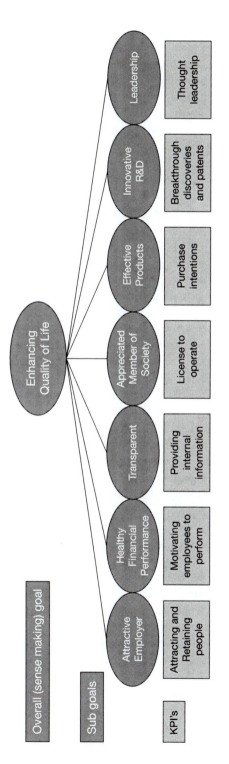

FIGURE 8.9 An interpretation of KPIs per goal

organization reward employees in a fair manner? Is it committed to employee well-being and does it provide each with equal opportunities?'.

The main goal 'enhancing quality of life' focuses on the RepTrak™ dimension of leadership and turns operational with such things as a 'well-organized company, appealing leader, excellent managers and a clear vision on the future'. This concept is elaborated in the D-row boxes in Figure 8.10. These are followed by the E-row boxes, which can be completed in an organization-specific way. Although this degree of detail may not always be necessary, it will increase the impact of KPIs if managers ask for the nuances.

The next step in building a dashboard that reveals the added value (or the lack of it) of all communication efforts is adding concrete quantitative indicators to each of the KPIs. Such an exercise can result in an overview that looks like Figure 8.11.

Using corporate communication KPIs in a dashboard in practice

In the previous sections of this chapter, I have discussed the use of KPIs as both implicit and explicit measures of corporate communication success. As explained in previous chapters, the expected contributions of communication managers are mostly implemented in conjunction with those of other managers in the firm, both in the C-suite and colleagues at staff level. Building and maintaining external and internal alignment have to be seen as the joint responsibility of all these groups. That is why it is quite logical to use KPIs such as reputation and employee alignment, not only for assessing the performance of the communication managers, but also at the executive level.

It is public knowledge that both KPN, the Dutch telecom market leader, and Eneco, a Dutch energy company, use RepTrak™ and the RepTrak™ Alignment Monitor as key performance indicators for the remuneration of their board-of-management members, impacting respectively 25 and 20 per cent of their total bonus. I will not reveal the details about how both companies use the two tracking tools in assessing a positive or a negative achievement in reputation management. What will be done here is showing a pure hypothetical way of using RepTrak™ and the RepTrak™ Alignment Monitor as remuneration KPIs for hypothetical companies X and Y.

Selecting the KPIs to determine success or failure in building reputation among key external audiences, using RepTrak™, can be done as follows: the first step is calculating which attributes impact reputation and supportive behaviour most. As is shown in Figure 8.12, five attributes appear to have the highest impact score. Three can be typified as *responsibility attributes*, and two can be labelled *ability attributes*. Based on a statistical analysis, combining longitudinal data for firm X (at least three years) with the global industry benchmark of the Reputation Institute, the predictions in Figure 8.12 can be made regarding a realistic increase in the five attributes in the coming three years.

Finally, a similar analysis can be done calculating the realistic increase of the Pulse score in the coming three years, combining inputs from the past three years

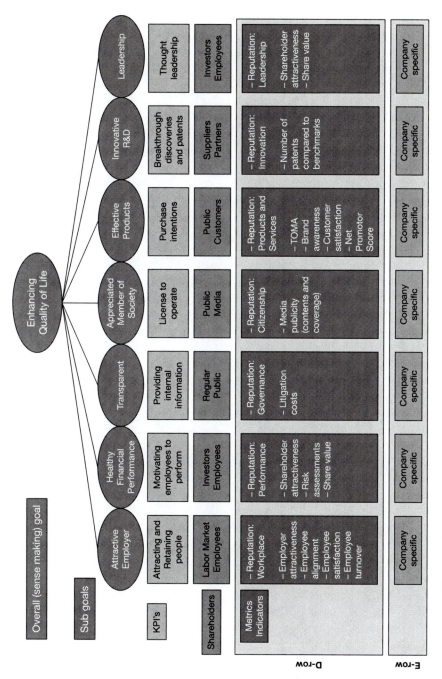

FIGURE 8.10 General and specific elaboration KPIs

KPI's	Stakeholder	Metrics	Scores	Benchmark*
Attracting and retaining key employees	Labor market Employees	Reputation: Workplace		Worldwide = >65; Industry = 59; Benchmark = 65
		Employer attractiveness		>60
		Employee alignment		
		Employee satisfaction		
		Employee turnover		
Motivating employees to perform	Investors Employees	Reputation: Performance		Worldwide = >65; Industry = 59; Benchmark = 65
		Shareholder attractiveness		Buy/Hold
		Risk assessments		
		Share value		Industry average
Providing internal information	Regulators Public	Reputation: Governance		Worldwide = >65; Industry = 59; Benchmark = 65
		Litigation Costs		
License to operate	Public Media	Reputation: Citizenship		Worldwide = >65; Industry = 59; Benchmark = 65
		Media publicity (content and coverage)		Negative <10%; Positive >20%; Share of vooice >35%
Purchase intentions	Public Customers	Reputation: Products & Services		Worldwide = >65; Industry = 59; Benchmark = 65
		TOMA		Public >20%; Customers >80%
		Brand awareness		Public >75%; Customers = 100%
		Customer satisfaction		>70
		Net promotor Score		Industry >15%
				Main benchmark >10%
Breakthrough discoveries and patents	Suppliers Partners	Reputation: Innovation		Worldwide = >65; Industry = 59; Benchmark = 65
		Number of patents compared to benchmarks		Industry average
Thought Leadership	Investors Employees	Reputation: Leadership		Worldwide = >65; Industry = 59; Benchmark = 65
		Shareholder attractiveness		Buy/Hold
		Share value		Industry average

FIGURE 8.11 Corporate communication dashboard

* Hypothetical figures

Step 1 – Identifying which attributes matter most

Longitudinal impact of attributes	
Products and Services	
High quality products	6.4%
Good value for money	7.5%
Stands behind its products	3.8%
Meets customer needs	7.1%
Innovation	
Is an innovative company	5.3%
Is generally first to market	3.3%
Adapts quickly to change	4.8%
Workplace	
Rewards employees fairly	4.1%
Concerned with employees	2.5%
Offers equal opportunities	3.1%
Governance	
Open and transparent	5.3%
Behaves ethically	4.3%
Fair in the way it does business	5.4%
Citizenship	
Environmentally responsible	4.7%
Supports good causes	2.6%
Positive influence on society	4.6%
Leadership	
Well-organized company	4.5%
Strong and appealing leader	2.1%
Excellent managers	3.7%
Clear vision for its future	4.0%
Performance	
Is a profitable company	5.1%
Performs better than expected	2.1%
Strong prospects for growth	3.6%

○ Ability
◑ Responsibility attributes

Step 2 – Examination of historical performance of own company and peers on key attributes

Performance own company on key attributes

ABILITY	2008	2009	2010	2011
High quality products	69.9	73.0	71.6	73.1
Good value for money	58.4	60.8	60.9	62.5
Meets customer needs	57.8	59.7	58.9	61.9
Is an innovative company	66.2	69.4	69.5	70.0

RESPONSIBILITY	2008	2009	2010	2011
Behaves ethically	63.2	66.0	63.0	64.9
Fair in the way it does business	63.5	67.2	65.7	68.5

Performance of peer group on key attributes

ABILITY	2008	2009	2010	2011
High quality products	70.5	72.6	71.5	73.9
Good value for money	69.0	70.5	66.4	72.0
Meets customer needs	73.9	77.5	75.0	75.4
Is an innovative company	71.9	75.7	73.2	74.9

RESPONSIBILITY	2008	2009	2010	2011
Behaves ethically	63.4	66.8	66.7	69.0
Fair in the way it does business	66.3	69.5	68.7	68.3

Step 3 – Extrapolating results to future KPIs

KPIs ABILITY	2012	2013	2014
High quality products	73.3	74.3	73.3
Good value for money	62.7	64.8	64.8
Meets customer needs	62.5	64.2	65.9
Is an innovative company	70.5	72.2	73.9

KPIs RESPONSIBILITY	2012	2013	2014
Behaves ethically	66.1	68.0	69.9
Fair in the way it does business	67.2	68.7	70.2

■ Maintain (≥70)
■ Improve (between 60–70)
■ Immediate action (<60)

FIGURE 8.12 Desired annual increase in reputation drivers for firm X

(monthly base), the global industry scores and the data in the key attributes. This results in the projections in Figure 8.13.

A similar exercise has been carried out for firm Y in the context of *employee alignment*. A similar analysis can be performed as was just illustrated for reputation. In this case, KPIs can be determined by using RepTrak™ Alignment Monitor data over three years, resulting in seven attributes divided between informing, motivating and capability development. Again, a statistical analysis has to be carried out on three years of data for the specific firm, compared with a global benchmark. This results in the increase in the key drivers of employee alignment, divided over informing, motivating and capability development in the coming three years, shown in Figure 8.14.

For the overall indicator for employee alignment, this implies the data shown in Figure 8.15 in the coming three years.

KPI PULSE			
	2012	**2013**	**2014**
Pulse	69.3	70.8	72.3

FIGURE 8.13 Desired annual increase in reputation for firm X

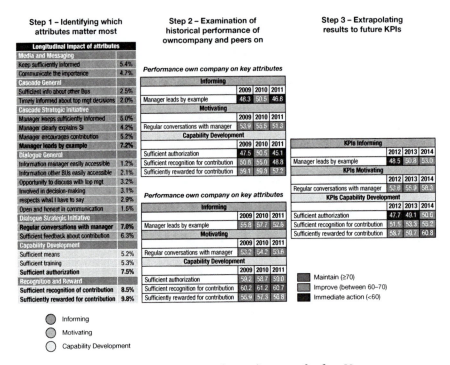

FIGURE 8.14 Key attributes impacting employee alignment for firm Y

KPI Employee Alignment			
	2012	**2013**	**2014**
Employee Alignment	55.9	57.2	58.5

FIGURE 8.15 Desired annual increase in employee alignment for firm Y

From metrics to motion

If communication is to earn its due respect within corporations, it is quite apparent that the function must use measurements that are identical, or similar, to those of other professions and disciplines. In the realm of religion, faith is the most important currency. In business, politics and almost all other endeavours, leaders want numbers. As they base decisions – and give respect, confidence and latitude – on key performance indicators, it would behove any and every communication department to develop a quantitative KPI in reputation or alignment for its company.

Like so many other elements of an organization, the most critical elements of such a set of KPIs will come from gaining agreement with senior management and are best developed with them in a cooperative manner, thereby almost guaranteeing legitimacy throughout the organization. The data have to prove whether or not the KPIs' objectives are being met, resulting in adequate actions closing the gaps between the desired and the actual situation.

Also like other functions, the performance of a communication function can be displayed on a dashboard. Showing a visual representation of performance will build confidence and earn trust among executives. And, with trust, a communication executive can start building an excellent department that best suits the organization's needs.

Notes

1 Euromonitor, 'Johnson & Johnson', *Global Market Information Database*, www.portal. euromonitor.com (accessed April 2011).
2 Datamonitor, 'Johnson & Johnson', www.datamonitor.com (accessed August 2009).
3 Johnson & Johnson, *Annual Report 2009*, www.jnj.com (accessed March, 2011).
4 Netpromoter website, www.netpromoter.com (accessed August 2010).
5 L. Patterson, *Marketing metrics in action: creating a performance driven marketing organization*, Chicago: Racom Communications, (2008).
6 M. Symonds, T. Wright and J. Ott, 'The customer-led bank: how to retain customers and boost top-line growth', *Journal of Business Strategy*, (2007), vol. 28(6), pp. 4–12.
7 Patterson, *Marketing metrics in action: creating a performance driven marketing organization*.
8 R. Kaplan, and D. Norton, 'Putting the balanced scorecard to work', *Harvard Business Review*, (1993), September–October, pp. 134–47.

PART IV

Epilogue

9

ALIGNMENT

Building and maintaining total stakeholder support

A positive and sustainable alignment with internal and external audiences facilitates smoother business operations. It buffers a firm against detractors and attracts investors, talented employees and customers. The ultimate aim of building alignment is to earn the trust that enables an organization to maintain an unrestricted licence to operate. The status is not a given, but is attained through excellent performance and strengthened by equally excellent communication. However, executives and individuals should recognize that, no matter how well they perform, or how expressive their communication might be, a misstep or a negative trend in their social environment could lead to restrictions on that licence.

Just ask Tiger Woods. Or the people of Toyota, which, in 2008, was found to be *the* most admired company in the world, as ranked in an international Reputation Institute study of the globe's 2,500 largest firms, with a Pulse score of 86.53. Not long thereafter, Toyota's score fell by nearly 11 points to 75.16 in 2009, a ranking not that bad, but still a harbinger of the body slam the social environment administered to the company. The decreases have continued since that year: 74.08 in 2010 and 71.26 in 2011. This seems to be the inevitable results of years characterized by a string of bad news stories and poor responses to accidents, complaints and scrutiny from the media and governments.

Perhaps Toyota was simply too slow to respond to sticking-accelerator problems in eight of its models, which have caused – as some claim – several fatalities and several dozen accidents over the past decade. However, at odds with all the well-considered, effective moves it has made over the decades, Toyota first blamed drivers and then floor mats, and finally recalled millions of cars to repair accelerator pedals. Then, brake issues forced Toyota to recall its 2010 Prius model, while steering issues threatened even more recalls. Finally, the company shut down production lines and focused all its attention on repairing the vehicles and communicating with the public, albeit late and slowly. Less than a month after the first recall,

Toyota's market value plunged $30 billion, or nearly 20 per cent. Some observers suggest that Toyota's global success and exceptional reputation allowed rust to form on its crisis-management skills. Others pointed to the firm's growth: in 2000, Toyota made 5.2 million cars, but now has the capacity to make 10 million. The rapid expansion made it difficult for executives to hear the 'weak signals' of problems on assembly lines. Analysts also described, 'a Toyota management team that had fallen in love with itself and become too insular to properly handle something like the current crisis'.[1]

US Congress vowed to grill Toyota executives in public hearings. Perhaps worse, a leading US transportation official promised that his agency would 'hold Toyota's feet to the fire' until it had proved that all current and future problems were fixed. In one of the company's most important markets, that is a restriction on its operational licence. Although its reputation capital will no doubt help Toyota's eventual recovery, the climb back for now looks quite steep, especially in light of the massive earthquake and the subsequent tsunami and nuclear power-plant disaster, a trifecta of terror that devastated Japan in 2011. With electricity in short supply in the summer, Toyota changed its factory 'weekends' to Thursday and Friday, closing plants on those days and operating instead on Saturday and Sunday, when power demand nationwide is lower – a socially responsible move that was beneficial to Japanese society. This was also a move by a company looking to rebuild its reputation, starting with its employees and home country.

Although Toyota alone was responsible for its predicament, the nature of reputation is such that a company doesn't have to be remotely responsible to get indirectly hurt by an unfortunate development. In 2009, salmonella outbreaks traced back to one US peanut-processing plant, for example, triggered renewed government regulatory scrutiny on all companies that use peanuts in consumer products. Also in the United States, ground beef tainted by a virulent strain of E. coli bacterium – blamed for at least sixteen outbreaks of illness in the most recent three-year period – has forced meat recalls from grocery stores and restaurants and in turn fostered a reluctance to eat hamburgers in a growing number of consumers. Many thousands of businesses that run clean, delicious and bacteria-free operations thus experience limits owing to the shoddy practices of others.

Alignment, then, is an ephemeral thing, only marginally controlled, no matter whether the damage is indirect or self-inflicted.

The basics, briefly

Building and maintaining sustainable alignment with key stakeholders require the professional application of three interrelated managerial efforts. 'Thinking before acting' is the first. This begins with gathering *relevant intelligence*. Internally, this requires understanding of the overall and specific identity traits, plus the degree to which employees support the new strategy in daily actions. Externally, it implies understanding public opinion, the nature and impact of industry-specific issues and reputation. This intelligence has to be shared with all relevant managers in the firm and used as input in decision-making about *the strategic road map*. Although this road map can either focus on negotiation or confrontation, both are aimed at persuading all relevant stakeholders to align with the company's strategic intents. In addition to the role of top management and a variety of staff and line managers, corporate communication specialists also have a key role in implementing the road map, including increasing familiarity with, understanding of, and appreciation for, the firm and its strategy.

The degree of success of the efforts made by corporate communication managers depends partly on themselves and partly on the attitude and behaviour of those in the C-suite. Top management has to enable the corporate communication department with a sufficient budget, good tools and integration of the department's head into the corporate leadership team, or what I've called the dominant coalition. The individual may be called vice president of communication or chief reputation officer. More important than the title is that the members of the dominant coalition perceive that the communication leader has a deep understanding of the business and is an effective partner/consultant in forming strategy.

The success of the corporate communication function also depends upon professionals within the department itself. The group must display obvious high ambition, aimed at gaining a respect from those in the dominant coalition. To win the department a decision-making seat in that coalition, a communication group should provide quantitative evidence of its value to the overall performance of the firm. Although all of its actions are in support of the corporation's strategy, communication managers should also analyse the context of perceptions and behaviours of all key internal and external stakeholders. The power and creativity of corporate communication are rooted in an ability to develop and distribute the right story, to the right people, and at the right time.

Creating total stakeholder support demands much from professionals. An *internal-alignment* assessment begins with an understanding of the organization's identity characteristics, a consideration that includes the industry; the firm's place within it; what senior management desires to project, versus what it actually projects; and how closely the identity perceived by employees matches the identity that's manifested in the daily behaviour of employees. Moreover, communication professionals need to realize that their success depends on the degree to which their work is embedded in the output of other departments, such as marketing, finance and human resources.

There is a clear structure to the process of building internal alignment: most organizations will start with a *negotiation-focused* road map, in an attempt to persuade employees voluntarily and enthusiastically to align with a new strategic objective. After consultation involving key persons and representative groups, a dialogue is started aimed at reaching mutually rewarding understanding about the benefits of the direction. Negotiation-focused activities are then complemented with a confrontation style of working, such as *mirroring* – through unavoidable corporate messaging – and *power play*, such as the introduction of new appraisal rules. Professional communication managers apply their skills to influence the negotiation and confrontation activities with four processes of internal communication – including *structure, flow, content* and *climate* – in such a way that all three managerial efforts – *informing, motivating* and *capability development* – work best in the specific paradigm of the firm, be it *bureaucracy, shared meaning, ideology* or *accountability*.

Creating *external alignment* requires a similar three-step flow procedure: *analysing, strategy development* and benefiting from corporate communication efforts in the *implementation of a new strategic objective*. Analysing the external context results in an elaborate understanding of the beliefs and actions of all relevant stakeholders, competitors and public opinion at large, on specific issues, their impact on society and what that means to the organization. Building bridges with external stakeholders can be distinguished again into *negotiation strategies* and *confrontation strategies*. External alignment boils down to (a) building lasting foundations of corporate communication, and (b) using them in a consistent way in specific communication programmes aimed at building enduring alignment with internal and external audiences.

Evidence of success in creating total stakeholder support is proven through KPIs that give clarity on measurable goals. A key lesson learned from professionals in areas that pioneered their use – such as marketing – is that KPIs will only be accepted if a chief financial officer or other senior executive takes responsibility for them. The finance department can be a critical relation for communication professionals. When finance is convinced there is monetary value in creating respect and trust among stakeholders, corporate communication shifts from a 'necessary expense' to an essential asset.

Petrobras: a case study from Brazil

A good example of a firm that has embraced many elements of modern stakeholder alignment over the past decade – and follows many of the fundamentals directly, indirectly or inadvertently – is Petrobras. The Brazilian giant is today among the top twelve energy companies in the world, with net revenues of US$183 billion and a global presence in thirty countries. It has a goal of being among the world's top five integrated energy firms by 2020. Although a publicly traded company, the majority stockholder in Petrobras is the Brazilian government, a most reasonable arrangement given that the company was created on behalf of the Brazilian people. Although no business could be as beloved as Brazil's World Cup football squad, Petrobras inspires an unusual degree of national pride.

Its origins are partly responsible. The company was born out of a popular campaign that started in the late 1940s, promoted by nationalists under the historic slogan, 'The oil is ours'. Petrobras was formally established in 1953 under the government of President Getúlio Vargas, with the support of both allies and the opposition party in the national congress, and it was set up as a monopoly designed to manage oil-industry activities in Brazil on behalf of the union. As *Time* magazine reported in 1955 (11 April 1955), the enabling legislation forbade the ownership

TABLE 9.1 The summary chart

Focus	Key Questions	Illustration
Basics of alignment	A mutually rewarding relationship between a company and its key stakeholders, which enables the firm to meet its objectives and to realize its purpose	Barclays
Gathering internal **intelligence**	Overall identity traits: *accountability, bureaucracy, shared meaning, ideology* Organizational specific identity traits: *desired OI, projected OI* and *perceived OI* Fit between strategic objectives, overall specific organizational identity trait and employee behavior	Eskom, FedEx, ING
Building **internal** alignment – developing a **roadmap**	Negotiation and confrontation	Philips case
Building **internal** **alignment** – corporate **communication** **support**	Informing, motivating, capability development Internal communication: structure, flow, content, climate Aligning internal communication with the four overall OI traits Four scenarios in building and maintaining internal alignment	TNT, FedEx, Gas Natural Fenosa, Repsol,
Gathering external **intelligence**	Issue scanning Public opinion Reputation Fit between strategy and stakeholder beliefs	Brent Spar case, La Caixa, Itaú
Building **external** alignment – Developing a **roadmap**	Negotiation: *consultation* and *consensus* Confrontation: *mirroring* and *power play* GM-food case: Frankenstein food or solving starvation problem? Telefonica, Unilever case, Monsanto case	
Building **external** alignment – corporate **communication** **support**	Foundations (*rules, intelligence, organization of corporate communication, corporate positioning* and *corporate branding*) Program support (*additional intelligence, program positioning, execution* and *embedding actions in primary process firm*)	Eneco, Unilever, Santander, BBVA
Assessing success of internal and external alignment with **KPIs**	Key Performance Indicators (KPIs) Internal and external success indicators Metrics in corporate communication KPIs for contributions of corporate communication in external and external alignment	Novartis, KPN

of shares by foreigners, or even Brazilians married to foreigners. The national sentiment behind Petrobras was evident in a speech given by Vargas: 'It is, therefore, with great satisfaction and patriotic pride that I sanctioned the bill approved by the legislature, which is a new milestone in our economic independence.'

The company held that monopoly over nearly all aspects of the oil and natural-gas industry – except for wholesale distribution and retail service stations – from 1954 until 1997. During those four decades, Petrobras has its ups and downs, as did Brazil. The first great 'oil crisis', caused by the Arab oil embargo of 1973, not only put a stop to the company's growth and nearly made it bankrupt, but it also stopped the rapid growth of the economy, which had been called the 'Brazilian miracle'. Petrobras weathered the second oil crisis in 1979 somewhat better, and, with the end of its monopoly status, began competing against other foreign and domestic companies, developing the muscle of a true multinational energy company.

Today, Petrobras is an integrated energy company operating in exploration, production, refining, oil and natural-gas trade and transportation, petrochemicals and derivatives, electricity and biofuels, besides other renewable energy sources distribution. By both market capitalization and revenue, it's the largest company in Latin America, where it has retail operations in five other nations. Perhaps most indicative of the company's emergence as a global energy power is its financial and operational participation in offshore deep-water fields in West Africa, the US Gulf of Mexico and elsewhere.

A world leader in developing technologies for deep-water exploration and production, Petrobras has made Brazil virtually self-sufficient in oil production. That status will probably continue as the company develops massive frontier fields of oil and natural-gas deposits trapped below a subterranean salt layer some 2 km thick, located 300 km off the Brazilian coast and at a depth of roughly 6 km below the sea surface. The so-called 'pre-salt' layer presents terrific technical challenges, the mastery of which only strengthens Brazil's domestic oil and gas supply and economic security. According to the director of corporate communication at Petrobras, Eraldo Carreira da Silva, manager of corporate communication planning and management, this is the challenge that makes Petrobras a major player on the international energy scene, which, of course, raises the issue of the complexities of building total stakeholder support.

Several studies suggest that Petrobras is on the right track. One respected survey finds that Petrobras is considered Brazil's most socially responsible company. In the Reputation Institute's 2011 study of the world's 100 most reputable companies, Petrobras ranked ninety-third, remarkable for a company in a sector that doesn't typically attract admiration, much less popular affection. In fact, it was the only energy company on the list, as well as the only Latin American firm.

Strategy, mission and a changing identity

Society clearly has a conflicted relationship with the energy industry, a sector that includes companies that produce oil, natural gas and coal; that manufacture

FIGURE 9.1 Petrobras truck

Source: www.petrobras.com

transportation fuels and other petrochemical products; and that generate electricity, in plants that burn coal or natural gas or use nuclear fuel, or from hydroelectric dams on rivers. Abundant energy is critical for the mobility of humanity, for the food that nourishes a planet of 7 billion people, and for the heat and light that developed nations take for granted. However, nearly all forms of conventional energy come at a price, be it particulate pollution, greenhouse-gas emissions or dammed rivers that no longer nurture fisheries. The poverty-stricken populations of resource-rich nations, in particular those in Africa, seldom see the benefits of oil and gas production, as wealth is all too often skimmed off by corrupt leaders. Still other populations feel as if they're hostages to the prices companies charge for energy.

Companies in this sector seldom have an opportunity to leverage *total* stakeholder support. The pursuit of alignment – so that companies win concessions and permits from governments to develop resources and sell energy with a relatively unrestricted operational licence – is an ongoing and ever-present demand. That major companies have productive operations that meet global energy needs and are financially stable is a testament to how well they build *partial* stakeholder support in what is often a hostile social and regulatory environment.

FIGURE 9.2 Petrobras logo

This new world of energy is highly evident in how Petrobras self-describes its strategy and vision. Only twenty years ago, stakeholder concerns were the last obligatory item in most oil companies' annual reports, right after the compulsory statement, 'employees are our most important resource'. At savvy energy companies such as Petrobras, stakeholders are addressed in the opening sentences of company literature, before any mention of oil production, market shares or other standard business issues.

For example:

> **Corporate Strategy**: Integrated growth, profitability, and socio-environmental responsibility are keywords in our corporate strategy. It is based on the performance on these three pillars that we built the 2020 Mission and Vision, transparently and with attentive eyes on what is going on in Brazil and in the world.
>
> **Mission**: Operate in a safe and profitable manner in Brazil and abroad, with social and environmental responsibility, providing products and services that meet clients' needs and that contribute to the development of Brazil and the countries in which it operates.
>
> **Values**: Described in the Strategic Plan, the values are the way the Company guides its strategies, actions, and projects. They must appear in how business is carried out and reflect Petrobras' way of being.
>
> **Sustainable Development**: We pursue business success under a long-term perspective, contributing to economic and social development and to a healthy environment in the communities where we have operations.
>
> **Respect for life**: We respect life in all of its forms, expressions and situations, and seek excellence in matters that involve health, safety and the environment.
>
> **Human and cultural diversity**: We value human and cultural diversity in our relationships with people and institutions. We ensure the principles of respect for difference, non-discrimination, and of equal opportunities.
>
> **People**: We turn people and their development into a performance differential of Petrobras.
>
> **Proud to be Petrobras**: We are proud to belong to a Brazilian company that makes the difference no matter where it operates, for its history, achievements, and for its capacity to overcome challenges.

In a document that richly describes the many operational units in Petrobras, from conventional oil exploration and refining to making biofuels and producing energy from renewable sources, the fourth paragraph contains this remarkable statement:

> As a member of the United Nations' Global Compact, defending its principles (related to human rights, labour force, the environment, and transparency), the company has established guidelines for its actions. Due to the commitment

to sustainable development, it has been included in the Dow Jones Sustainability Index, which is used as a parameter by investors who are socially and environmentally responsible regarding their decisions on investments.

These few examples suggest a very detailed road map that includes buffering and an extraordinary number of negotiation strategies. Although there is some mirroring involved, confrontation is quite muted. Such an overall alignment strategy inherently involves a great deal of communication. The Petrobras institutional communications group, for example, reports directly to the company's president.

Building and maintaining internal alignment

With more than 80,000 employees, Petrobras has a typical spread of people found in a multinational oil company, with a culture dominated by engineers and scientists. In a company that earns most of its money by producing and refining oil, reservoir, mechanical, chemical, electrical, civil, design and petroleum engineers are the coin of the realm. And yet, each is no more important to the firm's success than safety inspectors, accountants, auditors, traders, ship captains, drilling operators, attorneys, truck drivers, geophysicists, IT experts and computer programmers, to mention a few of the many disciplines required for such complex operations. It also involves the many skills required in a communication group, including writers, artists, lobbyists and executives, who can work closely with senior operational management – the company's dominant coalition.

A workforce that includes such disparate skills, from blue-collar workers to highly educated scientists and business-school graduates, obviously features myriad cultural traits. However, as Petrobras was founded as a national company, its overall identity for most of its existence probably best fits into bureaucracy, with strong shadings of the accountability identity found at most independent oil corporations. Because of the national pride built into Petrobras, bureaucracy would be an identity both projected and perceived among employees. Alignment then followed along a fairly natural path.

The high levels of centralization and formalization, typical of both an energy company and a state-owned one, also tend to suggest bureaucracy. As an engineer-driven company, it's also very important that clear and detailed directives are established, so that there is a high predictability of operational outcomes, hence diminishing any operational risks that compromise success in this industry. Another bureaucratic feature would be that task-oriented corporate communications are abundant; nevertheless, it would be unfair to state that these are the main drivers of employee alignment.

Studies conducted with the RepTrak™ Alignment Monitor methodology have demonstrated that employees at Petrobras have probably one of the highest levels of *identification* with their company in the world. More specifically, employees have a strong sense of belonging and an extremely high level of pride (above 90 points on a 0–100 scale) to be working for Petrobras. But what is it about the company that these employees are identifying with? In the early days of 'The oil is ours', working for the nation's sole energy company certainly had its psychological rewards. Today, however, Petrobras means so much more to Brazil, which changes how the employees identify with the corporation.

I suspect that Petrobras is in transition from a bureaucracy to more of a shared-meaning organization. In most cases, what typifies a shared-meaning organization is a strong identification with the president of the company. That could be one of the causes for Petrobras, but maybe more important is the identification that employees develop with the company's mission and inspiring vision, which are about deeper issues and meaning than simply producing and selling energy products. This corporate mission and vision statement is publicized on the Petrobras website, is an underlying theme of corporate advertising, and is laced into every community and social action taken by the firm. The *raison d'être* for Petrobras is the Brazilian community, together with the promise of development that the company has been delivering to society. It is a powerful statement of shared meaning.

However, meaning is shared to quite different degrees in widespread business units. Employees in a business unit that produces oil and is hugely profitable may feel equally positive about themselves and the company, whereas a unit that is shrinking because of market conditions or changes in a government regulation may not be as aligned as others. The Reputation Institute was asked to conduct three small studies of different business units and found *alignment* rates moderate at best, and not strong as the overall corporate number. (One must imagine that the Petrobras managers already knew of the problem and needed quantitative proof; hence the reason for the research.)

When overall Petrobras alignment drivers are analysed, it can be easily noticed that employees are highly aware of the company's strategic goals, proving the efficiency of Petrobras' internal media and messaging in conveying the company's main issues and goals. At the same time, it is also clear that employees in specific business units sometimes hit a block that keeps them from having a better understanding of the strategy, owing to insufficient face-to-face dialogue opportunities. However, such intelligence-gathering is essential if a company is to rebuild alignment in pockets that need improvement.

In fact, one of the units identified strategic lack of understanding as the main block to employee alignment. The challenge was to make sure that employees at the very bottom of the cascading process had an opportunity to talk about how they related to the corporate strategy and goals. To respond to that, programmes were organized to develop communication and leadership skills in those managers in charge of employees who worked on production sites, enabling a more open communication climate in the organization and, hence, a better connection with, and understanding of, the corporate issues. The company also established a 'Talking with the general manager' programme. This was an initiative led by employee communications and human resources together, in which the general manager received a group of employees every quarter to discuss matters that were important to them and to the company.

FIGURE 9.3 Petrobras oil platform

Source: www.petrobras.com

Such attention to detail speaks volumes of how much store Petrobras sets by internal alignment.

Building and maintaining external alignment

Petrobras self-represents itself as a provider of energy that is capable of driving development in a sustainable way. This is made very clear in the statement of values projected by the company in its communications and is also very much aligned with the perceptions that Brazilians in general have of the company. Nevertheless, there are other characteristics that are not so much projected by the company, but that help constitute its perceived identity. Frequently, these features are associated with government liabilities.

In looking for external alignment, Petrobras is taking a multi-pronged approach, but in two major directions. The first is operational. Some employees believe the company is staking its reputation on the pre-salt oil and gas formations, and that failing to deliver on its promise would cause the government to look unfavourably on Petrobras. Others see the danger of another BP Macondo well-style accident in ultra-deep water, which is exactly where the 'pre-salt' layer of potentially prodigious oil reservoirs is found.

Consequently, Petrobras launched an integrated communication programme to build alignment for the offshore developments, linking the opportunity to the company's past, present and future. It was synthesized into two short and simple sentences: 'Petrobras has made history. And is building the future.'

Nevertheless, opposition and potential threats to operations can arise quickly. In 2009, the Brazilian Senate established a Parliamentary Inquiry Commission to investigate five issues related to corporate administrative actions that had been reported in the national media. Faced with an emerging stakeholder crisis and acting on a decision that came from the company's CEO – to demonstrate total transparency to the Brazilian government and public – Petrobras' communication professionals created an interactive online environment outside the company's portal, called the Facts & Data blog.

The blog triggered a wide discussion throughout Brazilian society about the relationship between the media and their sources, with a lot of space provided for all points of view. Although the Parliamentary Inquiry lasted six months, the process had a favourable result for Petrobras. What's more, the blog has since been maintained as a corporate channel directed at Brazilian society as a whole, the company's workforce, the press, investors, public power, suppliers and partners, groups organized in social networks and virtual communities. Through it, the company has been promoting diverse themes – such as reviews of oil and gas market rules – by expressing its positioning and engaging audiences in this discussion.

With its ambitions to be a top five integrated energy company by 2020, I believe Petrobras will continue to deliver operational excellence across its many business lines, from conventional oil to gasoline, lubricants, shipping and distributing products and serving consumers at petrol stations throughout South America. Operational excellence deals with a hard, tangible performance that wins alignment from governmental permission-givers, but the soft stuff is perhaps much more powerful, especially when one considers what Petrobras does for Brazilian society and culture.

Indeed, when the nation's motion-picture industry went bankrupt, and no bank would help out, it was Petrobras that stepped in, financed studios and helped make 500 movies over fifteen years, which essentially resurrected the industry. The company's notion of sustainability, which is guided by the directives in its social-responsibility policy, is a clear road map to external alignment.

The economic axis that moves around Petrobras is clearly stated. Through taxes, royalty payments and social contributions, the company provides major support to federal and state governments in Brazil. It generates direct and indirect jobs, including nearly 60,000 agricultural workers in the semi-arid hinterlands, growing and harvesting plants that are converted into biodiesel fuel. The company funds educational programmes for all ages, including professional and technical offerings that promote 'digital inclusion'. It supports the rights of children and adolescents, especially in developing regions, so that children have adequate physical, mental and social development. Petrobras is by far the largest supporter of Brazilian culture, a diverse blend of native peoples – Portuguese, Africans, Germans, Italians and Japanese.

Sustainability also touches on alternative energy, environmental concerns and climate change. Petrobras works with numerous water-resource entities, to encourage improvement in managing the vital resource. The Petrobras environmental programme is involved in initiatives throughout the country. One such project, called Tamar, focuses on the preservation of sea turtles. Over a thirty-year partnership with Tamar, more than 10 million baby turtles have been released into the sea along the Brazilian coast, and there is much more.

Asking which stakeholders matter most to Petrobras is no doubt like asking a mother to choose her favourite child. Certainly, government holds the most sway over the company, but I tend to think the company's leadership and employees think of Brazil as its primary stakeholder, and that's the reason RepTrak™ studies find it's the most reputable firm in the country.

FIGURE 9.4 Petrobras Tamar Sea Turtle Project

Source: Petrobras Image Bank, reference no. 24389, by André Valentim

Using KPIs to assess alignment

Petrobras uses a set of sophisticated methodologies to assess and track both internal and external alignment, all of which are considered KPIs. Internally, besides climate studies and the RepTrak™ Alignment Monitor for employees, Petrobras has a customized tool called *Sistema de Monitoramento de Imagem Corporativa*, or SISMICO, which translates loosely into English as system to monitor the corporation's image. It measures a variety of aspects, including energy, vision, competitiveness, growth, profitability, management, ethics, environmental responsibility, social support, communication and transparency with society, positioning abroad, quality of products and technology.

This very same tool is also applied externally, in addition to the global RepTrak studies. Together, these KPIs help Petrobras better understand stakeholders' expectations and perceptions of the company. This also shows the firm's communication department whether it is meeting its strategic objectives. These include: raising the corporate reputation of Petrobras; creating and reinforcing bonds of trust between the publics of interest and Petrobras; and obtaining understanding and a favourable disposition of the stakeholders toward Petrobras' position on new regulations resulting from the discovery of pre-salt reserves.

In building alignment for the pre-salt exploration and production, Petrobras CEO Jose Sergio Gabrielli has participated in diverse communication actions. These include live presentations to employees in an auditorium, which were also broadcast through web television; a 'president's letter' sent by e-mail to the employees; articles published in *Petrobras* magazine; press conferences around the globe; and international events and local seminars addressed to government representatives and opinion leaders. With the numbers in the KPIs showing the power of communication, the leaders of Petrobras will probably continue their policy of transparency and active stakeholder engagement.

The authentic alignment factor

Alignment has been described as 'a mutually rewarding relationship between a company and its key stakeholders, which enables the firm to meet its objectives and realize its purpose'. Such a relationship will only survive when, in the long run, both parties benefit more or less in a comparable way. Given the power of many firms, especially those that operate on a large scale, companies sometimes barely avoid losing sight of the degree to which they do depend on external, but also internal, stakeholders.

If there's any great message to take away from the core vision expressed in this book, it's that nothing is ever completely certain. What's more, no company can afford to undertake major stakeholder engagements, internal or external, without measuring a set of beliefs before and after. Reputation and trust itself are gossamer, although building the web requires flint-eyed surveyors and interpretations by the most cold-hearted attorneys. And, no matter how admired a corporation might become, it behoves that firm's leaders to remind themselves constantly that they are nothing more than frail humans – although perhaps smart, talented and lucky humans – but not an almighty and invincible power.

Hans Christian Andersen's short story, *The Emperor's new clothes*, offers an appropriate analogy. As the well-known fable goes, a vain emperor who cares for little but his wardrobe hires two weavers, who promise him the finest suit of clothing ever made. Actually swindlers, the weavers promise the ruler that they will use a fabric invisible to anyone who is unfit for his position, or who is 'just hopelessly stupid'. The Emperor cannot see the cloth himself, but, for fear of appearing less than intelligent, he pretends that the garments are beautiful. His ministers, fearing the wrath of the sovereign, praise the clothing, even though it is invisible to them, too.

In other words, the emperor has no one in his court with the gumption to speak the truth, not unlike executives who just don't like bad news and weed out 'negative' voices on their staff.

Naked and unaware of it, the Emperor begins to march in a procession. A child in the crowd calls out that the king is wearing nothing at all; children, after all, have a great capacity to comment, unfiltered, on exactly what they see. Others join the cry, and, while the Emperor cringes in the suspicion that what the crowd is saying is true, pride causes him to stiffen his spine and continue.

In his first draft of *The Emperor's new clothes*, Andersen intended to have the crowd quiet, admiring the non-existent garments. Many theories exist as to why he made the change. One of the best concerns his own experience as a child in a crowd waiting to see King Frederick VI. When he appeared, Andersen said loudly, 'Oh, he's nothing more than a human being!'. Andersen's mortified mother tried to silence him, but the idea that monarchs are anything more than human has long made them a target for satire and mockery.[2]

And so it is that we in the academic profession should not be *overly* praiseworthy of corporations with trusted reputations. We admire their efforts and even champion

"I'm arresting you for bringing the Emperor into disrepute."

FIGURE 9.5 *The Emperor's new clothes*

practices that build total stakeholder alignment, for this is frequently beneficial to both internal and external groups and societies as a whole. But, given the dynamics of economic and social life, we cannot go so far as to praise the Emperor's clothing, when there is really nothing of real substance covering his body. All companies have the capacity to rise and fall. Some exceed in their efforts, but all share a path that crosses often precarious and shifting ground.

Authentic communication efforts orchestrated by professional corporate communication managers can make a substantial difference in establishing perceptions among stakeholders that do persuade them to become believers instead of opponents. Top management will gain when they support communication professionals taking on this challenge. Communication specialists will be accepted into the dominant coalition when they understand one of the basic notions of this book: corporate communication is first corporate, and only then communication.

Notes

1   B. Saporito, M. Schuman, J.R. Szczesny and A. Altman, 'Toyota tangled', *Time Magazine*, (2010), February 22, pp. 26–30.
2   Wikipedia website, http://en.wikipedia.org/wiki/The_Emperor's_New_Clothes (accessed 22 February 2010).

BIBLIOGRAPHY

Albert, S. and D. Whetten, 'Organizational identity', in L.L. Cummings and B.M. Shaw (eds), *Research in Organizational Behaviour*, Greenwich: JAI Press, (1985), pp. 263–95.

Allport, G.W., *Personality: a psychological interpretation*. New York: Holt, Rinehart, & Winston, (1937).

Argenti, P.A., 'Collaborating with activists: how Starbucks works with NGOs', *California Management Review*, (2004), 47, 91–116.

Bandura, A., *Self-efficacy: the exercise of control*, New York: Freeman, (1997), p. 604.

Berens, G.A.J.M., C.B.M. van Riel and G.H. van Bruggen, 'Corporate associations and consumer product responses: the moderating role of corporate brand dominance', *Journal of Marketing*, (2005), 69(3), 35–48.

Bosch, F.A.J., van den, and C.B.M. van Riel, 'Buffering and bridging as environmental strategies of firms', *Business Strategy and the Environment*, (1998), 7(1), 24–31.

Brouwer, M., 'Mass communication and the social sciences: some neglected areas', *International Social Science Journal*, (1962), 14(2), 303–19. (Reprinted in A.L. Dexter and D.M. White (eds), *People, society and mass communications*, New York: The Free Press/Collier-Macmillan, 1964, pp. 547–67.)

Brown, T.J. and P.A. Dacin, 'The company and the product: corporate associations and consumer product responses', *Journal of Marketing*, (1997), 61(1), 68–84.

Buchholz, R.A., *Essentials of public policy for management* (2nd edn), Englewood Cliffs, NJ: Prentice Hall, (1990).

Cable, D.M. and D.B. Turban, 'The value of organizational image in the recruitment context: a brand equity perspective', *Journal of Applied Social Psychology*, (2003), 33, 2244–66.

Cameron, K.S. and R.E. Quinn, *Diagnosing and changing organizational culture*, Reading: Addison-Wesley, (1999).

Carmichael, H.L., 'Reputations in the labor market', *American Economic Review*, American Economic Association, (1984), 74(4), 713–25.

Carroll, C.E. and M. McCombs, 'Agenda-setting effects of business news on the public's images and opinions about major corporations', *Corporate Reputation Review*, (2003), 6(1), 36–46.

Chauvin, K.W. and J.P. Guthrie, 'Labor market reputation and the value of the firm', *Managerial and Decision Economics*, (1994), 15, 543–52.

Childs, H.L., *Public opinion: nature, formation, and role*, Princeton, NJ: D. van Nostrand, (1965).

Clampitt, P.G. and C.W. Downs, 'Employee perceptions of the relationship between communication and productivity: a field study', *Journal of Business Communications*, (1993), 30(1), 5–28.

Coldwell, D.A.L., Billsberry, J., van Meurs, N. and Marsh, P.J.G., 'The effects of person–organisation ethical fit on employee attraction and retention: towards a testable explanatory model', *Journal of Business Ethics*, (2008), 78, 611–22.

Collins, J. and J. Porras, *Built to last: successful habits of visionary companies*, New York: Harper Business, (1994).

Cookson, R., 'Employee fraud causes on the increase as bad times fuel crime', *Financial Times*, 11 May 2009.

Cordeiro, J. and R. Sambharya, 'Do corporate reputations influence security analyst earnings forecasts?', *Corporate Reputation Review*, (1997), 1, 94–8.

Dell, D., Y. Tsaplina and R. Kramer, *Forging strategic business alignment*, New York: The Conference Board, (2003).

Dorsett, L., M.A. Fontaine and T. O'Driscoll, 'Redefining manager interaction at IBM', *Knowledge Management Review*, (2002), 5(4), 4–8.

Dutton, J. and J.W. Penner, 'The importance of organizational identity for strategic agenda building', in J. Hendry and G. Johnson (eds), *Strategic thinking: leadership and the management of change*, New York: Wiley, (1993).

Eccles, R.G., R.M. Grant and C.B.M. van Riel, 'Reputation and transparency: lessons from a painful period in public disclosure', *Long Range Planning*, (2007), 69(4), 353–9.

Elstak, M.E., C.B.M. van Riel and M.G. Pratt, 'Why identify? Self-enhancement and self-consistency motives in organizational identification', *Working Paper*, Rotterdam School of Management, (2010).

Fombrun, J. and C.B.M. van Riel, *Fame and fortune. How the world's top companies develop winning reputations*, New York: Pearson Publishing and the *Financial Times*, (2004).

Fryxell, G.E. and J. Wang, '*Fortune*'s corporate "reputation" index: reputation of what?', *Journal of Management*, (1994), 20(1), 1–14.

Gatewood, R.D., M.A. Gowan and G.J. Lautenschlager, 'Corporate image, recruitment image, and initial job choice decisions', *Academy of Management Journal*, (1993), 362), 414–27.

Goldberg, M. and J. Hartwick, 'The effects of advertising reputation and extremity of advertising claim on advertising effectiveness', *Journal of Consumer Research*, (1990), 17(2), 172–9.

Graunt, J., 'Natural and political observations made upon the Bills of Mortality', in Charles Henry Hull (ed.), *The economic writings of Sir William Petty*, vol. 2, (1899), pp. 321, 370, 379.

Greening, D.W. and D.B. Turban, 'Corporate social performance as a competitive advantage in attracting a quality workforce', *Business and Society*, (2000), 39, 254–80.

Grunig, J.E. (ed.), *Excellence in public relations and communication management*, Hillsdale, NJ: Lawrence Erlbaum Associates, (1992).

Grunig, J.E. and T. Hunt, *Managing public relations*, New York: Holt, Rinehart and Winston, (1984).

Gürhan-Canli, Z. and R. Batra, 'When corporate image affects product evaluations: the moderating role of perceived risk,' *Journal of Marketing Research*, (2004), 41(May), 197–205.

Hambrick, D.C., 'The field of management's devotion to theory: too much of a good thing?', *Academy of Management Journal*, (2007), 50(6), 1346–52.

Handy C., *Gods of management: the changing world of organizations*, London: Souvenir Press, (1978).

Heugens, P.P.M.A.R., F.A.J. van den Bosch and C.B.M. van Riel, 'Stakeholder integration: building mutually enforcing relationships', *Business & Society*, (2002), 41(1), 37–61.

Hunter, M.L., L.N. van Wassenhove and M. Besiou, 'Stakeholder media: the Trojan horse of corporate responsibility', *Working Paper*, INSEAD, (2009).

James, C., 'Global status of commercialized biotech/GM crops: 2009', (2009), www.isaaa.org (accessed 9 May 2011).

Johnson, J.D., W.A. Donohue, C.K. Atkin and S. Johnson, 'Differences between formal and informal communication channels', *Journal of Business Communication*, (1994), 31, 111–22.

Judge, T.A. and D.M. Cable, 'Applicant personality, organizational culture and organizational attraction', *Personnel Psychology*, (1997), 50, 359–94.

Kaplan, R. and D. Norton, 'Putting the balanced scorecard to work', *Harvard Business Review*, (1993), September–October, 134–47.

Kaplan, R.S. and D.P. Norton, *Alignment. Using the balanced scorecard to create corporate energies*, Boston: Harvard Business School Press, (2006).

Kilman, Scott, 'Monsanto sues Dupont over biotech patents', *Wall Street Journal*, 6 May 2009.

Kilman, Scott, 'Monsanto, Dupont escalate patent fray', *Wall Street Journal*, 19 August 2009.

Maathuis, O.J.M., C.B.M. van Riel and G.H. van Bruggen, 'Using the corporate brand to communicate identity: the value of corporate associations to customers', *Abstract Conference on Corporate Reputation, Identity and Competitiveness*, Amsterdam, (1998).

McCauley, D.P. and K.W. Kuhnert, 'A theoretical review and empirical investigation of employee trust in management', *Public Administration Quarterly*, (1992), 16(2), 265–84.

Milliken, F.J., E.W. Morrison and P.F. Hewlin, 'An exploratory study of employee silence: issues that employees don't communicate upward and why', *Journal of Management Studies*, (2003), 40, 1453–76.

Mintzberg, H., *Organisatiestructuren*, Schoonhoven: Academic Service, (1992).

Morrison, E.W. and F.J. Milliken, 'Organizational silence: a barrier to change and development in a pluralistic world', *Academy of Management Review*, (2000), 25, 706–25.

Neubauer, Chuck, 'DuPont, Monsanto trade barbs over competition', *Washington Times*, 28 August 2009.

Neubauer, Chuck, 'Monsanto chief accuses rival DuPont of deceit: seed business giant decries tactics as beyond competition', *Washington Times*, 18 August 2009.

Noelle-Neumann, E., 'Turbulences in the climate of opinion: methodological applications of the spiral of silence theory', *Public Opinion Quarterly*, (1977), 41(2), 143–58.

Orlitzky, M., F.L. Schmidt and S.L. Reynes, 'Corporate social and financial performance: a meta-analysis', *Organization Studies*, (2003), 24(3), 403–41.

Patterson, L., *Marketing metrics in action: creating a performance-driven marketing organization*, Chicago: Racom Communications, (2008).

Perrott, B.E., 'Strategic issue management: an integrated framework', *Journal of General Management*, (1995), 21(2), 52–63.

Ponzi, L.J., C.J. Fombrun and N.A. Gardberg, 'RepTrak™ Pulse: conceptualizing and validating a short-form measure of corporate reputation', *Corporate Reputation Review*, (2011), 14(1).

Ramzy, A., 'Heroic identity profile', www.narrativity-group.com, 2000.

Redding, W.C., *Communication within the organization: an interpretive review of theory and research*, New York: Industrial Communication Council, (1972).

Riel, C.B.M., van, 'Top of mind awareness of corporate brands among the Dutch public', *Corporate Reputation Review*, (2002), 4(4), 362–73.

Riel, C.B.M. van, G.A.J.M. Berens and M. Dijkstra, 'Stimulating strategically aligned behaviour among employees', *Journal of Management Studies*, (2009), 46(7), 1197–227.

Riel, C.B.M., van and C. J. Fombrun, *Essentials of corporate communication*, Abingdon: Routledge, (2007).

Roberts, P.W. and G.R. Dowling, 'The value of a firm's corporate reputation: how reputation helps attain and sustain superior profitability', *Corporate Reputation Review*, (1997), 1, 72–6.

Rosenberg, R.D. and E. Rosenstein, 'Participation and productivity: an empirical study', *Industrial and Labor Relations Review*, (1980), 33(3), 355–67.

Saporito, B., M. Schuman, J.R. Szczesny and A. Altman, 'Toyota Tangled', *Time* magazine, (2010), 22 February, pp. 26–30.

Smidts, A.Th., H. Pruyn and C.B.M. van Riel, 'The impact of employee communication and perceived external prestige on organizational identification', *Academy of Management Journal*, (2001), 49(5), 1051–62.

Stuller, J.K., *Ink-Stained Amazons and Cinematic Warriors Ink-Stained Amazons and Cinematic Warriors: Superwomen in Modern Mythology*, London: I.B. Tauris & Co., 2010.

Symonds, M., T. Wright, and J. Ott, 'The customer-led bank: how to retain customers and boost top-line growth', *Journal of Business Strategy*, (2007), vol. 28(6), pp. 4–12.

Thompson, J.B. (ed.), *Political scandal: power and visibility in the media age*, Cambridge: Polity, (2000).

Trombetta, J.J. and D.P. Rogers, 'Communication climate, job satisfaction, and organizational commitment', *Management Communication Quarterly*, (1988), 4(1), 494–514.

Varona, F., 'Relationship between communication satisfactions and organizational commitment in three Guatemalan organizations', *Journal of Business Communications*, (1996), 33(2), 111–40.

Wang, Y., G. Berens and C.B.M. van Riel, 'Managing reputation rankings: a crucial step for attracting equity investors?', ERIM: *Working paper*, (2011).

Weber, M., *Economy and society. An outline of interpretive sociology*, vols. 1–3, eds G. Roth and C. Wittich, New York: Bedminster Press, (1922/1968).

Zimmermann, S., S.B. Davenport and J.W. Haas, 'Communication meta myths in the workplace: the assumption that more is better', *Journal of Business Communication*, (1996), 33(2), 185–203.

INDEX